KU-373-918

EVE'S CENTURY

A sourcebook of writings on women
and journalism 1895–1918

Edited by Anne Varty

London and New York

First published 2000 by Routledge
11 New Fetter Lane, London EC4P 4EE

Simultaneously published in the USA and Canada
by Routledge
29 West 35th Street, New York, NY 10001

Routledge is an imprint of the Taylor & Francis Group

© 2000 Edited by Anne Varty

Typeset in Garamond 3 by Keystroke, Jacaranda Lodge, Wolverhampton
Printed and bound in Great Britain by TJ International Ltd, Padstow, Cornwall

All rights reserved. No part of this book may be reprinted or
reproduced or utilised in any form or by any electronic, mechanical,
or other means, now known or hereafter invented, including
photocopying and recording, or in any information storage or
retrieval system, without permission in writing from the publishers.

British Library Cataloguing in Publication Data
A catalogue record for this book is available from the British Library

Library of Congress Cataloging in Publication Data

ISBN 0–415–19544–6 (hbk)
ISBN 0–415–19545–4 (pbk)

UNIVER.   .__GE
V.

828.
9104   020318|7
VAR

For my daughter Caitlin Rose

Let the woman's work in the coming century be to face the fact which is ever the germ of tradition, to find the seed, as it were, from which Eve's apple-tree grew, and so right herself for time and eternity.

(*Gentlewoman*, 5 January 1901)

CONTENTS

CONTENTS

ILLUSTRATIONS

ACKNOWLEDGEMENTS

The preparation of this book took place during a period of domestic upheaval and biological chaos brought about by the birth of our daughter Caitlin and the demolition and rebuilding of our house to accommodate her. Thank you to my parents who generously supported this project in every way imaginable. Thank you to my partner Danny Carrick for his persistence in unearthing and arranging the typescript from the depths of various computers. Friends who have helped me include Charlotte Purkis and Marc Middleton-Heath, and neighbours Aline and Bruno, Mim and Bill. Thanks to Lindsey Newark for last minute typing. Thanks also to Siobhan Foley for unflappable computing skills (and her partner Pete for doing the plastering). Thank you to Talia Rodgers for her vision and unfailing support, and also the rest of the team at Routledge including Sophie Powell, Jason Arthur and Rosie Waters. I am grateful to the English Department at Royal Holloway for sabbatical leave to complete the work, and to Pembroke College, Oxford for helping me to meet the deadline. Special thanks to my children Joseph and Caitlin for sharing me with this book.

INTRODUCTION

What does the next century hold for woman? Is there agreement amongst women on how to project a future of their own? How will the achievements of women be assessed a hundred years from now? Who, and what, will manipulate women's choices and debates? These are not new questions. These questions were asked of women, and of society at large, in newspapers, magazines and journals a hundred years ago, at the advent of the twentieth century.

Answers – forecasts, fantasies and farewells – are illustrated here. Examples of British and American journalism for and about women, drawn from the period 1890 to 1918, allow us to situate ourselves as readers at the dawn of the twentieth century. We can read the past as though it were the future, revisiting the moment when our century was unveiled. With hindsight we can assess whether the distance women have travelled over the past hundred years was predictable, and gauge the continuities and discontinuities between women's experiences today and those of the past.

Three areas of popular discussion occupy this anthology: prospecting for women's future, appraising their past and exploring their present. The book opens with a chapter to set the scene, with material about when and where the twentieth century began, how the status of women was assessed at its outset, and how one significant women's magazine, the Philadelphia based *Ladies' Home Journal*, viewed its policy in relation to the confluence of the centuries. A record of the New Year's Eve service at St. Paul's Cathedral in London is a reminder of the Christian foundation of the calendar. Chapters two and three, 'Futures' and 'Retrospects', contain the Janus-faced core.

Configurations of the past and projections into the future were made relative to women's immediate political situation at the moment of transition in 1901. The supporting chapters of the volume represent key aspects of this situation, grouped thematically as 'Politics', 'Colonials', 'War', 'Girls', 'Christmas' and 'Advertising'. The chapters on war and girls contain material from later in the twentieth century to give some indication of how these issues developed. Together they afford today's reader a glimpse of what the editor of the *Lady's Pictorial* foresaw as he hailed the new century on 5 January 1901:

1

It may be that this twentieth century shall see the revolution of the world's history; but it is very certain that, whatever else may happen, those who bid it farewell will stand in a very different position from that which we, who are welcoming it, now occupy. Politically, socially, scientifically, everything will have altered greatly within the next hundred years: but those who come after us will like to learn what was our attitude, what were our views and aspirations when we came to the threshold of this new epoch, and it is therefore with a feeling that we are speaking to three generations ahead that we raise our voices to welcome the twentieth century. They who come after will find when they refer to our journals and books that we did somewhat dip into the future.

Continuities between women's position today and that of a century ago are plain to see from this anthology. The major discrepancy between eras is illustrated by the chapter 'Colonials', which shows a chilling confidence in imperialism alien from that of the present. This in turn reinforces the ideological bias of all the material from which this selection has been made. Women's journalism a hundred years ago was unashamedly white and predominantly middle class in perspective.

In the course of airing this material the anthology serves another purpose which is to suggest the ideological and stylistic range of journalism targeted at women a century ago. The 'new journalism' of the late nineteenth century was largely shaped by women's interests and often written by women. Its style is marked by the use of first person accounts, interviews and biographical profiling, all of which are illustrated here. Simultaneous with the commercial boom in women's journalism which gathered pace as the nineteenth century wore to a close, came the development of newspapers that espoused a cause, whether of temperance, suffrage, or of Christian missions. These offered a more severe noticeboard style and layout, and are represented here by the Boston *Woman's Journal* and the London *Woman's Signal*.

Not all of the items in this collection have been taken from journals produced exclusively for female readership. The American *North American Review* and the British *National Review* were monthly periodicals treating a broad range of intellectual topics, while *Cassell's Magazine* was a British monthly designed for family reading and *Great Thoughts and Christian Graphic* was a weekly paper that also catered for family readership. The *Humanitarian* and the *Monthly Packet* were also intellectual monthlies, both edited by women and angling their subjects for the woman reader. Otherwise the selection has been taken from weekly papers and monthly magazines designed specially to cater for a specific niche in the increasing female market. For example, *Queen*, the *Gentlewoman* and the *Ladies' Home Companion* competed for the upper middle class and aristocracy; *Woman's Life* for the lower middle class; *Womanhood*, launched in 1899, advertised itself as 'the only ladies' paper primarily intended for intellectual women'.

For journalism targeting women, this period afforded a special opportunity for reassessment. The nineteenth century had seen the first mass production of newspapers designed exclusively for the female market, for the soliciting and airing of women's views with masculine concerns ostensibly marginalised. The transition into the twentieth century permitted women's journalism a consolidation of its own position and that of its readers. In Britain this had a commercial dimension, as the editorial of the newly launched *Lady's Magazine* made clear in its first issue in January 1901:

> A magazine for the home, full of light, bright stories and entertaining articles, beautifully illustrated, well produced, and appealing in particular to women – that is what I mean the LADY'S MAGAZINE to be.
>
> There is at present no monthly magazine for women in this country with one-tenth the circulation of the most popular magazine of the kind in the United States, for the simple reason, I believe, that exactly the right sort of magazine has not yet been produced here.
>
> This is the opportunity for a new publication . . .

The model was the *Ladies' Home Journal*. In America celebrations were more idealistic in tone. The suffrage paper the *Woman's Journal* announced on 5 January 1901:

> It is proposed to celebrate the opening of the Twentieth Century by raising a fund to place the WOMAN'S JOURNAL in the reading room of every college of the United States. . . . The colleges and universities are now educating the future leaders of thought. . . . Now is the time to convert them.

Whether converting the pockets or the minds of new readers, journalism for women was a flourishing industry by the end of the nineteenth century. There were competing ideas about why this should be so. The eminent British editor of the *Pall Mall Gazette*, W.T. Stead, maintained the cynical view that this was simply to make money, predicting that:

> The Press of the Twentieth Century . . . will tend more and more to be homely, easy to read, commonplace, and full of pictures and stories. It will constantly seek to cater for fresh readers and for readers who will command advertisers. That is to say, it will tap the unreading ocean of womanhood.
>
> (*Great Thoughts*, March 1895, p. 363)

Alternatively, Evelyn March-Phillips argued in her article 'Women's Newspapers' in the *Fortnightly Review* in November 1894, that as women played an increasing role in public life so it was no longer acceptable to marginalise reporting of their activities in the existing newspapers:

No doubt the intellectual woman will habitually turn for her news to the ordinary paper, but the diverse subjects with which she is now specially connected in this country demand a fuller treatment than the ordinary paper will give them.

(p. 669)

Detractors and promoters of the value of journalism for women were agreed on one issue, namely that whatever its purpose, 'all these . . . publications must exercise a strong influence' (March-Phillips, p. 669). Christabel Coleridge, also writing about women's newspapers in the *Monthly Packet* of April 1894 went so far as to suggest:

In almost all there is an endeavour to maintain a standard, so that the readers in matters of opinion, conduct, intellect, or even taste, may look a little up rather than down. That is surely, hopeful for the future of woman, or of Woman on the whole.

(p. 458)

Common features of the women's press were the promotion of pages for correspondence and competitions. These invited the active participation of readers in the production of the magazine, an easy way for editors to generate copy and to confirm reader loyalty, but which had the perhaps unforeseen consequence of affording women of all social classes a public voice which was otherwise denied them. March-Phillips saw this as an aspect of major signifi-cance in her outline for an ideal paper for women, which should 'bring forward in an interesting and proper way some of the more important matters which today affect women, offering a field for correspondence and intelligent discussion' (ibid., p. 670). The letters page became a way not just of securing individual relationships between editor and reader, but of generating a community of women amongst readers turned writers. It could construct the subculture of an alternative women's parliament at a time when Britain and most American States denied women a legitimate political voice. *Womanhood* even called its letters page 'Woman's Parliament'; and the *Gentlewoman* published a complete list of Cabinet Officers polled by readers on 5 January 1901 (the Prime Minister was the Countess of Aberdeen); the editor of the *Ladies' Home Journal*, flagging the introduction of his 'Question Box' in October 1901, wrote:

I want readers of THE JOURNAL to feel that this is a wide-open magazine: wide open to them, their views, their perplexities, their questions . . . their manuscripts. It bars its doors to none. It has never been influenced by color, race or creed. If you have a message to this magazine or to its public send it along.

(December 1901, p. 18)

The measure of control held by women over the contents of their papers is a point of debate. But that the twentieth century augured well for women was widely agreed across journals for men as for women. The specially commissioned frontispiece for the January 1901 issue of the *Nineteenth Century (And After)* depicted the head of Janus from a Roman coin: the backward looking face was that of a man, the forward looking face was of a woman. And so began 'the preface to the descent of man' (*Gentlewoman*, 12 January 1901).

"SHOULD CLEVER WOMEN MARRY?"—VI

1 'Woman's Parliament: "Should Clever Women Marry?"'

1

THE NEW CENTURY

In January 1900 controversy about whether the twentieth century had begun raged throughout the world press. Laborious counting exercises were rehearsed, and it was finally agreed across Britain and America that the moment of transition was at midnight on 31 December 1900. Only the German Kaiser celebrated the start of the twentieth century on 1 January 1900. There was discussion too about the international date-line, and John Ritchie explains to readers of the *Ladies' Home Journal* in January 1900 the precise latitude and longitude of this, and where, consequently, the sun would first rise in the twentieth century. He notes how stories of political struggle are inscribed in the calendar. Consensus about the status of women at this time was just as unstable, and no less driven by ideology, as that about dates and places. Elizabeth Cady Stanton's typically reformist article from the *North American Review* (a journal for general readership) of December 1900 is the last word in a debate which began the previous month with a profoundly reactionary piece by Flora McDonald Thompson, 'Retrogression of the American Woman'. Thompson is appalled by the degeneracy of her contemporaries, and takes as the cornerstone of her argument what De Tocqueville wrote about American women in *Democracy*:

No free communities ever existed without morals; and as I have observed, morals are the work of woman. Consequently, whatever affects the condition of women, their habits and their opinions, has great political importance in my eyes.

(*North American Review*, November 1900, p. 749)

Thompson accuses her contemporary women of moral corruption, of too much divorce, of striving for economic and political independence, and of eroding the traditional structure of family life and values. She claims that the Americans are now no better than the Europeans whom De Tocqueville accused of 'confounding together the different characteristics of the sexes, [to] make of man and woman beings not only equal but alike' (ibid. p. 759). Elizabeth Cady Stanton fights off these arguments in the course of putting forward her own fresher vision.

Stanton's piece is one of many which appeared at this time. For example, two articles appeared in the *Temple Magazine* (for general readership but catering largely for women); the first, by Lady Violet Greville, 'Woman and the New Century' in August 1901, gave an account of educational and professional opportunities made available to women in the course of the nineteenth century. She asks 'are women happier, better, more healthy for all this storm and stress, this endless business and worry?' (p. 949). Its companion piece, 'Woman at the Dawn of the Twentieth Century,' by Mrs Hirst Alexander in the November issue of 1901, gives detailed information about career and social prospects open to women. These are framed by an expression of conventional piety: 'Women are awakening everywhere to the high work lying to their hands in the near future . . . work that shall be an instrument, under God's guidance, in His own divine evolution of eternal order out of original chaos. . . .' (p. 95).

It was not just material for Sunday reading which struck a note of piety on heralding the twentieth century. A poem, 'The New Age', by Sir Lewis Morris from the *Gentlewoman* on 5 January 1901 sounded in similar tones:

Bring Thou the full enfranchisement which can
Make of the Woman a new precious Force,
The Partner, not the Parasite, of Man,
A strong stream welling from a purer source.

Then shall the World's long agony give place
To gentler aims which seek the better part,
Peace, Mercy, Purity, abounding Grace,
Born of the wedded powers of Mind and Heart.

A purer life, a higher Destiny,
A nobler Art, a deeper love of Right;
Rise, Woman, fit thyself for what shall be,
Ascend, soar upward in the new-born Light.

Wit rather than sentiment was to be found in the competition pages. The *Gentlewoman* announced competition winners for epigrammatic definitions of the new century on 12 January 1901. The winning entry was 'the title page to a sealed book', while runners up included: 'The last century in the score. A new starter for the 2000 (Two Thousand)'; 'The future of the past'; 'The latest thing in cycles, with great improvements in the running'; 'A new cycle on an old track. Time on a new cycle'; 'The infant prodigy of Progressive parents'; 'Preface to the Descent of Man'.

'The So-Called Twentieth Century,' editorial, *Queen, The Lady's Newspaper* (London), 6 January 1900, p. 2

The Question as to whether we are or are not now in the twentieth century of the Christian era is one which is at the present time exercising many minds and exciting in some quarters much acrimonious discussion. Mere academical questions which are not capable of any very definite solution are precisely those on which disputants are apt to differ most strongly, and the subject under discussion is one of these.

In the first place, the data on which to argue are most unsatisfactory. The commonly accepted Christian era was not definitely fixed until the sixth century, and then it is well known that its founders were four or five years wrong in the date they assumed as that of its commencement. Then, again, comes the question as to whether they began with the year 0 or the year 1.

A century cannot possibly be completed until a hundred years have been completed, and the year 1900 is only the last year of the nineteenth century, which cannot terminate until the year is complete, consequently the twentieth century will begin at midnight on Dec. 31, 1900. It cannot possibly be otherwise unless we begin with the year nothing or 0, but no one believes in such a year or uses such an expression. We write of the years of the Christian era as AD1, or AD 1844, but never of AD 0. In the same manner, if we are writing of the years antecedent to the Christian era we never write or speak of BC 0, or of BC nothing; the idea is too absurd to be reasoned about.

Again, let us argue from the precisely parallel case of the age of children. When is a boy ten years old? Or, in other words, when has he completed his first decade? Obviously on his tenth birthday. But those who maintain that the twentieth century has now begun must, to be consistent, maintain that the boy is in his teens on his ninth birthday, if they maintain that the twentieth century begins with 1900. No mother regards her child as a year old on the day of its birth. She has to wait until the first year of its life is complete before making such an announcement, and she has to wait until ten years are completed before she can say her boy is now ten; and in the same manner we must all wait until the nineteenth century is complete before we can say we are in the twentieth. Again, illustrations may be taken from tangible objects. If a sum of one pound is to be paid in separate shillings, the debt will not be liquidated until the creditor has received twenty shillings; he will not allow the debtor to stop short with nineteen. This transformed into centuries is what those who maintain the twentieth century has begun are wishing us to receive. It is quite true that the 1900th year of the Christian era has commenced, but it must be concluded before the nineteenth century is finished, and then, and not before, shall we enter upon the twentieth century. . . .

But the anniversary of the penultimate Christmastide, the last one of the nineteenth century, has come and gone. The almost forgotten Christmas day of the olden time, namely, Twelfth Day, will soon have passed away. The New

Year, which must be regarded as the last of the present century, is in progress, and we can but wish its termination to be brighter than its commencement, and that the Christmas immediately antecedent to the twentieth century may be characterised by the recurrence of the "Peace on earth and goodwill to all men," a hope that we trust all our readers will live to see fulfilled.

'Where the New Century Will Really Begin,'
John Ritchie, Jr., *Ladies' Home Journal* (Philadelphia),
January 1900, p. 7

There is a good deal of sentimental interest attaching to the opening of a new century. Which land will see it first? Whose eye will be the first to note its advent? Whose hail will usher in its earliest moment? Like so many of the phenomena, such as the eclipse and the transit of the planets, the incoming of the twentieth century will be in a region so sparsely settled as to be almost devoid of human life.

The first moment of the twentieth century, the first second of January 1, 1901, will occur in the midst of the Pacific Ocean, along a line conforming in general to the meridian of one hundred and eighty degrees east and west longitude from Greenwich. There is here no land of consequence to salute the new century; no human eye, save, perchance, that of the watch on board some tiny ship, will be there to see its entrance, and its only welcome will be, perhaps, the last strokes of the eight bells marking midnight on board some steamship or vessel which, by chance, may cross the meridian at that instant.

The first people to live in the twentieth century will be the Friendly Islanders, for the date-line, as it may be called, lies in the Pacific Ocean just to the east of their group. At that time, although it will be already Tuesday to them, all the rest of the world will be enjoying some phase of Monday, and the last day of the nineteenth century. At Melbourne the people will be going to bed, for it will be nearly ten o'clock; at Manila it will be two hours earlier in the evening; at Calcutta the English residents will be sitting at their Monday afternoon dinner, for it will be about six o'clock; and in London, "Big Ben," in the tower of the House of Commons, will be striking the hour of noon. In Boston, New York and Washington half the people will be eating breakfast on Monday morning, while Chicago will be barely conscious of the dawn. At the same moment San Francisco will be in the deepest sleep of what is popularly called Sunday night, though really the early, dark hours of Monday morning, and half the Pacific will be wrapped in the darkness of the same morning hours, which become earlier to the west, until at Midway or Brooks Islands it will be but a few minutes past midnight of Sunday night. . . .

The Spaniards going west from their possessions in America carried their day to the Philippine Islands. The Dutch sailing east took their day with them to the adjacent islands of Borneo, Sumatra and Java, and to China. The circuit of the earth having thus been completed, there was the difference of a day between Manila and its neighbours, Manila being behind. As the business interests of the different islands brought them into closer relationships the absurdity of having different day-names in places so close together was the more striking. Accordingly, about the middle of the century the authorities arranged for a unification of dates, and a day was skipped by the Filipinos, the day being December 31, 1844. They went to bed on the evening of December 30, 1844, and awoke the next morning on January 1, 1845.

'Progress of the American Woman,' Elizabeth Cady Stanton,
North American Review (New York), December 1900, pp. 905–7

An article, by Flora McDonald Thompson, entitled 'Retrogression of the American Woman,' which was published in the November number of the REVIEW, contains many startling assertions, which, if true, would be the despair of philosophers. The title itself contradicts the facts of the last half century.

When machinery entered the home, to relieve woman's hands of the multiplicity of her labors, a new walk in life became inevitable for her. When our grandmothers made butter and cheese, dipped candles, dried and preserved fruits and vegetables, spun yarn, knit stockings, wove the family clothing, did all the mending of garments, the laundry work, cooking, patch-work and quilting, planting and weeding of gardens, and all the house-cleaning, they were fully occupied. But when, in course of time, all this was done by machinery, their hands were empty, and they were driven outside the home for occupation. If every woman had been sure of a strong right arm on which to lean until safe "on the other side of Jordan," she might have rested, content to do nothing but bask in the smiles of her husband, and recite Mother Goose melodies to her children.

On that theory of woman's position, men gradually took possession of all her employments. They are now the cooks on ocean steamers, on railroads, in all hotels, in fashionable homes and places of resort; they are at the head of laundries, bakeries and mercantile establishments, where tailor-made suits and hats are manufactured for women. Thus, women have been compelled to enter the factories, trades and professions, to provide their own clothes, food and shelter; and, to prepare themselves for the emergencies of life, they have made their way into the schools and colleges, the hospitals, courts, pulpits, editorial chairs, and they are at work throughout the whole field of literature, art, science and government. We should hardly say that the condition of an intelligent human being was retrogressive, in teaching mathematics instead of making marmalade; in instructing others in philosophy, instead of making pumpkin pie; in studying art, instead of drying apples. When hundreds of girls are graduating from our colleges with high honours every year, when they are interested in all the reforms of their day and generation, super-intending kindergarten schools, labouring to secure more merciful treatment for criminals in all our jails and prisons, better sanitary conditions for our homes, streets and public buildings, the abolition of the gallows and whipping-post, the settlement of all national disputes by arbitration instead of war, we must admit that woman's moral influence is greater then it has ever been before at any time in the course of human development. Her moral power, in working side by side with man, is greatly to the advantage of both, as the co-education of the sexes has abundantly proved. When the sexes reach a perfect equilibrium we shall have higher conditions in the state, the church, and the home.

Matthew Arnold says: 'The first desire of every cultivated mind is to take part in the great work of government.' That woman now makes this demand is a crowning evidence of her higher development. For a true civilization, the masculine and feminine elements in humanity must be in exact equilibrium, just as the centripetal and centrifugal forces are in the material world. If it were possible to suspend either of these great forces for five minutes, we should have material chaos, – just what we have in the moral world to-day, because of the undue depression of the feminine element.

Tennyson, with prophetic vision, forecasts the true relations between man and woman in all the walks of life. He says:

Everywhere
Two heads in council, two beside the hearth,
Two in the tangled business of the world.
Two plummets dropped for one to sound the abyss
Of science and the secrets of the mind.

The first step to be taken in the effort to elevate home life is to make provision for the broadest possible education of woman. Mrs Thompson attributes the increasing number of divorces to the moral degeneracy of woman; whereas it is the result of higher moral perceptions as to the mother's responsibilities to the race. Woman has not heard in vain the warning voice of the prophets, ringing down through the centuries: 'The sins of the father shall be visited upon the children unto the third and fourth generations.' The more woman appreciates the influences in prenatal life, her power in moulding the race, and the necessity for a pure, exalted fatherhood, the more divorces we shall have, until girls enter this relation with greater care and wisdom. When Naquet's divorce bill passed the French Chamber of Deputies, there were three thousand divorces asked for the first year, and most of the applicants were women. The majority of divorces in this country are also applied for by women. The higher intelligence woman has learned the causes that produce idiots, lunatics, criminals, degenerates of all kinds and degrees, and she is no longer a willing partner to the perpetuation of disgrace and misery.

The writer of the article on the 'Retrogression of the American Woman' makes one very puzzling assertion, that the present superiority of the sex immortalizes woman, but demoralizes man. Does she mean that a liberal education can only be acquired at the expense of one's morals? 'The American woman to-day,' says the writer, 'appears to be the fatal symptom of a mortally sick nation.' This is a very pessimistic view to take of our Republic, with its government, religion, and social life, and its people in the full enjoyment of a degree of liberty never known in any nation before! In spite of this alleged wholesale demoralization of man, we have great statesmen, bishops, judges, philosophers, scientists, artists, authors, orators and inventors, who surprise us with new discoveries day by day, giving the mothers of the Republic abundant reason to be proud of their sons.

Virtue and subjection, with this writer, seem to be synonymous terms. Did our grandmother at the spinning wheel occupy a higher position in the scale of being than Maria Mitchell, Professor of Astronomy at Vassar College? Did the farmer's wife at the washtub do a greater work for our country than the Widow Green, who invented the cotton-gin? Could Margaret Fuller, Harriet Beecher Stowe, Frances E. Willard, Mary Lyon, Clara Barton have done a better work churning butter or weeding their onion beds on their respective farms than the grand work they did in literature, education and reform? Could Fannie Kemble, Ellen Tree, Charlotte Cushman or Ellen Terry (if we may mention English as well as American women) have contributed more to the pleasure of their day and generation had they spent their lives at the spinning-wheel? No! Progress is the law, and the higher development of woman is one of the important steps that have been achieved.

There are great moral laws as fixed and universal as the laws of the material development going on all along the line, bringing the nations of the earth to a high point of civilization. True, as the nations rise and fall, their great works seem scattered to the winds. For example, Greek art, it is said, has never been equalled, but we would not change our ideas of human liberty, our comforts and conveniences in life, our wonderful inventions and scientific discoveries, the telegraph, the telephone, our modes of travel by sea, land and in the air, the general education and demand for better conditions and higher wages by the laboring masses, the abolition of slavery, rapid improvement in woman's condition, the emancipation of large classes from the religious superstitions of the past, for all the wonderful productions of beauty at the very highest period of Greek art. In place of witchcraft, astrology and fortune-telling, we now have phrenology, astronomy and physiology; instead of famine, leprosy and plague, we owe to medical science a knowledge of sanitary laws; instead of an angry God, punishing us for our sins, we know that the evils that surround us are the result of our own ignorance of Nature's laws. He who denies that progress is the law, in both the moral and material world, must be blind to the facts of history, and to what is passing before his eyes in his own day and generation.

The moral status of woman depends on her personal independence and capacity for self-support. 'Give a man a right over my subsistence,' says Alexander Hamilton, 'and he holds a power over my whole moral being.'

De Tocqueville cannot be impressed into the service of the writer, nor fairly quoted, even inferentially, as saying that the moral status of the American woman in 1848, owing to certain causes at work, was higher than it would be in 1900. Progress is in the law, and woman, the greatest factor in civilization, must lead the van. Whatever degrades man of necessity degrades woman; whatever elevates woman of necessity elevates man.

'The Two Centuries and This Magazine,' Edward Bok,
Ladies' Home Journal (Philadelphia), January 1901, p. 16

This magazine and the nineteenth century were not very old friends. When the LADIES' HOME JOURNAL first saw the light the century was already eighty-three years old. This left only seventeen years of actual acquaintance, and as it requires that length of time to season a magazine, it stands to reason that the part which the JOURNAL played in the nineteenth century was limited. Of course, it must have played some part. No magazine can issue and circulate ninety-five million copies (or, to be exact, 95,237,523), as has this magazine from its first number up to this present issue, without creating some impression or exerting some influence. Naturally, its conductors like to feel that this influence, be it greater or smaller than they believe, has been for good. Still, as the old negro preacher said in his farewell sermon, 'It's for dem what has bin dun good to say how good they have bin dun.'

[. . .]

It started with a determination to be clean and wholesome, and in that one respect, at least, it feels it has succeeded. It may not always have presented what is technically called 'literature' – albeit exactly what constitutes 'literature' has never been clearly defined even by its most ardent and accomplished votaries. But, at least, what the JOURNAL has printed has been free from unclean phrase or innuendo. It has thus demonstrated that a popular periodical can adhere to a clean, wholesome literature and receive the support of a large part of the American public. It is a popular impression in some quarters that this is not possible. Pessimists are wont to say that only the sensational and suggestive in literature can succeed: that only the unclean plays prosper on the stage: that only the hotels which have a bar as a prominent feature can have a profitable patronage. But the American public constantly refutes these allegations and shows their fallacy.

[. . .]

But a success of any kind invariably brings with it some thing more than gratification. If success is anything it is exceedingly impressive. There come moments when one can stop and feel an exhilaration in a successful accomplishment, but there are a far greater number of moments when the attention is directed and absorbed by the responsibilities which go along with success in any field of human endeavour. The easiest part of success is making it: the hardest part is maintaining it. It is after a success has been made that the real work begins. And that is the point at which the LADIES' HOME JOURNAL finds itself as it emerges from the old century and enters the new. It is a success: no doubt of that. But it is a success which must be kept. The only substantial gratitude that a magazine can show its public, which has brought success to it, is the proof that it can carry out a success and maintain it. In other words, it must justify the confidence reposed in it. For the public's part in a magazine is that of pure faith and confidence. It pays a subscription in advance in pure faith that it will receive twelve issues of that magazine, and that the contents will be such as to justify both the investment and the confidence. For a whole year that obligation rests upon the conductors of the magazine. During that year others have subscribed with the same confidence, and thus the magazine is constantly under the highest obligation which one human being can place upon another: that of trust, of confidence. Now, if any one has the idea, as some have, that such an outward expression of confidence carries with it nothing more than to enjoy one's self, and to go to the office occasionally to cut off some coupons from gilt-edged securities, the opportunity is in this office to test the question. I am not saying that those who conduct this magazine do not get pleasure out of their work. They do. Lots of it. If they didn't they couldn't do their work. But ever present is an obligation to discharge – a confidence to justify.

The most satisfying phase of editing this magazine is the bond of close personal relation which has been cemented between those who read it and those who make the LADIES' HOME JOURNAL. No corps of editors was ever in closer personal touch with its readers. This was the intent of the conductors of the magazine when it started, and the hope has been fully realized. It may interest those who do not know it that the editors of this magazine receive each year more than thirty thousand personal letters from their readers. And never is one of these letters intentionally slighted. Not one ever goes unread. The vast majority are acknowledged. This has always been esteemed a privilege; never a burden. An editor's mail is, of necessity, a large one, but it is never so large that he has not time to enjoy a word of praise or hearken to a suggestion or to a warning uttered in the spirit of honest criticism. The readers of this magazine have pointed the way to its editors in innumerable instances, and much of the success attained is directly due to this personal touch [. . .]

Now it is always difficult, in fact impossible, to say what a magazine will do a year ahead. It makes arrangements in advance, of course, and such as it can make it announces. But read any magazine's announcements at the beginning of the year, and follow its issues through that year, and one will at once see how much it publishes which it could not announce in advance. This must be so. A magazine must keep itself fresh in interest, and its pages open to material which comes along. Conditions change radically during the progress of a year, especially in such a country as ours, and the magazine must change with them. For, as the newspaper is, or should be, the picture of a day, the magazine is, or should be, the reflector of thought. To say that So-and-So edits a magazine is always a mistake. It is the public that edits a magazine. The editor simply edits the public's thought as it comes to him for expression through his magazine. In the manner in which he presents that thought he may stamp his personality upon it, and so we know that there is an individuality behind the printed page. But the thought remains that of the public, whether edited by the editor in manuscript or expressed with his own pen. He remains simply a medium placed in control of a channel of expression. That channel represents certain principles, and those principles become what is called the policy of a magazine. This policy determines whether certain questions shall be discussed in the affirmative or the negative, or whether the questions are important enough to be discussed at all. For instance, the LADIES' HOME JOURNAL believes in everything that will make a woman's life simpler, more restful and more cheerful. That is its policy because it is the principle of its conductors – that principle being based upon observation, experience and conviction. On this policy the magazine either ignores altogether or opposes anything which its conductors are convinced, for well-grounded reasons, will complicate the lives of women or make them restless, and therefore less happy. Such a policy, one might say, is the backbone of a magazine. Upon it, it rests, and this it reflects in its opinions. Of course, no such policy can meet the approval of all. Hence come dissension from its opinions: disagreement with its attitude: dissatisfaction with the magazine itself. Sometimes this leads to irate letters: at other times to a withdrawal of support: in further instances, to public attacks. All this is, of course, inevitable. In a sense, it is expected. The magazine's policy is based upon human opinion and conviction, and, being human, it may be faulty. Its opportunities of wider observation, of course, give it an advantage to get closer to the heart of things than is generally possible for the individual. Yet even then it may misinterpret the truest and wisest signs. It simply reflects what, after observation, investigation, experience and conviction, its conductors believe to be the truth, and the highest wisdom, according to their lights.

[. . .]

What the twentieth century holds out for this magazine no one can tell. The probability is that the measure of success will be proportionate to the magazine's merits. . . . The best thing to do in this world is to devote every moment to our very best effort, and then it is very probable we shall find that the results will take care of themselves. They have had a habit of doing so thus far since the creation of the world, anyhow, and it is extremely doubtful whether any change will occur in that respect during the new century. And until a change is made it is safer and better to accept such things as they are.

At least, that is the plan upon which this magazine will be conducted during the time of its existence in the century before it. It will simply strive to do its best, influencing by actual accomplishment rather than by promise. It will reach out wherever the minds and hearts of men and women have something to say or give which will benefit womankind. Its past will be valuable to it only from the experience it has taught. In this respect it enters the first year of the new century better equipped than it entered the last year of the old cycle. It is a year older in experience. Its conductors have prepared twelve more numbers, and each has taught its lesson.

The one dominant feeling of all connected with this magazine is that of gratitude to its readers – those who have made it possible for us to do and to progress. That this magazine has been singularly favored in the patronage extended to it is recognized, felt and appreciated. This marvellous expression of approval and confidence finds no suitable return in simple thanks, sincere and direct from the heart tho' this may come. One cannot adequately thank so vast an army of supporters and friends. The least and best one can do is to remain humble and use every endeavour to merit what has been so generously given: to prove worthy of confidence: to justify the trust. And in that spirit we hail the new century and every man, woman and child that enters it with us. May what is best for each come to each! None of us, reader or writer, will see its close. But we see its beginning, and we are thus made part of it. And standing on its threshold, it lies with each to do our allotted part as we will. For our lives are what we make of them ourselves.

'The Last Day of the Nineteenth Century. The Form of Prayers used at St. Paul's,' unsigned, *Queen, The Lady's Newspaper*, 5 January 1901, p. 9

Messers Novello and Co. send us the Form of Prayer chosen by Dean Gregory to be used in St. Paul's Cathedral at the crowded service which took place at seven o'clock on the last day of the nineteenth century, which they have published, with music, at sixpence a copy, and with words alone at twopence. It consists, in the following order, of the hymn 'Now thank we all our God' (music by Charles Macpherson), sung in procession. (2) The Lord's Prayer. (3) Collect from the Commination Service, 'O Most Mighty God and Merciful Father.' (4) Antiphon, 'Remember the Days of Old' (music by George C. Martin). (5) Psalms XC (Hervey), CIII (Elvey), and CXV (Tonus Peregrinus). (6) Lesson from Revelations, chap. xxi. (7) The hymn 'O God of Jacob' (music by Charles Macpherson). (8) Antiphon, 'Unto us a Child is born' (music by George C. Martin). (9) The Magnificat (Stainer). (10) The Apostles' Creed. (11) The Lord's Prayer; the Collects, 'Almighty God, who hath given us thy only begotten Son to take our nature upon him,' etc.; 'Almighty God, who through thine only begotten Son Jesus Christ has overcome death, and opened unto us the gate of everlasting life,' etc.; 'Grant, O Lord, we beseech thee, that the course of this world may be so peaceably ordered,' etc; 'O Almighty God, who hast knit together thine elect in one communion and fellowship,' etc.; 'O God the Father of our Lord Jesus Christ, our only Saviour, the Prince of Peace, give us grace seriously to lay to heart the great dangers we are in by our unhappy divisions,' and the Doxology. (12) The hymn 'Guide me, O Thou Great Redeemer' (music by George C. Martin). Then followed the sermon by the Rev. Canon Mason, and the service concluded with the hymn 'A few more years shall roll,' to the tune written by Sir George C. Martin, the organist of the Cathedral.

'Greetings for the New Century,' *Englishwoman's Review*
(London), 15 January 1901, pp. 1–2

To Our Readers

> The tender heaven, the bounteous earth,
> The ceaseless round of Death and Birth,
> The stars that pace their fixéd span,
> And heart of man to heart of man,
> As sentinel to sentinel
> Cry through the ages – 'All is well.'
> A. W.

Century unto century uttereth speech

The scroll of the Eighteenth Century – The Seventeenth Century as it passed out, handed on this charge – Let women be useful in the Home! Therefore I, the Eighteenth, have sheltered them from the burden of much learning, and have kept away all weight of care for aught beyond the garden wall.

Thereby they have learned that they have no independent will, the keynote of their lives is to Please.

The young Nineteenth took the scroll and pondered. – 'No independent will, then these pleasing creatures can have no place in my Reform Acts – for they mean to sweep in all who are not of so mean value as to have no wills of their own, according to the holy custom of our ancestors.'

Presently murmurs sounded in the ears of the Century, low, few at first, but growing louder, fuller till a great cry arose all around.

'Enough, enough of difference of conduct and knowledge. Let us all concern ourselves with the things that concern us all, the common needs of human beings.'

The old Century listened and pondered and passeth on this charge today.

The charge of the Nineteenth to the Twentieth Century. – Know that none are made useful by the with-holding of learning. Know that none are sheltered by the denial of wider duty. And none become more pleasing by the narrowing of understanding. The note this, the Nineteenth Century, leaves to the future, is the old yet ever new note – Communion of Labour. Set thereto they hand and seal, the secure seal of the Franchise.

H. B.

2

FUTURES

For some the future was an extravagant fantasy, thought of as radio messages from Mars (*Lady's Pictorial*, 12 January 1901); others refrained from picturing the unknown at all. The first three articles in this section about woman and the future life are taken from the weekly paper *Great Thoughts and Christian Graphic* of 1895. All three are responses to a prophetic article by Rev. Joseph Parker on 5 January 1895, 'The Twentieth Century. A Forecast' in which he addressed many aspects of likely social change. On the subject of women he stated:

The position of Woman in the Twentieth Century will be in happy contrast to that which she now occupies. It is now customary on the part of weak men to lower the conversation so as to bring it within feminine capacity. I have been immensely amused by the superhuman condescension of sundry masculine idiots. The moment a lady enters the room the subject drops from even a very moderate intellectual level to the baby, the weather, the crops, and the newest thing in umbrellas. There is the softened murmur of maudlin consolation in respect of rheumatism and a feebly energetic protest against any woman caring, or daring, to have an opinion of her own. Recent University successes have shown that women can go to the top without losing one atom of grace or gentleness, of simplicity or childlikeness, of sympathy or affection. All that has been taken away from the region of fancy, and squarely settled down in the region of indisputable fact. It must be very humbling to men of a certain cast of mind to know that girls take the B.A. degree in dozens and scores, and never stoop to wear the elementary and now humiliating decoration. But what are third-class men to think of girls who know mathematics and natural philosophy enough to build the Forth Bridge, and yet can laugh, and dance, and joke, and even take a hand in the kitchen?

In March of 1895 Mrs Lynn Linton replied for the opposition. She was notoriously hostile to the New Woman movement, and her piece is characteristically retrograde. The reformist article by the editor of the *Woman's Signal*, Lady Henry Somerset, was printed beside Linton's to balance the view. The last word was given to Florence Balgarnie the following week: her forecast is the most radical. Many of the changes in legislation and attitude for which she argues have not yet fully matured.

Lady Jeune's article about the future of society was the first of a series run by the *Lady's Realm* in 1902. Constance, Countess de la Warr and Susan, Countess of Malmesbury contributed the second and third pieces in February and March. Unlike Lady Jeune, their approach was narrowly aristocratic in interest. Their focus was on 'Society' as the Countess of Malmesbury had defined it in her September 1901 article 'Is Society Deteriorating?': 'the aim and object of Society is to enable persons of wealth and leisure to spend their lives agreeably together, guarded by certain unwritten laws and self-imposed restrictions.' Only Lady Jeune looks beyond the confines of her class to consider more generally how social fabric may be changed by the two major factors she identifies: the emancipation of women and the development of communication technology. Her interest in technology is shared with the author of 'What May Happen in the Next Hundred Years' for the *Ladies' Home Journal* of December 1900. Excitement at the advance of science is heedless of the concomitant ethical and environmental issues which occupy us today when many versions of Watkins' prophecy have indeed come into being.

An item of fiction concludes the chapter, taken from the Christmas issue of the *Gentlewoman* in 1900 which dated itself Christmas 2000 and the entire contents of which were projected a hundred years into the future. 'The Courtship of Lord Arthur Armstrong' by E.F. Benson is a remarkable blend of science fiction, romance, social satire and literature of ideas. The story, set in the summer of 2000, is governed by the simple conceit of total role reversal between women and men, and between middle class and aristocracy. Power is held by middle class women. Men are valued for their bodies, and as the moral standard bearers of society. Illustrations which accompany the text show women somberly dressed in trousers and tails, men with crimped hair and billowing cravats. The exposition allows for description of technological and social change (streets are air conditioned, news is flashed on hoardings, the Derby is a race for cars). Dialogue allows the rehearsal of ideas which present shifts in social attitude and expectation. Arguments for the disenfranchisement of men replicate those for the then continued witholding of voting rights for women. What function does this ideological cross-dressing serve? Does it point up the absurdity of those arguments, or does it confirm men as the only legitimate bearers of power? Does it anticipate the feminism of Mary Cholmondely's 1909 play *Votes For Men*? In 1892 the *Gentlewoman* had polled readers on whether women should be given the vote and found overwhelming support for the idea. Benson could therefore assume that readers would find his satire congenially subversive, but the overall message of the piece is unstable and ambiguous. The story contains much discourse of traditionally masculine domains – racing, betting, power politics: does this contribute to the immersion of women into a man's world, or is it simply a narrative weakness by a male author? Would it attract or repel the contemporary female reader? Similar questions surround the picture of responsiblity that goes with political power. Is the overall effect a nightmare vision of the future, or one which could command interest and some respect? The narrative ends with the heroine permitting herself to be pursued by the hero, and uttering the word 'love' in his arms. The image of race and pursuit that comprises the central dramatic episode of the story in the description of the Derby, suggests that women will not succeed without men to guide them, and that the race for victory can only be won if middle classes and aristocracy work together.

'The Twentieth Century Woman,' Mrs E. Lynn Linton,
Great Thoughts and Christian Graphic
(London), 23 February 1895, pp. 329–30

Dr. Parker's forecast is optimism of the rosiest and most perfect kind, equalling Utopia in beauty and realising the Millennium in holiness. What he foresees of the 'bodies of things to be in the houses of death and of birth' is a new human nature, with the animal obliterated and the savage civilised, with passions subdued and reason triumphant, vices forgotten as one forgets the ignorance of childhood, and virtue supreme in all the daily doings of men. And conspicuous in this sublime evolution stands woman, freed from all her frailties and purified from all her special sins, with the strength and know-ledge and breadth of man added to the charm and sweetness of her own ideal. We wish we could share in this rose-coloured hope; but we do not think that the New, as the germ of the Future, Woman makes that as yet undeveloped being a cause for much prophetic rejoicing. For to our mind the New Woman has sundry unpleasant characteristics which will have to be changed if she is to be as good as Dr. Parker's forecast would make her. She will have to get rid of her present rampant self-assertion and disregard of old-time modesties, and to reconsider the wisdom of her restless interference in things with which she has no business, mated with her neglect of all her hitherto assigned duties, before she can reach the standard of her moral possibilities. And she will have to make it clear to herself that her present aims are as impracticable as a ladder made of a bean-stalk and going straight up to the skies. For she wants to combine the irreconcilable conditions of both states – to have the freedom of a man while retaining the protection accorded to a sheltered woman – to learn life experimentally as a man, yet be treated with the chivalrous devotion, the supreme respect paid by men to pure women – to be the rival not the helpmate of man, yet to be loved as no one can love a rival, and to be given, beside the fair field of open competition, special favour and consideration. It does not seem likely that out of these discordant elements will be evolved the perfect being so ardently desired and so poetically described. Nor can the predominance of women, which is the real thing aimed at, lead to the advancement of society, unless the fairy tale of Hope should come true, and she of all things in creation, should be the sole bit of perfected work.

The predominance of woman in political life, which will come about by sheer force of numbers if given the franchise, would be a national disaster because of her very virtues and the character of her integral qualities. Say what the New Woman may, the *raison d'être* of the sex is maternity; and flout and flounce as the man-haters and children-contemners may, the mental and moral qualities which fit her for that function unfit her for political life. Attention to minor details and absorption in the present moment are absolutely necessary for a mother, if her children are to live and do well; so too, is that exclusive partiality which cares for her own rather than for the community, which would sacrifice both principles and individuals to preserve her own safe from harm. Have we ever known a living mother who would urge her son to lead a forlorn hope, or rejoice that he should place himself in positions of certain death for the good of others? In old Greek and Roman days, when patriotism was both a passion and a religion, we do read of women capable of this supreme sacrifice. In our own times, when some among us sneer at patriotism as worn-out superstition and but another word for egotism, we have not a trace of the sentiment. The excessive regard for the individual which has weakened even the stronger fibre of men, is naturally the dominant note with women; and the cowardly dread of pain which has invaded the whole modern civilised world, producing the most grotesque results in the way of sympathy and pity, is also naturally more pronounced with women than with men. In this circle, then, lies the difference between men and women, and in this difference must necessarily lie unlikeness of social duties, political power, and mental and moral characteristics, if the world is to go on harmoniously and society is to be righteously organised and conducted.

The rose-coloured prophets see otherwise. According to them the future woman is to be on an exact level with man in education, function, political power and political activity. She is to know classics, mathematics, physiology and pathology, the arts and sciences, imperial politics, and political economy; how to build the Forth Bridge and how to calculate eclipses, and at the same time to be able to trim a bonnet and cook a dinner. That is, she is to combine both masculine attributes and womanly qualities – masculine acquirements and womanly accomplishments. A few of the more ardent believers turn the thaumatrope the other way round, and add to this strengthening and enlarging of woman's sphere the corresponding weakening and restricting of man's, by which we should have an amalgam, where men would not be men nor women, women, but a kind of indeterminate third sex, with – *vide* the smoking, drinking, slangy wearers of knickerbockers and bowlers – but such minute differences in dress as will leave the sex still more obscure. Well, to some among us who hold by the old ideal of womanly distinction, that does not seem the highest to which the future can attain. We think we did better with our sweet Countess of Salisbury, our Lady Russell, our Lady Fanshawe, our Lady Granville, and that countless host of women, pure-hearted and innocent-minded, lovely, graceful, delicate and dutiful, who knew where their best strength lay, and who were content with the shaping force of motherhood and the unseen influence of womanliness.

People talk as if an educated and learned woman were a new invention – as if no woman before Newnham and Girton had ever known more than the mere rudiments of things for the most part useless, the most lady-like skimmings of intellectual futilities. There have been eras of learned women before now as there have been eras of masculine women. The later Bluestockings repeated the learned ladies of the Middle Ages, as they, the Bolognese professors for instance, repeated the Aspasias, the Distimas, the Hypatias of a still earlier school. We had Anne Ayscough and Lady Jane Grey, Lady Elizabeth Hastings – 'to love whom was a liberal education' – Mrs. Montague and even Caroline Herschel, and Mrs. Somerville closely touching the skirts of to-day, long before our crop-haired BA's jostled their brothers at the universities and held the ability to read Aristophanes and Juvenal in the original of more account than grace, beauty, or the sense of feminine delicacy and duty. But the learned woman of the present day is, after all, *sui generis*; and perhaps it is as well she should be. We have had, too, masculine women in the past – 'Homasses' who put on armour, of a kind, and went to the crusades, 'charming the seas to give them gentle press' and acting with the active ferocity of Amazons, not only the passive fortitude of ordinary women. They had their poetic apotheosis in Bramante and Marphisa, in Britomart and the Roaring Girl, and their historic and later impersonations in Joan of Arc, and Chevalier d'Eon, and the various unsexed females who have served in the ranks and before the mast, undetected till wounded or dead. Whether they were exactly one's ideal of womanhood, or 'sports,' which one was thankful were not to be continued to the race, is a matter for each to decide for himself. It may be that a section of the future womanhood will resolve herself into these 'Homasses' of the past under modern conditions. In which case our young men will become nurse-girls and lady's maids, and the travesty will be complete. No, the future woman will be admirable only so far as she shall forsake her present extravagant pretensions and return to her own more beautiful and more natural lines. As she is now, under her names of *Fin-de-siècle* and New Woman, she is all wrong from start to finish, and a national disaster rather than a domestic blessing and a social ornament.

'The Position of Woman in the Twentieth Century,' Lady Henry
Somerset, *Great Thoughts and Christian Graphic*
(London), 23 February 1895, p. 331

It is my cherished belief that in the Twentieth Century there will be no
artificial restrictions placed upon women by laws which hedge them out of
certain employments, professions, and careers, or by that public sentiment,
stronger than law, which now practically closes to them many paths of
usefulness for which they seem to me to be especially adapted. All that the
most progressive pioneers have ever dreamed of asking is that, in the case
of women, as in that of men, they should not be hedged about by barriers
made by the privileged classes, who, in political, ecclesiastical, professional
and business life have secured the power to say who shall come in and who
shall stay out. This power has crippled the efforts of men to develop according
to the utmost of their possibilities, but it is now universally conceded among
intelligent people that men are fast coming to their own in the sense of being
free to make the most of themselves in any direction to which their bent of
mind has predisposed them.

The same will be true of women in the Twentieth Century. I confidently
expect that they will win their greatest laurels in the realm of government.
Many of the great statesmen of the future will be women; many of the greatest
preachers will be women. The world has lost incalculably by the senseless
prejudice that has silenced the potent voices of the mothers of the world in
the aisles of prayer and the halls of legislation. The tact of woman would
have been of incalculable service to the peoples in the settling of disputes.
From the beginning a mother has been both statesman and diplomat in the
home; from morning to night it has been her work to settle disputes; in short,
to administer justice tempered with mercy. It has been well said that probably
the greatest loss humanity has suffered is from the fact that half the wisdom,
more than half the purity, and more than half the gentleness of human kind
have been missed from the mart, the camp, the court. We want the survival of
the most as well as of the fittest, the survival of others as well as of ourselves,
and we shall never have this principle carried to its complete conclusion until
every child that is born, whether boy or girl, shall from the first drink in the
inspiration of knowing and feeling that 'the world is all before them where to
choose.'

'Women in the Twentieth Century. A Forecast,' Florence
Balgarnie, *Great Thoughts and Christian Graphic*
(London), 2 March 1895, pp. 347–8

Dr. Joseph Parker never penned a sentence more pregnant with meaning than
when he wrote 'the position of women in the Twentieth Century will be a

happy contrast to that which she now occupies.' The full force of that contrast will be but gradually realised. The degree of progress will be measured by the declining prominence given to woman as woman.

In the year 1995, those who attempt forecasts of the twenty-first century will not be called upon to determine the position of woman as distinct from the position of man. In considering the future of commerce, politics, religion, and art, it will be as impossible to discuss them apart from woman as it is to-day impossible to discuss them apart from man.

The very fact that it is deemed necessary to-day to differentiate woman from these fundamentals of human existence, that she should be placed in a separate category, and that a special forecast should be made of her, affords silent but convincing proof that she has not yet found her proper sphere. In the twentieth century she will become a TRUE HELPMATE OF MAN, inasmuch as man, her mate, will have discovered what a comparatively helpless being he is without her help in all spheres of human existence. He will have at length realised that his insufficiency in the domestic round of duties when unaided by woman is but typical of his actual condition in public life. The larger house-keeping of the parish, the town, the county, the state, will require the aid of prudent and thrifty women as well as of enterprising and far-seeing men.

Woman will no longer need to clamour for her right to take her share in these larger affairs, they will be forced upon her by general public sentiment as part of the debt she owes her day and generation.

Woman will no longer be discussed as written with a capital W. The subject will have become as trite as the Rights of Man are to-day. What the eighteenth century was to man, and the nineteenth to woman, so the twentieth will be to the human. Men and women will have discovered that the right of one sex to keep the other sex in subjection, is so prejudicial, both to the one dominated and to him who dominates, that all thought of the mastery of sex will have disappeared.

In place of rivalry between the sexes there will be HEALTHY HUMAN COMRADESHIP. The ivy will no longer be a fitting symbol for womanhood. It is too apt to strangle the oak in its clinging embrace. Men, having come to a clear comprehension of their duties towards women, will echo the noble utterance of Mazzini in his address to the workers: – 'Consider woman, therefore, as the partner and companion, not merely of your joys and sorrows, but of your thoughts, your aspirations, your studies, and your endeavours after social amelioration. Consider her your equal in your civil and political life. Be ye the two human wings that lift the soul towards the ideal we are destined to attain.' It follows that the idea of a 'Woman's Party' will have been relegated to the limbo of forgetfulness. Women will have developed that last grand gift of Heaven, the saving sense of humour. This will enable them to discard as amiable foibles much that is struggled for to-day with an intensity of earnestness worthy of a more serious cause.

The dross will have been cast aside – the exaggerated, the hysterical, and the morbid – and from out of the refiner's melting-pot the gold of a truer womanhood will have emerged. Above all things women will have more courage. Such a creation as Evadne, of the 'Heavenly Twins,' would be an impossibility. The Twentieth Century woman will no longer allow Mrs. Grundy to stand between her and her highest ideals. She will not merely require AN EQUAL STANDARD OF MORALS in the man whom she marries, but she will see to it that she sets a higher standard for herself. Her finer perceptions will recognise that the intellectual immorality of small back bitings, petty tyranny, slanderous gossip, and half-truths may in the sight of God be as heinous as the political immoralities which she so justly condemns.

Purity of heart and of lip would be for herself as much a *sine qua non* as purity of life. Women requiring perfect chastity in their future husbands will refuse to do any man the irreparable wrong of marrying him merely for a home, or for a settlement.

Marriage will no longer be a profession – too often a poor one at that – in which women look to men to keep them.

No woman will marry unless she has found her ideal, for whom she cherishes a love, the light of which is so dazzling that all transient passion is eclipsed.

She would refuse, and a reformed church will no longer require the Twentieth Century woman to bind herself into slavery as she kneels at the marriage alter, and in the very act of making the most solemn vow to promise an obedience which ninety-nine women out of every hundred already disclaim. She will, like her partner, promise to love, honour, and cherish, for with true comrades MUTUAL OBLIGATION ECLIPSES OBEDIENCE. Under the collectivism of the twentieth century, inheritance will decrease. But what a child will lose materially it will more than gain mentally and morally.

The right of being well born will be claimed as inalienable for every child. Enlightened women, able to trace effects to causes, will regard it as a disgrace persistently to give birth to children diseased in body or in mind. If there be a decrease in the birth rate there will likewise be a very considerable decrease in infantile mortality.

That too often crass selfishness known as 'family affection' will have widened out into something more human. Hence, laws will be so changed that the absence of a formal marriage bond will not permit a man to discard the woman whom he has cherished as his wife, and the child whom he has brought into the world. No child will be damned at birth by the designation of 'illegitimate.'

She who would rob another woman of her natural husband and child of its natural father, be it under the guise of marriage in Hanover Square or Westminster Abbey, is one who can with but an ill grace draw her skirts aside from the wretched promenaders of Piccadilly and Leicester Square.

But this higher conception of the relations of the sexes must inevitably be preceded by the COMPLETE ECONOMIC INDEPENDENCE OF WOMEN. Pure marriages will be possible exactly in proportion as the consideration of financial advantage is eliminated.

Parents unable to dower their daughters will provide them with as adequate a training as they provide their boys. Women will no longer compete with men on unfair terms and undersell them in the labour market. Capacity, not sex, will be the standard for remuneration. Hence, if a woman consent to surrender her economic independence, in order to become a wife and mother, her husband will, as a matter of course, consider her his partner, entitled to an equal share in the disposal of the family income. A contrast this, indeed, to many a present-day man, who will spend thousands on his racers, or on enabling his sons to keep up a good appearance in the Army or in the Diplomatic Service, while wife and daughters are kept an allowance of pin-money so meagre that they are generally regarded as the mean appendages of a most lavish and generous-hearted being.

The economic independence of women will ensure wider opportunities in life. Girls will, like their brothers, look forward to a career. Some will find it in business, others in law, literature, art, the pulpit, in local governing bodies, and in the House of Commons. All adult women, as well as all adult men will have the Parliamentary vote. Marriage will no more disqualify a woman than a man from the rights of citizenship. While all human beings will have equal opportunity for exercising public functions, men will probably to the end of time remain in a majority in all offices. Nor will this in any way be to the disadvantage of women. They will not be ranged on one side in politics, and men on the other, but will permeate all parties, and chiefly the two main parties of the twentieth century, the collectivist and the individualist. When women have attained to an assured position in the labour field, when they are no longer subject to men in the home, the feverish restlessness which characterises so much of these latter decades of the nineteenth century will have vanished; and the majority of women, in the new dignity, added beauty, and deepened responsibility attached to the domestic sphere, will cherish it with a tenderness and a loyalty which those of to-day can scarcely comprehend.

Free in mind, body and estate, with every relic of servitude banished, women, having ceased to strive for personal emancipation, will with men seek to sanctify the family, the country, the world at large.

'The Twentieth Century Woman,' Charlotte Perkins Gilman, *Woman's Journal* (Boston), 5 January 1901, p. 2

We need most, in this age, the kind of brain that is capable of grasping large social conditions and solving the social problems which are gathering thick before us; also, the kind of heart which cannot rest in peace when the doors are shut on one household's fed contentment, but which aches for the other children who are not fed.

Further social development in brain and heart and conscience, – this alone can lead our civilization beyond the dangers which have wrecked the others.

And this is precisely what is coming to us from the change in the position of woman. The restriction on her growth has held back her son. Freedom and enlightenment for her is instantly shown in him.

Human qualities have grown in us through our human groups and activities. Women are beginning to enter those groups and those activities as never before.

New powers and aspirations will open to them, and they will see the world needs as well as the home-needs.

It is not that this century has discovered woman, but woman is discovering, at length, what century she is in, and coming forward to take her place and do her duty in it. As a citizen of the twentieth century, she will bring new light to the dark questions which vex us, both domestic and social.

Her broad and trained intelligence will simplify the manifold difficulties of home life to-day, and give us an educated childhood, – free and healthy and beautiful.

With great-hearted and great-brained mothers behind them, and as noble women for sisters, wives, and friends, men can face our social problems better prepared, and not alone.

That is the line of advance we are entering upon in 'the woman's century.' Larger social relations for woman means a larger development in the human creature, – and we need it.

A better people, stronger, healthier, clearer-headed, bigger-hearted, we can take hold of this good world of ours and put it in better order. It is better than it was; we can make it far better than it is.

No unsexed masculine creation of our timid fancy is coming to us; it is simply woman, beautiful and gracious, wise and tender, but of a nobler growth than now.

She who now makes home so comfortable, and who, when she comes bravely out into this 'harsh,' 'sordid,' 'weary,' 'bitter,' 'cold and cruel' world, will clean house promptly, settle and put it in order, and make it what it should be to us all, – our home.

'The Future of Society,' Lady Jeune, *Lady's Realm*
(London), January 1902, pp. 361–5

The past century has been so prolific in changes and extraordinary developments that it seems difficult to imagine the new one can be as remarkable. It is impossible that it will pass through a social revolution such as the one we have just witnessed, or that at the beginning of the twenty-first century the conditions of life will have altered to the same extent as those of the last fifty years. The great changes which have so altered English social life have arisen during the last half of the century, for the earlier part was almost as uneventful as that which preceded it. It would require the most daring of prophets to predict what the new century might bring forth; but however wonderful its changes may be, it cannot produce so complete a social upheaval as that which has been brought about by the two great events which changed the whole conditions of Society – namely, the increased facility of communication, and the emancipation of woman. Nothing so subversive can await us in the future. Much that is remarkable and novel will be evolved during its existence, but the consequences cannot possibly be so far reaching as those of the greatest social revolution which the world has ever witnessed, and which have been accomplished with the most perfect tranquillity. The facilities of communication which we now enjoy will probably be improved. Every part of England and its vast Empire will be brought into nearer communication, and in that way Society and all its interests will become wider, as every section of the community will be more able to participate in the national life. The monorail, if it possesses the powers ascribed to it, must operate enormously in the future, when railway-travelling will be possible at a hundred miles an hour or even more.

It is a curious contrast to what life was at the beginning of the nineteenth century, when there were but few roads, and the great highways of the country were only those on which people could travel with comfort. The crowded stage-coach was the only means of locomotion during the long, tedious, weary days, unbearably hot in summer, and cold to extinction in winter, whose passengers were packed in close proximity to each other and in the greatest discomfort. In the sentiment which hangs round the past we think only of the old coach, with its good team and smart-coated guard and coachman, who cracked their whip and blew their horn as it rattled over the stones of the widely separated towns, and drew up, hot and dusty, to have the steaming horses unharnessed and a fresh, spanking team put in their place. This was the one event of the day in many places on the main road; but to those who lived in the outlying districts, not even this excitement varied the monotony of their life. There were no newspapers, no penny posts; the genii of electricity had not developed the telegraph, and the world outside the large towns lived calm, quiet, even lives, with nothing beyond the local gossip to vary their existence. People were born, married, died, and never dreamed of leaving the village to which they belonged; and this was the life of every class in England, except the aristocracy or a few rich commoners, who were able to afford the luxury of a few weeks' stay in London or in the principal town of the county in which they lived. There was formerly a county Society, which was, however, limited exclusively to the locality; in towns like York, Bath, Exeter, Carlisle, Chester, and others in the Midlands there was, during the winter, a good deal of gaiety, and the great potentates came into the town, occupying their houses and dispensing hospitality. Bath, Cheltenham, and Leamington were also great centres of Society, for they possessed the double recommendation of being health resorts, and were very popular. But all this was the sole privilege of the rich, for the expense of living made it prohibitive to the poor or the professional classes.

When a nobleman went to London he was the leader of a huge cavalcade. His wife and children travelled with him in chariots, each often drawn by four horses; while his servants followed in carriages and carts, which tested the resources of the largest stable. The accounts of a Scotch family are still in existence detailing the cost of transit of a large household to London in 1816, which show that it cost over £800, and now the modest sum of three guineas enables a traveller to cover the same distance.

In 1825, when the first train ran from Stockton to Darlington, the greatest social revolution of the century began. It was not unattended with fear and misgiving; for the dangers of railway-travelling were viewed by the community as so great that many and evil were the prophecies as to its future. It is wonderful to look back now on that short railway journey and to realise into what it has grown and what the effect has been on our country. With the gradual growth of railway communication, every part of the kingdom has been brought into touch, and news which reaches London is transmitted within a few moments to the farthest part of Great Britain. We are now contemplating the result; and when we compare the past with the present it seems impossible to believe that any greater changes are impending. There will be developments, and possibly some of the theories of life which many consider visionary may be reduced to practice; but that any sweeping alterations from our present existence are likely to happen seems very improbable.

The changes of the last century have affected every class of the community, but they have had a wider influence on women than on any other; and as the influence of women today is supreme, and many of them hold opinions on social subjects which are not shared by the majority of their sex, they may endeavour to carry their projects and ideas into execution. It would be rash to prophesy failure, for after the experience of what changes the last fifty years have worked in the lives of women, it is possible that they may succeed in carrying out some of the innovations which many of them advocate. The independence of women seems almost absolute; and the freedom they enjoy, both as regards their career and everyday life, leaves little more for them to desire. There is now no limit to their professions and amusements, no restraint on their occupations, and no need exists for the safeguards of the past; while the camaraderie which exists between the sexes has abolished the necessity for any supervision or control.

It seems difficult to foretell what, if any, changes are likely to come in other directions. We seem to have reached the acme of luxury, enjoyment, and pleasure. In all matters pertaining to our everyday life there is a spirit of self-indulgence: we dress expensively, we live extravagantly, and our life is a pursuit of pleasure and amusement. With this qualification, however, it must be admitted that there is also a sense of responsibility, a deep feeling of charity, and a fervent desire to mitigate the sufferings of the poor. The luxury and extravagance which we see on all sides have stimulated the sentiment of humanitarianism, which is a strong characteristic of our day, and we witness the unusual spectacle of these two extremes meeting and co-operating on this one point. It is easy enough to inveigh against the riches, luxury, and ease of our time, to devise remedies for the destruction of the causes which pessimists declare are sapping our manhood and our moral sense, and to picture a new life in which we shall go back to the Spartan simplicity of the past. Such remedies are useless in combatting a state of Society which is brought about by the increase of wealth and the existence of a class richer and more powerful than any that has hitherto existed. The great fortunes of England are nothing in comparison to those of America; but whether our millionaires are English, South African, of American descent, or Jews, they are too powerful to be deposed, and they have done too much for the country of their adoption to be regarded with any feelings but those of gratitude.

The most important factor in the social life of the new century is the beginning of a new reign, and it is one which must exercise a great influence over a certain section of Society. The withdrawal of the late Queen from all social duties was mitigated by the example of devotion which she showed in her life of work and labour for her people. The loss of the Prince Consort to a woman in the position of Queen was a heavier loss than to one in a more lowly position of life. He relieved her of much work that was routine yet necessary; he undertook the organisation and supervision of the Royal Household; while in the graver and more important questions of her life his wisdom and devotion were of indescribable importance. The blow which fell with unsuspected suddenness on a warmhearted, impressionable woman with a highly strung nervous organisation like the last Queen's completely paralysed her; while her renunciation of the social part of her life deprived her of the personal influence which a sovereign enjoys who lives in touch with and in daily sight of his subject. The pathos and isolation of Queen Victoria's life deeply affected the country, for it understood, and sympathised with, her to the fullest extent, but it weakened her influence in an important direction.

There are some who believe that, considering the social changes which were impending, the late Queen did wisely in not again entering into the world and resuming her position as head of Society, and that in her position of isolation she exercised a stronger restraining influence on the new mode of life. That opinion must always remain conjectural, for at one period in her reign there was a strongly adverse feeling. That her people, however, never really misjudged her, but appreciated and admired her in a deeply passionate way, the last years of her reign conclusively proved.

It therefore followed, in the absence of the Queen, that from the time of their marriage and establishment at Marlborough House, the Prince and Princess of Wales became the accepted leaders of Society, though in a position which lacked the real authority of a sovereign.

It is not necessary to recapitulate the social changes of the forty years which nearly embrace the period which has elapsed since the day on which the beautiful Danish Princess took all our hearts by storm. Those years have seen an increase of wealth, a growth in Society of greater luxury, and a standard of living more lavish than any that has preceded it. The facilities of travelling have brought everyone to London, which has become the great centre of the world. The breakdown of the Imperial power in France and the nomadic habits of the American people have also tended to place London in the position once occupied by France; while the cosmopolitanism of to-day has made English Society welcome everyone of distinction and even notoriety. There is no modern Society, nor, indeed, has there ever existed any into which every class, every shade of opinion, and every profession have been admitted and welcomed as in England. The qualifications are not severe, nor is the standard unattainable. But Society, if not exclusive, is entertaining, from the variety of the elements of which it is composed, and which have been welded together by a variety of influences impossible of combination in any country but our own. The difference between it and that of 1837 – when Queen Victoria began her reign – is its rapid growth and enormous size, for Society in 1837 was a small clique composed of the powerful and wealthy families of two great aristocratic and political factions. The Whigs and Tories divided Society between them; and though the doors had been opened for the admission of other elements by the passing of the Reform Bill, no one, so to speak, belonging to the new order had passed its threshold. No one in trade or business was in Society, the literary world was just recognised, but neither the artistic nor dramatic world had found a footing there.

The middle-class men of the Liberal party had begun to exact their reward, and were received at the houses of the great political leaders; but that recognition had not then been extended to their womenkind, though it was not long withheld. Political claims have long ceased to constitute the sole right to social advancement, for the power of the purse has swept them aside.

The effect of a real Court on such a condition of Society will be interesting to observe. How far the hospitalities of Marlborough House will be renewed and carried on in Buckingham Palace remains to be seen. The residence of a Court in London, with its brilliant entourage, must have a beneficial effect on trade; and a revival of the gaieties and entertainments of the early part of the reign of Queen Victoria which an era of Royal hospitality and splendour must produce will give an impetus to production and revive many dormant industries. In all directions a Court will be welcomed, and it will be a boon to the workers who live on the amusements and luxuries of the rich. There will be Court balls and concerts, as well as the unusual spectacle of the King and Queen often driving in state through the streets of London; while the endless incidents which grow out of the revival of a Royal residence in the metropolis will add to the satisfaction and pride with which English people regard all such pageantry.

It is always the fashion to prophesy that sweeping changes must necessarily follow an important event like the beginning of a new reign, to imagine that the influences and interests which arise from its occurrence must be entirely novel and unexpected, and that in consequence all that has hitherto existed will be swept away and a completely new state of things arise. Nothing is more erroneous than such a supposition; for in a country so really Conservative as England, with its long-conceived theories and strongly rooted ways of life, the results of any event, however important, are more or less ephemeral. The people who compose what is generally spoken of as Society will see whatever may be the immediate consequences of such an event, but they are in reality so small a portion of what constitutes English Society that they have little or no influence on the great mass of people who live outside it. Those who represent what is called Society – namely, the people belonging to a certain set in London – who, while representing the highest and best-born classes, are but a fraction of the larger numbers who live there, making their home and finding their interests and amusements in it, – how few of these are affected by the fact that there is a King and Queen at Buckingham Palace! – nor are their lives altered or influenced by the gaieties which a Court brings in its train. They will not be invited to any Court functions, and in no way will it affect them. They have been their own amusements, their own occupations, and but that from time to time, some fortunate member of the society may make a fortune and so rise out of his humble to a more-exalted sphere, they will be unconscious of any change.

The size of London Society has become such that, with the exception of a comparatively small portion, the new reign will affect it but little. If we take the area in London inhabited by what we call Society, and measure it roughly by Oxford Street on the north, the House of Commons on the south, Alexandra Gate to the South Kensington Museum on the west, and Regent Street on the east, we easily realise how small a portion of that huge town is comprised in it. Outside that area are streets and squares of large houses inhabited by rich and well-to-do people, who are neither seen nor known by – and never go into what the papers call – Society. The inhabitants of the vast districts of Kensington, Bayswater, and Bloomsbury are those who fill the theatres, concert-rooms, and picture-galleries, who crowd the Church Parade; and yet how many of them go to Court or are ever likely to do so? and in what way are they likely to be influenced or affected by the new reign or any of the changes which may grow out of it? They will crowd the street and places from which the ceremonies of the Coronation can be seen; they will illuminate their houses; and then they will return to their life and amusements as if nothing had happened to disturb them.

The people on whom the influence of the new reign will fall will be that section known as 'Society,' and as it is parrot like in its adherence to the example set by those who lead it, it must be deeply influenced by its advent. Whatever the *met d'ordre* be, they will follow. If it be one in which the standard is high and what goes for economy, simplicity, and a higher rule of life, it will be welcomed by all who desire the welfare of their country and who feel that the present moment is a critical one in her future.

'What May Happen In The Next Hundred Years,' John Elfreth Watkins, Jr., *Christmas Ladies' Home Journal* (Philadelphia), December, 1900, p. 8

These prophecies will seem strange, almost impossible. Yet they have come from the most learned and conservative minds in America. To the wisest and most careful men in our greatest institutions of science and learning I have gone, asking each in his turn to forecast for me what, in his opinion, will have been wrought in his own field of investigation before the dawn of 2001 – a century from now. These opinions I have carefully transcribed.

America with Five Hundred Million People. There will probably be from 350,000,000 to 500,000,000 people in America and its possessions by the lapse of another century. Nicaragua will ask for admission to our Union after the completion of the great canal. Mexico will be next. Europe, seeking more territory to the south of us, will cause many South and Central American republics to be voted into the Union by their own people.

The American will be Taller by from one to two inches. His increase of stature will result from better health, due to vast reforms in medicine, sanitation, food and athletics. He will live fifty years instead of thirty-five as at present – for he will reside in the suburbs. The city house will practically be no more. Building in blocks will be illegal. The trip from suburban home to office will require a few minutes only. A penny will pay the fare.

There will be No C, X or Q in our every-day alphabet. They will be abandoned because unnecessary. Spelling by sound will have been adopted, first by the newspapers. English will be a language of condensed words expressing condensed ideas, and will be more extensively spoken than any other. Russian will rank second.

Hot and Cold Air from Spigots. Hot or cold air will be turned on from spigots to regulate the temperature of a house as we now turn on hot or cold water from spigots to regulate the temperature of the bath. Central plants will supply this cool air and heat to city houses in the same way as now our gas or electricity is furnished. Rising early to build the furnace fire will be a task of the olden times. Homes will have no chimneys, because no smoke will be created within their walls.

No Mosquitoes nor Flies. Insect screens will be unnecessary. Mosquitoes, house-flies and roaches will have been practically exterminated. Boards of health will have destroyed all mosquito haunts and breeding-grounds, drained all stagnant pools, filled in all swamp-lands, and chemically treated all still-water streams. The extermination of the horse and its stable will reduce the house-fly.

Ready-Cooked Meals will be Bought from establishments similar to our bakeries of today. They will purchase materials in tremendous wholesale quantities and sell the cooked foods at a price much lower than the cost of individual cooking. Food will be served hot or cold to individual houses in pneumatic or automobile wagons. The meal being over, the dishes used will be packed and returned to the cooking establishments where they will be washed. Such wholesale cookery will be done in electric laboratories rather than in kitchens. These laboratories will be equipped with electric stoves, and all sorts of electric devices, such as coffee-grinders, egg-beaters, stirrers, shakers, parers, meat-choppers, meat-saws, potato-mashers, lemon-squeezers, dish-washers, dish-dryers and the like. All such utensils will be washed in chemicals fatal to disease microbes. Having one's own cook and purchasing one's own food will be an extravagance.

No Foods will be Exposed. Storekeepers who expose food to air breathed out by patrons or to the atmosphere of the busy streets will be arrested with those who sell stale or adulterated products. Liquid-air refrigerators will keep great quantities of food fresh for long intervals.

Coal will Not be Used for Heating or Cooking. It will be scarce, but not entirely exhausted. The earth's hard coal will last until the year 2050 or 2100; its soft-coal mines until 2200 or 2300. Meanwhile both kinds of coal will have become more and more expensive. Man will have found electricity manufacture by water-power to be much cheaper. Every river or creek with any suitable fall will be equipped with water-motors, turning dynamos, making electricity. Along the seacoast will be numerous reservoirs continually filled by waves and tides washing in. Out of these the water will be constantly falling over revolving wheels. All of our restless waters, fresh and salt, will thus be harnessed to do the work which Niagara is doing to-day: making electricity for heat, light and fuel.

There will be No Street Cars in Our Large Cities. All hurry traffic will be below or high above ground when brought within city limits. In most cities it will be confined to broad subways or tunnels, well lighted and well ventilated, or to high trestles with "moving-sidewalk" stairways leading to the top. These underground or overhead streets will teem with capacious automobile passenger coaches and freight wagons, with cushioned wheels. Subways or trestles will be reserved for express trains. Cities, therefore, will be free from all noises.

Trains One Hundred and Fifty Miles an Hour. Trains will run two miles a minute, normally; express trains one hundred and fifty miles an hour. To go from New York to San Francisco will take a day and a night by fast express. There will be cigar-shaped electric locomotives hauling long trains of cars. Cars will, like houses, be artificially cooled. Along the railroads there will be no smoke, no cinders, because coal will neither be carried nor burned. There will be no stops for water. Passengers will travel through hot or dusty country regions with windows down.

Automobiles will be Cheaper than Horses are To-Day. Farmers will own automobile hay-wagons, automobile truck-wagons, ploughs, harrows and hay-rakes. A one-pound motor in one of these vehicles will do the work of a pair of horses or more. Children will ride in automobile sleighs in winter. Automobiles will have been substituted for every horse vehicle now known. There will be, as already exist to-day, automobile hearses, automobile police patrols, automobile ambulances, automobile street sweepers. The horse in harness will be as scarce, if, indeed, not even scarcer, than as the yoked ox is to-day.

Store Purchases by Tube. Pneumatic tubes, instead of store wagons, will collect, deliver and transport mail over certain distances, perhaps for hundreds of miles. They will at first connect with the private houses of the wealthy; then with all homes. Great business establishments will extend them to stations, similar to our branch post-offices of to-day, whence fast automobile vehicles will distribute purchases from house to house.

To England in Two Days. Fast electric ships, crossing the ocean at more than a mile a minute, will go from New York to Liverpool in two days. The bodies of these ships will be built upon the waves. They will be supported upon runners, somewhat like those of the sleigh. These runners will be very buoyant. Upon their undersides will be apertures expelling jets of air. In this way a film of air will be kept between them and the water's surface. This film, together with the small surface of the runners, will reduce friction against the waves to the smallest possible degree. Propellers turned by electricity will screw themselves through both the water beneath and the air above. Ships with cabins artificially cooled will be entirely fire-proof. In storm they will dive below the water and there await fair weather.

There will be Air-Ships, but they will not successfully compete with surface land and water vessels for passenger or freight traffic. They will be maintained as deadly war-vessels by all military nations. Some will transport men and goods. Others will be used by scientists making observations at great heights above the earth.

Aerial War-Ships and Forts on Wheels. Giant guns will shoot twenty-five miles or more, and will hurl anywhere within such a radius shells exploding and destroying whole cities. Such guns will be aimed by aid of compasses when used on land or sea, and telescopes when directed from great heights. Fleets of air-ships, hiding themselves with dense, smokey mists, thrown off by themselves as they move, will float over cities, fortifications, camps or fleets. They will surprise foes below by hurling upon them deadly thunderbolts. These aerial war-ships will necessitate bomb-proof forts, protected by great steel plates over their tops as well as at their sides. Huge forts on wheels will dash across open spaces at the speed of express trains of to-day. They will make what are now known as cavalry charges. Great automobile ploughs will dig deep entrenchments as fast as soldiers can occupy them. Rifles will use silent cartridges. Submarine boats submerged for days will be capable of wiping a whole navy off the face of the deep. Balloons and flying machines will carry telescopes of one-hundred-mile vision with camera attachments, photographing an enemy within that radius. These photographs, as distinct and large as if taken from across the street, will be lowered to the commanding officer in charge of troops below.

Man will See Around the World. Persons and things of all kinds will be brought within focus of cameras connected electrically with screens at opposite ends of circuits, thousands of miles at a span. American audiences in their theatres will view upon huge curtains before them the coronations of kings in Europe or the progress of battles in the Orient. The instrument bringing these distant scenes to the very doors of people will be connected with a giant telephone apparatus transmitting each incidental sound in its appropriate place. Thus the guns of a distant battle will be heard to boom when seen to blaze, and thus the lips of a remote actor or singer will be heard to utter words or music when seen to move.

Telephones Around the World. Wireless telephone and telegraph circuits will span the world. A husband in the middle of the Atlantic will be able to converse with his wife sitting in her boudoir in Chicago. We will be able to telephone to China quite as readily as we now talk from New York to Brooklyn. By an automatic signal they will connect with any circuit in their locality without the intervention of a 'hello girl.'

Photographs will be Telegraphed from any Distance. If there be a battle in China a hundred years hence snapshots of its most striking events will be published in the newspapers an hour later. Even to-day photographs are being telegraphed over short distances. Photographs will reproduce all of Nature's colors.

Grand Opera will be Telephoned to private homes, and will sound as harmonious as though enjoyed from a theatre box. Automatic instruments reproducing original airs exactly will bring the best music to the families of the untalented. Great musicians gathered in one inclosure in New York will, by manipulating electric keys, produce at the same time music from instruments arranged in theatres or halls in San Francisco or New Orleans, for instance. Thus will great bands and orchestras give long-distance concerts. In great cities there will be public opera-houses whose singers and musicians are paid from funds endowed by philanthropists and by the government. The piano will be capable of changing its tone from cheerful to sad. Many devices will add to the emotional effect of music.

How Children will be Taught. A university education will be free to every man and woman. Several great national universities will have been established. Children will study a simple English grammar adapted to simplified English, and not copied after Latin. Time will be saved by grouping like studies. Poor students will be given free board, free clothing and free books if ambitious and actually unable to meet their school and college expenses. Medical inspectors regularly visiting the public schools will furnish poor children free eyeglasses, free dentistry and free medical attention of every kind. The very poor will, when necessary, get free rides to and from school and free lunches between sessions. In vacation time poor children will be taken on trips to various parts of the world. Etiquette and housekeeping will be important studies in the public schools.

Everybody will Walk Ten Miles. Gymnastics will begin in the nursery, where toys and games will be designed to strengthen the muscles. It will be compulsory in the public schools. Every school, college and community will have a complete gymnasium. All cities will have public gymnasiums. A man or woman unable to walk ten miles at a stretch will be regarded as a weakling.

There will be No Wild Animals except in menageries. Rats and mice will have been exterminated. The horse will have become practically extinct. A few of high breed will be kept by the rich for racing, hunting and exercise. The automobile will have driven out the horse. Cattle and sheep will have no horns. They will be unable to run faster than the fattened hog of today. A century ago the wild hog could outrun a horse. Food animals will be bred to expend practically all of their life energy in producing meat, milk, wool and other by-products. Horns, bones, muscles and lungs will have been neglected.

Vegetables Grown by Electricity. Winter will be turned into summer and night into day by the farmer. In cold weather he will place heat-conducting electric wires under the soil of his garden and thus warm his growing plants. He will also grow large gardens under glass. At night his vegetables will be bathed in powerful electric light, serving, like sunlight, to hasten their growth. Electric currents applied to the soil will make valuable plants grow larger and faster, and will kill troublesome weeds. Rays of colored light will hasten the growth of many plants. Electricity applied to garden seeds will make them sprout and develop unusually early.

Oranges will Grow in Philadelphia. Fast-flying refrigerators on land and sea will bring delicious fruits from the tropics and southern temperate zone within a few days. The farmers of South America, South Africa, Australia and the South Sea Islands, whose seasons are directly opposite to ours, will thus supply in winter with fresh summer foods which cannot be grown here. Scientists will have discovered how to raise here many fruits now confined to much hotter or colder climates. Delicious oranges will be grown in the suburbs of Philadelphia. Cantaloups and other summer fruits will be so hardy that they can be stored through the winter as potatoes are now.

Strawberries as Large as Apples will be eaten by our great-great-grandchildren for their Christmas dinners a hundred years hence. Raspberries and blackberries will be as large. One will suffice for the fruit course of each person. Stawberries and cranberries will be grown upon tall bushes. Cranberries, gooseberries and currants will be as large as oranges. One cantaloup will supply an entire family. Melons, cherries, grapes, plums, apples, peaches and all berries will be seedless. Figs will be cultivated over the entire United States.

Peas as Large as Beets. Peas and beans will be as large as beets are to-day. Sugar cane will produce twice as much sugar as the sugar beet now does. Cane will once more be the chief source of our sugar supply. The milkweed will have been developed into a rubber plant. Cheap native rubber will be harvested by machinery all over this country. Plants will be made proof against disease microbes as readily as man is to-day against small-pox. Soil will be kept enriched by plants which take their nutrition from the air and give fertility to the earth.

Black, Blue and Green Roses. Roses will be as large as cabbage heads. Violets will grow to the size of orchids. A pansy will be as large in diameter as a sunflower. A century ago the pansy measured but half an inch across its face. There will be black, blue and green roses. It will be possible to grow any flower in any color and to transfer the perfume of a scented flower to another which is odorless. Then may the pansy be given the perfume of the violet.

Few Drugs will be Swallowed or taken into the stomach unless needed for the direct treatment of that organ itself. Drugs needed by the lungs, for instance, will be applied directly to those organs through the skin and flesh. They will be carried with the electric current applied without pain to the outside skin of the body. Microscopes will lay bare the vital organs, through the living flesh, of men and animals. The living body will to all medical purposes be transparent. Not only will it be possible for a physician to actually see a living, throbbing heart inside the chest, but he will be able to magnify and photograph any part of it. This work will be done with rays of invisible light.

'The Courtship of Lord Arthur Armstrong,' E.F. Benson: illustrated by Edmund J. Sullivan, *Gentlewoman Christmas Number* (London), 25 December 2000 [1900] p. 1–17

CHAPTER I

It was a warm, clear afternoon of early summer, and the sunshine which peered and filtered through the network of the innumerable cables and the lines and girders of the close-woven electric rails overhead, lay in ribands and patches of brilliant light on the crowded roadway. The streets were in full flood with their surging tides of women and men, and for the time being the noises more directly human quite overscored the hum and buzz of the myriad engines, locomotives and newsbearing, and the hiss of endless platforms which carried the crowds this way and that up and down the street was drowned in the babel of tongues from those who travelled thereon. To-day was the first of genuine summer weather, for spring had been hesitating and unclement, and to-day, for the first time since November, had the great furnaces which drove the hot sterilised air into the streets been allowed to go out, and, instead crowds lingered to catch a breath of freshness opposite the ventilating fans where, only yesterday, they had stood in order to warm themselves.

Year by year this natural, invigorating warmth of early spring makes the blood of a man to leap in his veins when first again he feels it after the sluggish passage of the winter months. However cunningly we heat our streets in the icy days, however temperately we cool them in the stress of a tropical July to the perfect mean, in spite of the utmost efforts of chemist and analyst, we cannot yet quite catch the fine quality of the air in these first days of definite summer. With her reasonable mind, a woman knows that down the great four-foot mains at every street corner pours air for which, in the matter of absolute chemical purity and freedom from microbes, you may hunt in vain on glacier or Pole, yet how many of us are there who, when first the true breath of summer pierces overhead lines and cables, and the yellow sunshine of our smokeless London lies like patches of primroses on the streets, are off for an hour or two, shamefacedly it may be, but with an instinct that will not be denied, to ruined towns of the Sussex seaboard, or to the daisy fields of Hampshire! Perhaps it is some curious survival of heredity which may account for this, traceable to the day when London was a town over which, as we see in the fast-fading canvases of the 19th century masters, there ever hung a yellow pall of fog and smoke, when every breath man drew was to inhale for certainty a hundred murderous microbes, when, as August drew near, as we read in authors of that date, 'all London' flew from the reeking and pestilential atmosphere to the purer air of seaside or moor. How strange that seems to us; London empty, a dead city for a couple of months every year! But whether it is heredity, the mother of every habit and inclination, which prompts our flitting, or not, the comparative emptiness of our streets on the first day of summer may be conceded as a fact, for it would be hard to find a woman or a man who has not observed it.

In this point, then, the day of which we speak was a notable exception to the rule. Summer had come, yesterday summer had not come, yet never had the streets been fuller or more busy. Something, it would seem, of sufficient moment to wean the citizens from their yearly hour by the seaside had happened, or rather, to judge by the crowds which thronged the news-boards at the street corners, and the size of type employed on what the news-boards recorded, was still happening. For the eyes of the crowds were fixed intently on the words as they were spelled out, and each line of print as it appeared evoked a murmur which sometimes rose to a roar; clearly the matter on which so many were curious was even now taking place.

Opposite the board in front of Burlington House was drawn up a motor of the very latest building and design. The whole framework of it was aluminium, it ran tricycle fashion on two huge spider-web wheels, with a small guider in front, and four pairs of sensitive antennae, the patent for which had only been taken out a month ago, protected it in front and behind, causing it automatically to alter its course if any other motor was approaching in the same line. Now, as it stood at rest, the antennae drooped like the leaves of a disturbed sensitive plant, but at this moment one of the women who sat inside touched the starting-lever, and, gathering speed, it rushed down Piccadilly in the direction of Charing Cross, its whistle getting shriller as the speed increased, with antennae alert and quivering.

The driver turned to the companion who sat beside her, a girl a little more than twenty.

'Really, Beatrice is a very bold woman,' she said. 'She told me confidentially, a month ago, that the Government contemplated something of the kind, and of course the subject has been in the air for four or five years. But I never thought they would actually attempt to pass it this year. Personally I don't believe they can, in which case out they go. The whole of the athlete class will be against them; they can't have squared them. Of course, sooner or later, the disenfranchisement of men must come, but I doubt, oh! I gravely doubt, whether we are ripe for it yet.'

'Well, I know nothing about politics,' said the girl, 'but I would back Beatrice in this, just as I would back her in anything she seriously took in hand. How clever, too, the time she has chosen for it. The House adjourns to-morrow for the Derby week. Well, if Beatrice's motor wins the Derby she will be just head and shoulders more popular than any woman in England. She is the most brilliant figure we have, and brilliance is the one quality we all respect.'

'And if her motor does not win the Derby!' asked Mrs. Torrington.

'I beg your pardon for saying "if it does." I ought to have said "when it has." My dear woman, such a thing has never been known before, a motor starting for the Derby at evens on. And accidents do not happen to well-regulated motors, and quite certainly they do not happen to Beatrice. I was down at her stables yesterday, and timed it as it was having a spin. Well, I can tell you it can take that hill as fast as yours can go on the flat; and it steers like a fish in and out of weeds. Flick! flick!'

Mrs. Torrington, prompted, it may be, by some half-conscious feeling of pique, pressed the lever over to full speed, and the girl, feeling the vastly increased motion, laughed aloud.

'But it can take corners also better than yours,' she said. 'Don't go that pace, Alice. How full town is! Really, I did not mean any reflection on your machine, which I think is delightful. The antennae seem to answer with extraordinary rapidity.'

Mrs. Torrington laughed also, and checked the speed.

'I put it on unconsciously,' she said. 'But when shall we get a racing track in London? Yes, the antennae do answer well. But, Evie, do you feel as certain about the Derby as that? I know there isn't in London a better judge of a motor than you, but think! Beatrice is going to drive herself – she told me so. Now, excellent driver as she is, she cannot help having this Bill on her mind. Will she be at her best?'

2 'The Debate in the House on the Bill for the Disenfranchisement of Men'

'The more she has on her mind,' said Evie Grimston, 'the better she does it all. If she wasn't the owner of the finest motor stable in England, and the Prime Minister, and – oh, well, never mind that – she would soon get as slack and desultory as a man. It is responsibility and work and interest which make her what she is. Oh, there's some more news! Just stop, there's a dear. What is it? "In answer to a telephonic question from the American Opposition, Miss Beatrice Chevening announced that the first reading of the Bill for the total disenfranchisement of men would take place on the 10th of June." Yes, you will see; that is the first business, then, after the adjournment. She will speak on that day, I suppose.'

They drove on slowly for a little way in silence. Then said Mrs. Torrington:

'You were saying just now, Evie, that it was work and responsibility which made Beatrice what she is – owner of the finest stables, Prime Minister, and – and then you stopped. What were you going to say?'

Evie Grimston did not at once answer.

'Nothing,' she said at length. 'A piece of gossip merely.'

'Can I guess what it was?'

'Probably, but I would rather you did not. Oh, I don't know that it matters.'

'There is no reason why we should not discuss it,' said Mrs. Torrington, 'since everybody else is doing so. We all know how busy Beatrice's head is; you were wondering whether her heart is not equally so.'

'Yes, that is what was in my mind,' said Evie. 'Now tell me – you are a friend of hers – can this rumour be possibly true?'

'I can't say. Beatrice is not a woman who shows even to her most intimate friends that which concerns herself only. It is true she is largely public, but I fancy there is a very big piece marked "private," and she does not tolerate trespassers. A priori, I should not have thought she was the kind of woman to marry at all. Half the fathers in London have been trying to catch her for their sons for the last six years, and there isn't an eligible young man in London who hasn't tried to catch her on his own account; but they have all failed so conspicuously that one has tended to put her down as a woman who will not marry.'

'Then would you contradict this rumour?'

'The only thing about Beatrice that I should ever contradict is if I was told that she had done something mean,' said Mrs. Torrington. 'That is the only thing of which I feel sure she is incapable. All the same, it does seem incredible that she should be thinking of marrying one of the old aristocracy. What is the man's name? Lord Arthur Armstrong, is it not?'

'Yes: the second son of the Duke of Ireland. Of course, it is not the man's fault that he has been born into that class. He can't help it. But there he is. Nor would it have been his fault if he had been born with four or five mouths and no nose, yet that, no less than the other, would be a very good reason for not marrying him. All the same he is an athlete, one of the first in the country, and a man who is that may hope to lift himself out of the titled class, just as a century ago a man who really had brains could lift himself into it. Really, the Victorian period is the most fascinating to study. All the forms of the old civilisation, or barbarism you may call it, are retained, but there underlies it a great deal of the spirit of the new age.'

'What do you mean?' asked Mrs. Torrington.

'Really, Alice, you ought to be better up in recent history. Personally, I have just taken that age up for my Fellowship at Oxford. It is the greatest mistake only to study the big eras, and leave out the intermediate and apparently unimportant years. It would be far more reasonable to study the intermediate times, and infer from them, as you would be able to do, the great eras that followed. For instance, if you knew the Victorian times well, you could easily deduce our own day. Oh! in a way they were great; they were the smooth, quiet-looking egg out of which to-day was hatched.'

'A Russian war,' said Mrs. Torrington, 'an Indian mutiny, a South African war, the partition of China; those were the only events. I know them as well as you, in spite of your Fellowship. But, socially speaking, as regards the great revolution which has taken place since, I don't see that the Victorian times have anything to do with ours. Oh! there was a sort of New Woman movement, it is true. I read quite a quantity of contemporary literature about it the other day. Women apparently took to smoking cigarettes and travelling third class. But it doesn't appear to have led to anything in particular. In fact, the movement disappears after a time like a stream in the desert.'

Evie Grimston laughed.

'How like you,' she cried. 'How exactly like you! I do not believe there is a woman in England except you, the State historian, who would think of going to contemporary literature for a picture of the times. What a hopeless quest. It is not we who know what our own age is, it is the succeeding age only who can form a real idea of it. It has to be focussed, like looking through a telescope, before you can judge it. Does the battery which supplies your carriage know about electricity? Certainly not; it is the carriage which is sent along by it which knows what electricity is. In the same way it is we who should be able to form an adequate idea of the Victorian age. Contemporary writers know nothing about it.'

Mrs. Torrington laughed at the vivid and shallow paradoxes.

'Well then, you authority on the Derby and the Victorian age, be far less discursive,' she said. 'Come back and toe the line. You said just now that in Victorian times all the marks of the old civilisation were preserved, and that much of the spirit of the new underlay it. At any rate, your words were to that effect.'

'Yes, that is a fair statement of what I meant, and I was talking of the way in which a man with brains might lift himself into the aristocracy, comparing it with the way in which now a man with muscles may lift himself out of it. Brains, you will allow, are getting rarer now. That is why we make so much of our athletes; the demand is greater than the supply. In Victorian days a man with wits used to make beer, or tea, or something, and as soon as he had made enough they ennobled him: that is the first point: the old titles, baron, earl, marquis, were retained, but they were not given on the principles on which Richard Coeur-de-Lion gave them. The old form was retained, but the honours were for successful mercantile transactions. Do you see?'

'Well?'

'Nowadays a man has only to get his county colours at football or golf to stand a good chance of marrying into the upper class, the class with brains and power, our class, the class the Victorians called the middle class. Now, utterly unlike as these two processes sound, you will find exactly the same principle underlying them. We are both bolstering up our upper class. Nowadays they have brains, and our efforts are directed to giving them muscles. In the same way in Victorian days the royal and aristocratic classes waited with trembling avidity for any of the middle class to show himself a man of brains and ability, and forthwith they hoisted him into the upper class. That shows a certain shrewdness. They were constantly fortifying their upper class with the best brains of the middle class, the class that even then they saw must soon be predominant.'

'Their shrewdness did not have exactly the effect they desired,' remarked Mrs. Torrington, drily.

'No; they overdid it,' said Evie, 'and the middle class took the bit between its teeth, as the Victorians used to say. Titles became too common, and thus nobody wanted them. Again, so many men in those days as soon as they got their titles ceased to do any work at all, and lived with their coronets, so to speak. There sounds the note of mortality! A man – you will correct me if I am wrong – before he was made a peer had to settle so much a year, on his death, on his eldest son. What an extraordinary blunder of policy on the part of those who wished to bolster up the aristocracy! They only thought of keeping up the dignity, or so they called it, of their titled class, their powdered footmen, their dinners, their parties, and they never saw that this was striking a death blow at the vitality of the class. If only a new peer had been compelled to leave his eldest son absolutely penniless, there might have been some chance of the inheritors of the titles being fit for something. Instead, they almost made it necessary that they should be fit for nothing. The eldest son became a soldier, or a sailor, or a man about town, and it occurred to nobody that in a hundred years there would no longer be any army or navy.'

'Ah, that could not have been foreseen,' said Mrs. Torrington. 'Even forty years ago who could have told that America would have united again with England, and that when the five other Powers went to war with her, they faced a navy that was unfaceable? What happened? Famine in France, in Italy, in Germany, famine everywhere but in America and England. Nonesense, Evie, who could have foretold that?'

The girl laughed.

'You speak as if there was such a thing as foresight,' she said. 'Indeed, there is not. What you mean by foresight is simply the due appreciation and estimate of what has already happened. The coalition of England and America was years ago a logical necessity of the future. If I knew and could correctly estimate all that has happened on the earth to-day, I could tell you for certain all that will happen to-morrow. Prophecy is simply an affair of sound judgment based on knowledge. But to return to the point. I don't know enough about either Beatrice or Lord Arthur to say whether she will marry him. And, what is far more important, I don't know what will happen to her Bill for the disenfranchisement of men if she does.'

Her companion pulled up, for the self-closing traffic gates at the bottom of Northumberland Avenue were against them.

'How do you mean exactly?' she asked.

'I mean this. Beatrice with one hand, so to speak, tears up man's franchise, the other she offers to a man. Now that does not make a good picture. A woman who disenfranchises men ought not to recognise their existence at all. That is the more consistent attitude.'

'Ah, you make a mistake,' said Mrs. Torrington. 'She only refuses to recognise them as a political factor. During all the years in which women had not the franchise politicians were not necessarily celibate. Besides,' she added, hesitating a moment, 'there may be far more behind her marriage than you allow for.'

'What more can that be?' asked Evie.

'My dear girl, is it possible that you do not see what Beatrice may be driving at? No, not driving at: it is too strong a word; but do you not see what a wonderful opportunity her falling in love with this aristocrat gives her? Her bill for the disenfranchisement of men comes on after the Derby, you tell me, you who know, that she is certain to win. If she wins, driving herself on that difficult course, she will propitiate half the aristocracy, and if after her victory she marries one of the foremost athletocrats, aristocrat that he be . . .'

'He went round Mitcham in sixty-eight this morning,' said Evie in parenthesis.

'Sixty-eight, good gracious! Well, if she marries him, or is known to be engaged to him, she will carry with her three-quarters of the athletocracy. Now they are the class who may, and I believe do have it in their power to wreck this bill. But they will vote for any proposal that the winner of the Derby and the *fiancée* of Arthur Armstrong chooses to make. That is the way a really clever woman works, she makes all she does pull in one direction.'

Evie considered this a moment in silence, then shook her head.

'No, you are ingenious but astray.' she said. 'Personally I only just know Beatrice Chevening; you are her best friend, and so in a way I know her better than you . . .'

'You may explain as you go on,' remarked Mrs. Torrington.

'Surely it needs no explanation. She dazzles all those who know her well, like you, and the woman in the street . . . I, that is . . . probably forms a juster estimate of her. Now I do not believe she is like that. She would not for the sake of her ambitions, or for any other sake, make so sorry a plaything of a man. She would not be engaged to Lord Arthur for the sake of catching the athletocratic vote. She has a low opinion of men from a political standpoint, I grant you that, for otherwise she would not stand godmother to the bill of their disenfranchisement, but she is not the kind of woman to propose to a man for any reason except that she loves him. It is here you make your mistake; for you think of her as the most advanced product of the human race, but in some ways she is the most old-fashioned. Now you married Torrington for his money; he was the only child, and he had a good temper. You have often told me that it is impossible for a husband to have more than those two good points. Personally I applaud you; I am modern too. But Beatrice would never have done that.'

'She doesn't need to: she is well off.'

'That is feeble, dear. Yes, politically it would be a master-stroke to marry him, and it would more than counterbalance the *mésalliance*, which in itself would be deplorable. As you say, she would capture the whole of the athletocratic vote. But if she marries him I do not believe that she will do it for that reason.'

They had drawn up on the Victoria Embankment, close to the weather-worn spike of stone which archaeologists are for ever trying to prove was once the so-called Cleopatra's Needle. On their left ran the glorious river, clear and sparkling in the succession of pool, rapid and shallow. Half a hundred salmon-fishers, women for the most part, but with a certain sprinkling of men among them, were casting their lines over the string of pools extending from Westminster round the bend of the stream at Charing Cross, and like a benignant genius the great aluminium statue of Sir Herbert Maxwell, the pioneer of the salmon-fishery of the Thames, seemed to smile encouragingly on their devotion. On their right ran the long lines of the felt-faced houses, with every window open to catch the cool breeze of sunset, and the steady throb of the ventilating fans made a soft pulsation in the rustled air. From time to time a crowd would gather to look at a horse driven down the street, and roll away again like spilt quicksilver at the hoot of an approaching express motor. Already at the cafés the tables were beginning to grow populous, and waiters hurried about with little dishes of steaming protein, boxes of meat capsules for the less leisurely who would swallow their food and be gone, and jugs of hot sterilised water scented with lemon or violet for those who were going to sit with friends and discuss the evening meal and the news together. A new capsule combining the nutritive qualites of fish and meat, had lately come out with the encomium of the state-analyst, and there were many this evening who called for it. Some would swallow it and pass; elsewhere the new food was the subject for maturer deliberation, and a woman after taking a couple of the capsules would sit and chat for ten minutes waiting for the appetite to declare its satisfaction. A revival of Wagner's 'Ring' was also on the boards of the opera house this week, and the motors of the curiously and archaeologically inclined were disgorging their passengers at the door of the state-house.

The curtain rose on an admirable performance. The actors had caught with wonderful correctness the note of *naïveté* which fitted the old-folk legend, while the phonographs were of wonderful timbre and fullness. Especially soothing and refreshing was the third act, the awakening of Brunnhilde, and the awakening of her straightforward unsophisticated love. It had all the tenderness and the purity of a summer dawn, and the audience, whose lives hurried along in the swift van of time, were insensibly charmed back to childhood by these fragments of early gentle days, when civilisation was still uncomplicated, and the large airs of rudimentary emotion still swept coolly over the yet unfevered race of man. Yet even in this old-fashioned drama a thoughtful and imaginative spectator might discern the seeds of the great revolution in the relations between the sexes which has been the notable feature of these last hundred years. The quaint old German master had, though unconsciously, foreshadowed this in the mastery of the woman over Siegfried, in the fiery quality of her love as compared with the slower burning passion of the man. Perhaps, even, so thought Evie, fantastically enough, the ring of flame in which Brunnhilde had been put to sleep symbolised this. For centuries woman had slept, the fire of her own nature playing round her, and at last she had awoke, dominant. Certainly, so it seemed to her, there was a pretty fitness in the presentation of this opera on the night on which the approaching disenfranchisement of man had been authoritatively announced. Like Brunnhilde, woman had awoke.

CHAPTER II

Park Lane is, with the exception of two or three monuments, such as the Hippodrome, which are maintained at the public cost, the only remaining portion of old Victorian London not pulled down at the rebuilding in 1960. It lies in that network of intricate streets which extends from Burlington House to the Albert Memorial, and it has a curious old-world air of its own. Scarce a house therein is more than four storeys in height; it is irregular and cottage-like in appearance, built of brick, of stucco, of brown stone, without symmetry of precision or plan; there is not a square foot of asbestic felt in the whole length of it, nor a single aluminium roof, yet somehow it has a quaintness and a charm, surrounded as it is and drowned, one may say, by the artisan dwellings which surround it and tower for twelve storeys above its topmost roofs. Yet poor Park Lane, stagnated backwater as it is, once commanded higher rents than perhaps any street in London. Here dwelt millionaires, brewers, railroad kings of America, dukes and marquises of our own obsolete aristocracy. Here once crawled the horse-carriages of those who

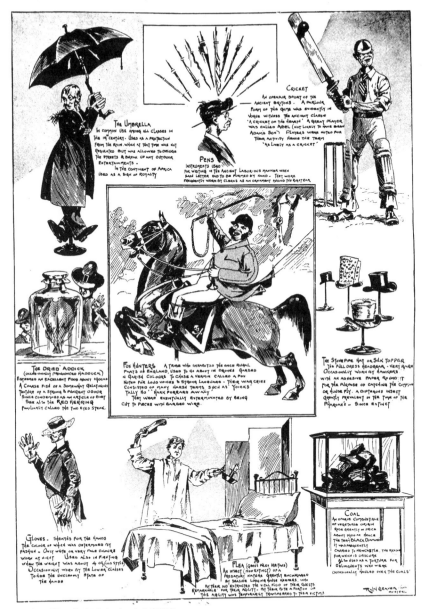

COMMON OBJECTS
OF THE YEAR 1900.

3 'Common Objects of the Year 1900'

were born at the helm of England, its Upper House of wealthy peers, its even wealthier commoners, and here night by night in those dead years, when men and women of the upper class used to sit over heavy dinners, swilling wine the while, for a couple of hours, and dance about ball-rooms in pairs together afterwards, would be heard the shiver of violins and the rhythmical throb of cellos, until smoky dawn looked in through the narrow curtained windows, and beheld rows of empty champagne bottles, and pails of half melted ices compacted of deadly cream or yet deadlier water, and flavoured with fruit picked by the hands of none knew who, and sent, as likely as not, uncooked, and perhaps unwashed, into the kitchens of these unhygienic hovels.

About half-way down Park Lane stands a house of somewhat more habitable aspect than the rest, built, we may suppose, some eighty years ago, and though nowadays not the most conservative of urban councils would pass a plan which showed so little window space, and was so full of inflammable material as its wooden doors and wooden window frames implied, yet from the paucity of its chimneys we might guess that it had been erected at a time when the old fashion of coal fires was beginning to die out. It belonged at the time which this story treats to the Duchess of Lincoln, a woman of good middle class birth and breeding, whose marriage into the very lowest class of the aristocracy had, some twenty years before, roused in London so great a storm of scandalous surmise. Not content with this, she had availed herself of the old custom, even then growing obsolete, and now illegal, of taking her husband's name instead of bestowing her own on him, and from a perversion, as it were, of independence, went to live in his house, this brown-stone hovel in Park Lane, and sold her own excellent flat on the twentieth storey of the Westminster Bridge Road mansions. It was but natural that many of her old friends gradually dropped her, for who could be expected to stretch friend-ship to such lengths as these? Others gave inevitable *sequelae* to her mistaken marriage, or else it was an instance of incredible impertinence, so it appeared to the recipients, that she continued to send her old friends cards of invitation to her phonograph or cinematograph parties. She was devoted to her husband and they had nine healthy children, all models of health and stupidity. Two of the boys, however, had already shown a great aptitude for golf, and one of the girls was a perfect fiend of precision at croquet.

These things, especially the probability of her family rising high in athleto-cratic circles, were sufficient to make their mother more than content; so also would her husband have been, had not an ulcer of snobbishness eaten deep into his heart. Born as he was in the very dregs of the aristocracy, his marriage was of almost romantic character, and the desire that ruled his life was to move at ease in the clear-brained, hard-working circles in which his wife had been born and bred, and it was partly through this alliance, partly by growing hope that three at least of his children would rise to real eminence in the world of athletics, that he looked forward to attaining his ambition. Yet the very fervour of his desire to be at ease in Zion left him ill at ease, and the mere vicinity of the happy men, and yet happier women, whose birthright it was to live by their brains, tended to produce in him a trembling and nervous utterance. It may be mentioned finally, with regard to the Duchess's marriage, which had caused so great a commotion among upper circles, that it was a love-match on both sides.

To-night the house was a blaze of lights, for the Duke held one of his 'at homes,' and by nine o'clock the drawing-rooms were already full of people who had elbowed their way up, and the stairs of those who had not yet succeeded in doing so. Athletocracy was bravely represented, and county football and golf colours were as numerous as the stars in heaven. Two internationals were there, dressed in shorts and jersey, with the lion thereon, and also the amateur golf champion of the year before, in knickerbockers and Norfolk jacket, on which were pinned not less than sixty or seventy medals, gold and silver.

Lord Arthur Armstrong, chaperoned by his father, had been among the first to arrive; he was an intimate here, and a great friend of the Duchess, who, leaving the duty of receiving to her husband, got ten minutes' chat with him. His score that day at Mitcham coupled with the thrilling rumours which had begun to circulate through London about Miss Chevening's great admiration for him, made him for the moment at least a man whom even the most exclusive would have been glad to see at their houses. But apart from this he was a young man of great personal charm, courteous in manner, agreeable in conversation, and of most prepossessing exterior. His chief defect, socially, so women found, was that he was a shade inclined to be reserved and stand-offish, and met the ordinary drawing-room advances in a way which the most self-satisfied man-killer could not interpret as encouraging. Also it was difficult, except for the tallest woman, to shout little compliments into his ear, which was some foot above the average height of his admirer's mouth.

He had been there some half hour, when the Duchess, taking advantage of a lull in the throng of arrivals, left her place at the top of the stairs, and came to where he was standing.

'Do let me take you to a seat, and talk to you for ten minutes, Lord Arthur,' she said. 'What a horrible squash, is it not: Lincoln insisted on asking everybody he had ever heard of and I asked everybody I had ever seen. So we are having a real sardine-time of it. Take my arm, won't you? You must know we are all envying you, you are the white elephant of the moment. How nice to be a White Elephant! Don't you find it charming? Really it was a wonderful score of yours at Mitcham. Tell me, what was the strong point of your game? Were you dead on the approach, or driving terrifically, or what?'

'Oh, things went right,' said he. 'But please excuse me Duchess. I have played every one of those sixty-eight strokes three times over since I got here. I almost wish I hadn't done it at all. But come to lunch tomorrow. There was a cinematograph on me the whole time, and they will send a copy in tomorrow morning, so you can see it all. But tonight, no. Besides I want to ask you a question or two.'

'Yes, I can come tomorrow,' said the Duchess, 'and I shall be delighted to. Wait a minute, though – no, it's only a county council affair, and I can leave early. Now, what are your questions?'

'Probably my questions are as stale to you as my golf is to me. At least if what I have heard is true, everyone in London must be talking for some hours about the subject, I mean, of course, this proposal for our disenfranchisement. Is it true then that Miss Chevening has pledged herself to introduce a bill for it directly after the Derby week?'

The Duchess gave him a quick look out of her black, rather bird-like eyes. Her nickname at the clubs was the Jackdaw, and certainly at this moment there was a brisk, shrewd inquisitiveness about her face that made the sobriquet very apt. This question bordered closely on a subject that interested her deeply.

'I should have thought it would have been you who was better fitted to pronounce on Miss Chevening's intentions,' she said.

Lord Arthur raised his eybrows, and treated the Duchess to a long and rather disconcerting stare.

'Why?' he asked.

'My dear Lord Arthur,' cried the Jackdaw, in some little confusion, 'you are very close friends, are you not, with Beatrice? You are constantly about together, and I, why I hardly ever see her now. You are much more likely to be able to answer any questions about her than I.'

'Am I to understand then that you do not know whether she has pledged herself to do this?' asked he.

'Oh, as for that, she said she was going to introduce the bill,' answered the Duchess. 'But who knows what that enigma will do?'

'But she made a public statement to that effect?'

'Certainly; it was on all the newsboards. But I half expect her here to-night. You can ask her all about it.'

'Please let one of your maids tell me when she comes,' said he.

'Why?'

'Because I do not wish to see her to-night.'

The Duchess stared in blank amazement.

'What do you mean?' she asked. 'Have you quarrelled with her, Lord Arthur? Come, I am a great friend; at least, I hope you so consider me, of yours, and I have known her all her life. What is the matter? Cannot I help in any way?'

'Many thanks, I am afraid not. But I wonder that you ask me if we have quarrelled.'

'But what has she done?' cried the Duchess, 'or what have you done? Do you mean' – and a sudden light struck her – 'do you mean the introduction of this bill?'

'What else should I mean?' asked he, rather hoarsely.

The Duchess lit a cigarette.

'I had no idea, indeed I had no idea that you felt about it like that,' she said. 'I could not conceive that you cared in any way or the other about that question.'

'Nor do I care about the question,' he said, hotly; 'but that she should have introduced it' – and he stopped suddenly, conscious that he had said more than he meant to say.

There was a moment's silence, which he broke by rising quickly from the alcove in which he and the Jackdaw were sitting.

'I need not tell you how entirely I trust you to keep this matter secret,' he said. 'My words were spoken without thought; indeed, I do not think they express what I really feel,' and without another word he turned away.

The Duchess rejoined her husband at the head of the stairs with her head in a whirl of excited perplexity and conjecture. Shrewd and sharp as she was, she had never dreamed of the possibility of such a complication, and lamented bitterly that her intimacy with the two actors prevented her putting the situation in her next Society novel. Anyone could see how much Lord Arthur admired Beatrice, how charming he found her, how brilliant the match was for him. Truly that entrancing riddle called man was yet far from solved, and the most extensive knowledge of the sex could never have deduced or forseen that if the marriage did not take place, it would be the man's undoing. Yet it was in things like these, things utterly unexpected and inconjecturable, that the charm of the sex lay. It was idle to attempt to follow the workings of a man's mind; it snowed on a midsummer day, it thundered from the blue; these things were unaccountable, and the reward of the study of man was simply the observation of such phenomena, not the attempt to reduce them to a law. Yet in this case she began by degrees to think that she could deduce the steps that led to the result, and as she somewhat absently shook hands with the crowd that came up her staircase her mind was busy over it. He did not care whether men had the franchise or not, he had said so himself, yet the fact that Beatrice had pledged herself to introduce the bill for its abolition bitterly affronted and offended him. Clearly then there was one explanation to cover the facts. He must be deeply, genuinely in love with her, for thus only would the thought that this woman should put the sex to which he belonged so low, should declare that it was unfit to take any part in the Government of the State, be distressing to him. His pride, that dim but imperishable part of man, was in revolt. Beatrice thought thus of men, and he was a man. How unreasonable and childish, but how curiously fascinating.

Lord Arthur meantime had wandered on through the congested rooms in a vague quest for his father, who was supposed to be chaperoning him. Soon there was a crowd of women round him, and he found himself discussing every subject under the sun with a sort of feverish gaiety which he knew was but false and hollow, but which served the purpose of the minute.

'Yes, that is Lord Hotspur,' he was saying, in answer to a question of his cousin, Lady Kitty Liverpool, 'the man with the suspiciously sunburnt face.'

'You don't mean to say he is painted?' asked she. 'How wonderfully done! I could never have told.'

'Surely it is obvious. Look, he is quite brown up to his hair. That can't be real. One's skin is always less tanned beneath one's cap. His shoulders are padded too, do you see? When he moves his arms, they go into soft creases, instead of hard lines. Those golf medals are not real either. Oh, an artificial man.'

'I rather like artifice, at least in a man,' said Lady Kitty. 'Most people are so distressingly real. But it is horrible when a woman makes herself up. Look at Lady Kent there, I'm sure those curls are not natural. Good gracious, how disgusting women who make up, are. Luckily that sort of thing is rare, for just now we are all doing our best to copy Miss Chevening, and certainly there is nothing artificial about her. She is almost brutally herself, mind and body alike. What do you think about this new bill?'

Lord Arthur laughed. His recklessness no longer needed any effort, it was becoming automatic.

'We ought to give her a testimonial,' he said. 'She has removed, or has at least pledged herself to try to remove, the last bar which stands between us and the delectable life. With one's vote gone, one will no longer have any excuse for a sense of duty towards anybody. The last shred of authority is to be taken away from us; for the future we shall feel no interest whatever in any question which concerns mankind as a whole. Disenfranchised! At last we shall be like animals again; that is the true evolution, we shall sleep and be fed, and have no longer any reason for worrying about anything under the sun.'

'You will like that?' asked his cousin.

'I shall revel in it. All my life women have been reminding me of the dignity and the glorious destiny of the human race, and bidding me act up to it. Well, it will be sheer puerility on their part if they continue to remind me of it any longer. A woman, the foremost of her sex, whom you all copy, as you told me just now, has pronounced that we are not fit to influence the destinies of the human race in any matter, large or small. We are to be released from all responsibility. For the future, when once this bill is passed, we shall be emancipated. We shall shrug our shoulders at all serious people and laugh in their faces. I do that a good deal now; I shall do it more then. Indeed, I do not see how I shall find time for anything else.'

Lady Kitty frowned; there was a cynical defiance in her cousin's words which was altogether unlike him, and at the same time belied their lightness.

'But the vote is a very small matter, Arthur,' she said. 'You still retain all that on which men's power really rests. Indeed, I should not wonder, now that men will be – pardon me – restricted to their proper sphere, that that power will be infinitely increased.'

Lord Arthur raised his eyebrows.

'What power do you mean?' he asked.

'All your real power. Your power over women, over the home, over the moral standard without which the world can neither progress nor exist.'

He laughed.

'Really, you are an ingenious woman,' he said, 'and I am sure you are persuaded that you are speaking quite straightforwardly. But to me it sounds a sophistical argument to say that, by taking away any little power we certainly have, you increase the power which personally I do not think we have got.'

'You think anything subtle is sophistical,' said she, 'and you have made a great mistake. Miss Chevening, I am sure, does not desire to extinguish men's power; she wants, rather, as I believe, to increase it by confining it to its proper channels.'

'You speak as if I were in need of consolation,' said Lord Arthur, 'as if I resented what Miss Chevening proposes to do. I have given you no grounds to suppose that. But to argue the question on your own lines, do you think it will increase the respect in which girls hold their fathers when they know that their mothers have just determined that they are unworthy to govern at all? Of course to all of you Miss Chevening appears as a sort of goddess with the wisdom of the original serpent added. But if she only knew how men will laugh at her! If she only knew how wonderfully shortsighted she has been!'

'Shortsighted?'

'Yes,' cried Lord Arthur, excitedly, 'shortsighted and stupid. Of course all women will worship and adore her for her bravery and her statecraft. But there are men as well in England. In time she may learn that. You say that the disenfranchisement will heighten the legitimate influence of men over women, over the home, over the moral standard. She has knocked away the supports by which the moral standard stood, I tell you. That is what she has done. She has told men that women as a body despise them, think them unworthy of a voice in national affairs. Now is that likely to help them to respect themselves? Good God, I have heard Miss Chevening spoken of as the great respecter of morals. I consider this bill likely to cause more immorality in a month than would otherwise have occurred in a year. "Get into your kennels," she has said to men.'

Lady Kitty rose as the crowd near them suddenly opened a lane.

'I am sorry if I have offended you,' she said. 'But I have nothing to do with this bill. Here comes a person more directly responsible.'

Right down the centre of the room, towards the sofa where they were sitting, advanced the Duke of Lincoln, leaning on the arm of Miss Chevening. He hardly knew what he was saying to her, or she to him, so excited and elated was he by the extraordinary honour she had done him in coming here. Five minutes ago he had hungered for the presence of any almost of her class: now he would scarcely have noticed the arrival of the whole House of Representatives. She was in full State dress, wearing the long trained, low-cut gown of an earlier age, which still, strangely enough, lingers among us, just as in Victorian days men used to attend a levée in the costume of a century before;

a collar of magnificent pearls was clasped round her neck; on her head, perched high in the dusky masses of her hair, she wore a great diamond star. Her manner, ever regal and commanding, had to-night the most winning touch; she talked to the Duke with all the deference due from a well-bred woman to a man, yet not a hint of condescension marked the difference of her class. She nodded and smiled right and left to the greeting of women whom she knew, stopped every now and then to shake hands with some man whom she had seen, perhaps, only once before, but whom her marvellous middle-class memory had never forgotten.

Lord Arthur had risen hastily when he saw her, and taking the arm of Lady Baringdale, who presented herself at this moment, went out through the far door of the room, past the phonograph stand hidden behind banks of artificial flowers, to the supper room, where the coloured sprays of iced carbolised water set against the walls made an aromatic coolness in the air. But in the doorway he could not help lingering to look just for one moment at that wonderful face and form, the beauty of which made his heart beat fast and thick. Yet when he was with her he hardly thought of it; she might have been a hunch-back, and yet her charm would have been unimpaired. And she of the imperial beauty, in the charm of her brilliant womanhood, had to-day only made known exactly how low she held men in her esteem. And the man looked at her in bitter revolt at the chain which bound him. Then he turned without meeting her eye and passed into the supper room.

Here chairs were set out in twos and threes round the revolving tables of labelled capsules, and neat waitresses hurried to and fro with trays of hot lithia water and tempting glasses of iron and sparkling quinine tonic.

'What will you have?' asked Lady Baringdale. 'I can recommend an iron and soda with just a dash of bromide in it. It is a wonderful thing if you have been out all day taking exercise, sustaining and at the same time slightly soothing.'

'Thanks, but I don't need either the one nor the other,' said he. 'Please get me just a protein biscuit and a glass of seltzer water. And, Lady Baringdale, you might just put a dash of whisky instead of the bromide.'

Lady Baringdale smiled.

'I know you like those old-fashioned drinks,' she said, and left him to go and struggle with the crowd at the bar. Being a firm, strong kind of a woman, she soon ploughed her way in, and in a very short time returned to him with refreshments.

'Did you see Beatrice Chevening?' she asked, after swallowing a fruit capsule in a glass of rather stiff lithia. 'I expect this is the first time she has been to Park Lane. And her coming to-night after her speech was really an extraordinary compliment to the Duke. And now tell me, Lord Arthur, exactly what you think about this bill.'

'I think she will very likely pass it,' said he.

'Ah, then, it is not true what I heard,' said she, inventing a rumour of which she had heard nothing whatever, 'that you were going to take up the cudgels for your sex. For you are the only man in the world who has the smallest influence with Beatrice.'

'And how small that influence is you may judge from the fact that she introduces the bill,' said he.

'That is interesting. Did she often talk to you about it?'

'We often used to discuss the position of man as it is and as it ought to be,' he replied. 'But perhaps,' and his bitterness welled up again within him, 'perhaps I misunderstood her altogether, and she was only drawing me on to satisfy herself of our utter inadequacy.'

Lady Baringdale was surprised at this vehemence.

'I should not have thought you would have cared a straw about the matter, either one way or the other,' she said.

'That, I know, is the general opinion.'

Lady Baringdale was too well-bred a woman to question him further on a matter about which he evidently did not mean to speak, and she drank the rest of her lithia in silence.

'Let us go,' said Lord Arthur, when she had finished. 'Perhaps you would look about for my father; I am tired; I want to go home.'

But going was not a simple matter, for the rooms were very full, and close to the door a stationary group had collected which made exits almost impossible. But suddenly, in the unexplained fashion of crowds, it began to melt, and straight in front of them stood Miss Chevening. Her eye brightened as she saw him.

'Ah, Lord Arthur', she cried. 'A thousand congratulations. You are the hero of the hour, the last record-breaker.'

He bowed, not shaking hands.

'I have a hundred things to say to you,' she went on, in her low, beautiful voice. 'Have you supped? Yes? Do let me have ten minutes with you.'

He looked at her, and his resolution faltered; then, ashamed of his weakness, he braced himself again. At any rate, he could not talk to her now.

'I am just off, I fear,' he said.

'How unkind you are. Well, one question, then. I have to carry twenty-two stone for the Derby, so won't you come in the motor with me for the race? You and I and a couple of bars will just make the weight. It will be delightful if you will come.'

Lord Arthur could not help hesitating. He had only twice driven in the Derby, and never in an even possible winner, and he longed to say 'Yes.' But his hesitation was brief.

'It is too kind of you,' he said, 'but I am not intending to go to the Derby this year.'

'You do not usually miss the Derby,' she said.

'No, not usually.'

All the light and gladness had died out of Beatrice's face, and a cloud of anxious misgiving settled there, contracting her eyebrows in a frown of pain and wonder. But the woman's redoubtable courage came to her aid, and she smiled naturally at him.

'I am very sorry for that,' she said. 'I hoped I should see you here tonight, and that you would be able to come: but – woman proposes. Good night. You look a little tired after your feat.'

Lord Arthur smiled also.

'You, on the other hand, look quite fresh after yours,' he said. 'Good night.'

'I want to talk to you,' she said, hurriedly. 'May I come to see you to-morrow? Please let me.'

Again he tried to steel himself against her charm and her loveliness, but now he failed.

'Yes, come at twelve,' he said.

CHAPTER III

Beatrice Chevening stopped on some half hour after Lord Arthur had left, for though the dominant desire in her nature was to do things which should be of fine and striking quality, this aspiration was wedded to a fixed horror of doing anything which should be merely eccentric. She had come, so she knew herself, and so, for all she cared, everyone else was saying, simply because she was likely to meet Lord Arthur here, but it was quite another matter to leave the house in an obvious hurry, because he had gone away. But she was glad when her conventional self told her that she could go without making her departure conspicuous, and drawing her gold thread cloak, lined inside with the skin of the almost extinct rabbit, closely round her, for the cooler air outside struck somewhat chill after the atmosphere of the hot and crowded rooms, she waited in the porch for her motor to disengage itself from the long line of waiting vehicles.

As long as she had been with people, obliged by the mere rule of politeness to say a hundred trivialities to her acquaintances, and meet their response with a suitable lightness, she had been able to stifle, almost without effort, the bat-like flittings of misgiving which her two minutes' conversation with Lord Arthur had caused to swarm round her. Never had he been so cold and unresponsive, never had his manner to her, or, as far as she knew, to anyone, bordered so closely on positive rudeness. Yet she felt instinctively that it could not be a mere failure of politeness that had made him so *brusque*: his was a gentle nature, incapable of shallow discourtesy. What then, had caused this? And she was afraid that she knew.

She had intended to go home and get through an hour's work before going to bed, but she knew that her brain – usually so obedient a servant to her will – was in revolt; that she was incapable of applying herself to those political affairs which demanded a cool and undivided attention. So instead of going up the Strand to her flat in Temple Chambers, she turned down off

Northumberland Avenue, and drew up at the doors of the Catherine, a small and exclusive club, of which she was President. Here, at least, she would find some friend with whom she might distract her mind in conversation; she might even find someone to whom she could confide her trouble. Again and again she told herself that Lord Arthur was just a man; an ill-fitting coat, a pinching shoe, an annoyance on some money matter, was sufficient to cause this lack of cordiality; perhaps even she was unwittingly a party to what was called a lovers' tiff. In any case she was going to see him tomorrow. No thinking would mend what had happened, and it was the part of wisdom to dismiss what had occurred from her mind. This was most easily done by the presence and conversation of other people

A somewhat noisy party of women about town held the smoking-room, and as she passed through it, it amused her for a moment to hear high betting going on about her own motor for the Derby. A shout of derision greeted some magnanimous offer of three to four on, and it was carefully explained to the layer that the market odds were evens on, and would probably be three to two on to-morrow.

But the noise and vapidness of the talk were but little to her liking to-night, and she went on into the library. Here she found Mrs. Torrington with Evie Grimston, just out from the performance of 'Siegfried,' engaged, it would appear, in a somewhat heated discussion with the two sisters, Edith and Joan Hutchinson, who were members for Liverpool. These, known respectively as Speech and Silence, were perhaps the most formidable members of the Opposition, but the Catherine was avowedly a non-political club, and most women of real culture belonged to it, agreeing to sink, when once within its hospitable doors, all subjects on which they raved at each other from the benches. Silence, at the moment when Beatrice entered, wore a sneering smile, her most effective weapon, and Mrs. Torrington was apparently in a difficulty. She looked up with evident relief at the *dea ex machina*.

'And now you can defend yourself,' she said, leaning back in her chair.

Beatrice laughed: any sense of opposition always roused her intellectually, and it was with a feeling of temporary escape from her private hell that she threw off her cloak, and sat down.

'Let me hear the accusation,' she said. 'Good evening, all of you. Silence, that sneer is only to be used at Westminster. My dear, try to look genial. Now what have I done?'

'Oh, we all agree about the wisdom of what you have done,' said Mrs. Torrington, 'we differ about the motive that prompted you.'

'You mean the Disenfranchisement Bill?' asked Beatrice. 'Surely the motive is clear enough. But this is politics, by the way. We are bound not to talk politics here.'

'But nobody will know,' said Speech.

'Possibly not, but the obligation is one of honour.'

'Ah, I said so, I said so,' exclaimed Mrs. Torrington; 'we can talk about this, though, Beatrice. It does not concern politics, it concerns your honour. There is no rule against personalities in the club.'

'My honour?' said Beatrice.

'Yes, dear,' said Mrs. Torrington, 'horrible things have been suggested about you. But, perhaps after all, it is too personal; let us drop it.'

Beatrice laughed.

'I'm afraid I can't allow that now,' she said. 'Oh, you need not mind. My feelings are incapable of being hurt. People who do not know me do not hurt my feelings, simply because they do not know me, and people who do know me cannot hurt my feelings, because they do know me. So please go on.'

Speech cleared her throat with a rasping sound, as if her vocal chords were files.

'So that is all right,' she said. 'We were talking about the bill, Chevening. I ventured to say that you looked beyond the actual bill itself, as every woman must, and contemplated the state to which men would be reduced in say, twenty years' time. Now years ago, in the East of Europe, men used to keep harems – the multiplicity of their wives is not concerned with my point – and women lived behind bars, the slaves of their masters. Now, that I maintain will be the logical outcome of the disenfranchisement. Men will live behind bars, the slaves of their wives. Then, to be quite frank, your personal honour comes into question. It is supposed that you are contemplating matrimony.'

For a moment anger and disdain flashed in Beatrice's eyes, but the next, sober dialectician as she was, the personal element vanished; she became interested merely in the point at issue.

'I am not given, as you know,' she said, 'to make speeches, except when I am obliged; but this accusation cannot be met by a "yes" or "no." As Alice said, this is not really a political question, it concerns my honour, as you will see. So give me a minute.'

She leaned forward in her chair, with her head sunk between her hands, and stayed thus for a space. Then she sat upright again.

'No, I do not think of a man, or their relations to women, in that way,' she said, 'but for years past the dominant power in the land, in all practical questions, has been in the hands of women. Now, I am not a woman who goes in for flirtations and intrigues, but I have known many men well. Without exception they have recognised this, and the natural consequence has been that they are ceasing to take any vital interest in these questions. That being so, they are, in my opinion, unfit to have a voice in them, for no one ought to be able to influence in however small a degree, deliberations on subjects which are not vital to him. Now disenfranchisement means exactly that and no more. Men will retain all the immense influence they possess over us, they will only be deprived of power to affect those things about which they do not really care.'

The sneering smile had returned to the wide and ugly mouth of Silence, and her sister gave it utterance.

'They will be banished into strictly private life,' she said. 'I put it coarsely, perhaps, but that is exactly what I meant by the harem-system.'

Beatrice flushed.

'No, no,' she said, 'indeed it is not so, for it lies in the power of men to say whether our civilisation and progress shall be sound or not.'

'Then the Lord help our civilisation,' said Evie, from the depths of her armchair.

'My dear girl,' said Beatrice, 'if you are going to be cynical, I should advise you to go to bed, for it is infinitely better to be asleep than to be cynical. Oh! I dream of a civilisation higher and more splendid than any which has yet appeared on this beautiful planet. I do not say I am right in the means by which I now think we shall advance. But men, with all their power and strength, have shown themselves to be incapable in certain ways. When they ruled the world, when they made the laws, they were also the great lawbreakers. If you examine old prison registers, you will find there are five men to one woman in jail. Their system, then, so far, was a failure. We, too, failed in the part that was allotted to us, to keep the moral standard high. But now these parts have been reversed; it is to men we look to keep our moral standard high, and how much more admirably they do it than we did. And it is the inspiration they give us which spurs us on to practical deeds. Ah, there is no doubt, whatever we may say, that it is the love of man which helps and encourages us. That is our inspiration, but woe to us if our inspiration produces nothing. An energy that does not find some fruition, that is the poisonous thing. Instead of being a spring of good, it becomes a suppressed disease.'

'Yes' she went on, 'that is what men can do for us, and without them we are helpless, lacking in inspiration. For years I have been without the inspiration, blindly groping on, wondering how it was that others no wiser than I had a fire about them which was wholly lacking to me. Then in me, too, the fire was kindled, and what humbleness it brings one, what distrust of one's own feeble efforts, but what a passionate determination to work and work. Oh, I doubt very much if we can care for the human race, if we can feel the glorious necessity for progress and enlightenment, unless we are very deeply attached, ah, why should I not say it? Unless we are in love. Until the sun comes out, we see only grey levels and brooding clouds, difficulties and dulnesses are on all sides of us. Then comes illumination, the rainbow is athwart the cloud, beyond the level flats lies a sapphire sea, or the rosy tinted snows of the summits that overlook the world. Oh, my poor girl,' she said, turning suddenly to Evie, 'never say the sort of thing you said just now. You said it in ignorance, of course, and it is better to feign cynicism than to feel it, but it is a poor thing to feign.'

Speech laughed.

'You are the only orator I know,' she said, 'you alone, while you speak make me feel that what you say must be true.'

Beatrice shook her head.

'I am sorry for that,' she said, 'because indeed I have nothing to do, so to speak, with what I am saying. But about the eternal truth of what I say, I have no manner of doubt. Oh, it is a glorious thing to be alive. But how much more alive we ought to be! With this deathless feeling in one's soul, one's body should never grow old. Nor, I think, would it, if we never allowed ourselves a moment's doubt of the greatness and splendour of our destinies. Doubt, cynicism, dulness, those are the three enemies of mankind, it is they which make us women old at forty.'

'I should have thought the nerves were more responsible,' said Speech.

'Yes, and what makes our nerves to play us tricks, to reduce us to mere jumping jacks at one time, to mere lumps of flesh at another? These three things, as I have said, which bring discords into us, making us inharmonious with ourselves and all the world.'

Speech rose.

'Well, you are delightful,' she said, 'whether what you say is true or not. But there is one more point . . .'

'Yes, I know,' said Beatrice, 'the point on which my honour is concerned. It is true that to-day I declared that in my opinion men are not fit to share in practical politics. It is true also, as you said, that I contemplate matrimony. But I assure you that no array of terms can tell you how deeply I love and honour – a certain man. And for no consideration in the world would I ask any man to be my husband unless I loved and honoured him so and no less. There is my assurance on the point; it is impossible for me to offer proofs beyond my mere word. I wish I could.'

Speech held out her hand.

'Thank you,' she said, 'that is sufficient. I must go to bed. I have to go down to Liverpool tomorrow morning to open the new wing of the Infants' Institute.'

'Ah, yes,' said Beatrice. 'I am interested in that. You take the babies, do you not, when they are a week old, and rear them for six months? How do the mothers take to it?'

'It is an immense success. On so large a scale it can be done very cheaply, and the babies thrive most wonderfully. A baby ought always, I think, to be treated with the same precision and regularity as an invalid. It has its food at regular hours in the Institue, it has bright objects danced before it at other regular hours, a doctor visits every baby twice a day, and if there is the slightest ailment, you see, it is taken at once to the infirmary. The play hour is really the prettiest thing, Chevening. Six hundred babies all crowing and laughing together at the bits of dancing tinsel paper. You should come down to see it.'

'Indeed I will,' said Beatrice, 'as soon as the House rises. I shall remind you of your invitation. Good-night.'

The two sisters went out, and Beatrice and the others strolled across to the window, and sat ruffle-haired to the mellow summer breeze.

'Regularity and precision,' she said, at length, 'what excellent qualities! How necessary! Necessary even for babies, perhaps. But somehow I don't want to see that unfortunate Infants' Institute the very least.'

'Isn't it a good thing?' asked Evie.

'I feel sure it is. I feel sure also that babies are much healthier if they are treated like that. But somehow it does not correspond with one's idea of baby-hood – that laughter at stated intervals, the regularity of food and medical inspection.'

'My dear Beatrice,' said Mrs. Torrington, 'what has come over you?'

'I don't know. A fit of old-fashionedness, I suppose. To-night it seemed to me that those two women were no more than animated machines, something like the sensitive antennea of your motor-car. I respect them, as you know, but they seem to aim at nothing higher than perfect health for human beings, completely sanitary conditions, and all the things that will produce material happiness. I wonder if half of us, after all, are not mere materialists? We have done away with all poverty, supposing we should do away with all disease and crime! I am afraid lots of us would be satisfied.'

Evie looked up quickly.

'You would not,' she said, 'I am glad you would not. But what is it you would be satisfied with?'

'Ah, if I knew what would satisfy me, I should be a materialist, too,' said Beatrice. 'I dread ever knowing what would satisfy me.'

Mrs. Torrington laughed.

'Decidedly, you are in love,' she said.

Evie rose.

'O, most fortunate woman,' she said. 'Dear me, if I was Prime Minister and owner of the Derby favourite, and in love, I think I should commit suicide. It would be so much safer. One would guard against all disappointments. Good-night.'

The two others sat for a little while in silence, Beatrice with a smile on her lips at the girl's words. But the smile soon faded; the mention of the Derby and her love affair together reminded her of her trouble, and in a moment down came the shining temples in which her mind had wandered for this last half hour, and she was just love-sick and apprehensive again. Mrs. Torrington noticed the change in her face.

'I have just read your speech,' said she. 'It seemed to me remarkably lucid. But where have you been this evening in all your fine clothes? Oh, by the way, did you hear that Lord Arthur went round . . .'

Beatrice made an impatient gesture of assent.

'I have been at a party at the Duke of Lincoln's' she said; 'I saw him there.'

She lit a cigarette with a quick nervous movement, blew out three or four hurried breaths of smoke.

'Oh, what do our wretched politics matter,' she cried, 'or his wretched golf either? An attack of the nerves (it is nerves, perhaps, that ails me to-night) rides rough-shod over all one's schemes, and aspirations, and ambitions. One moment I am up in the clouds, one moment in a slough of bottomless mud. Indeed, I came here to look for someone who could tell me what is the matter with me. You will do excellently. What can it all mean?'

She turned her dark eyes on her friend with the beseeching air of some dumb animal in pain.

'My dear Beatrice,' she said, 'how can I tell you what is wrong, unless you tell me what you think is wrong. Your high flight just now seemed to be the lark-song of a happy lover: your moans seem to be the moans of the uncertain lover. Or is it your speech to-day that is bothering you? If so, indeed, it need not; it was admirably moderate and firm as a sketch of your policy. Perhaps you are feeling the reaction after the excitement of it, for it must have excited you.'

Beatrice shook her head.

'Oh, that is not it,' she said. 'Hours after my speech was over I was in excellent spirits. I went on to this party at Lincoln House in excellent spirits.'

Alice Torrington for answer caught hold of the girl's bare arm, and drew her fingers gently up and down it from elbow to wrist. After a few moments Beatrice leaned back against the sofa arm and half closed her eyes.

'Ah, that is nice!' she said. 'You have the real mesmeric touch; you would make your fortune as a witch-doctor. Go on doing that while I tell you what has happened; I can speak quite calmly while your cool finger-tips do that. Well, I went to the Lincolns', of course, to meet Arthur. He was there, looking perfectly splendid, brown with the sun, and cool and big. You know he always makes other men look weak and flabby when he is there. I asked him to ride on my motor in the Derby; he said he was not going to the Derby. I asked him to let me talk to him for ten minutes; he said he was just off. I told him he looked a little tired with his feat; he replied that I did not look at all tired with mine. Finally I asked him if I might come and see him to-morrow; he hesitated, and then said I might.'

'And have you made up your mind exactly what you are going to say to him to-morrow?' asked the other.

'I had, but I don't know now if I shall have nerve enough. Oh, Alice, it is an awful thing to feel that one's whole life and happiness depends on a monosyllable from a man! Yes, in spite of all my big words and fine dreams, the intimate, the middlemost Me cares for nothing else. It is awful, I tell you, this feeling that one does not belong to oneself, that one has to pour oneself into another, as a river pours itself into the sea. And this is I, the ice-woman, as they used to call me. She was proud of the name! Oh, Alice, I am very far from proud to-night.'

There was the clear bell-like ring of truth about her voice which it is impossible to mistake, and Mrs. Torrington, feeling it hopeless to reiterate banalities about reaction and excitement, just waited for what she should say next. Only that afternoon she had talked, she remembered, with Evie Grimston as to the possible motive which might be prompting Beatrice to contemplate this extraordinary marriage, but now the Prince of Doubters could not question what the motive was. Here was Beatrice, the aloof, the ice-woman, caught in the grip of that mysterious passion, the feeling of man for woman, of woman for man, which hitherto had been so alien to her nature. Passionately, but utterly powerlessly, she revolted and strove against it; it held her tight.

'Excited, a feeling of reaction, do you say?' she went on. 'Excited if you like. Every nerve and atom of power in me protests against this. I would do any-thing in the world to get rid of this feeling – except get rid of it,' she added. 'My heart beats when I see this man; it hangs in my throat, throbbing; my mouth is a hot cinder. And it is the sight of a man – of a man, Alice, that thus turns me dumb and stupid. I give you my word, I did not think it possible that such things could happen to me. O, the degradation and the glory of it! I am like the women of a hundred years ago – a shade more frank, perhaps. Look, I am dressed as if to receive the American members, or to celebrate the jubilee of our enfranchisement. I put on my pearls, I put on a dress I have never worn before. I put on my gold-thread cloak. I looked tired about the eyes and I darkened them with antimony; there is rouge upon my cheeks. I have done these disgusting things! And all because I thought I might meet a man. I met him; he did not care. Oh! I am a child; I am not fit.' – a sob caught in her throat and choked her.

Again Mrs. Torrington took hold of the beautiful outflung arm, and with deft fingers soothed and stroked it.

Beatrice drew it away impatiently.

'No, I must do without that,' she said. 'I have to look this thing fairly in the face, and judge myself soberly. I am a coward, I think; I am honest. So let me tell you all, for it is better to say a thing than only think it: speech gives a definiteness to one's thought, and if one does not speak one may gloss a thing over in the mind. I love this man, here is the sum total of it, in a way that I cannot understand. I am a throw-back, I must suppose; my great-grand-mother lives again in me. To-night I have felt jealous, yes jealous of those absurd women at the party. Lady Kitty Liverpool was there; she was talking to him when I first saw him, and I was jealous of that little suburban doll. Afterwards I saw him with Lady Baringdale, and I was jealous of that bald Niebelung. Yes, she is bald, and she wears a wig. I was glad of that; I was glad that Arthur must have known it was a wig. Merciful heaven, that I should care whether Lady Baringdale's hair is her own! But why Alice, did he behave to me like that? Was this one of those lovers' tiffs one reads about in novels? They are always represented as pleasantly exciting, a kind of rapture of despair. I assure you I felt no rapture. My heart simply fell with a thump into my shoes. I remember wondering if anyone had noticed it.'

'No, it doesn't seem to me like a lovers' tiff,' said Mrs. Torrington. 'But I am a bad judge; I never loved anybody. And I never by any chance have a tiff with anyone.'

Beatrice sat suddenly upright.

'Tell me,' she said with a curious concentration, 'do you think it has anything to do with the Disenfranchisement Bill?'

'Ah, that has occurred to you, then.'

'What does not occur to me at such moments? But who would have guessed that Arthur would have cared a capsule for his vote?'

'A child does not very likely care a capsule for a toy his nurse takes away. It is the taking away he minds. And have I not heard you say men are so like children?'

'A toy? To the nurse what she takes away is a toy – but this is no toy to me. Besides, Arthur has told me he does not care a straw about any political question.'

Mrs. Torrington was silent for a moment.

'I cannot advise you,' she said at length. 'You do not really face the question. Supposing, for instance, that Lord Arthur has taken deep offence at your speech; supposing, for instance, that he refuses to marry you if you are still determined to introduce the bill, what will you do? You say you are honest. What will you do?'

Beatrice did not reply at once, but Mrs. Torrington saw she had heard the question and did not repeat it. At last she rose, still silent, and threw her cloak over her shoulders.

'Honestly, then,' she said, 'I have not the slightest conception what I shall do.'

CHAPTER IV

Beatrice was punctual to her hour when she drew up next morning at the old-fashioned wooden door where Arthur lived with his father. The excitement of her nerves had quieted down, the tumult at any rate no longer broke on the surface; it was as if oil had been poured on a tumbling sea, and though the depths still stirred and were troubled, the flying spray and foam had been stilled. She was, in fact, mistress of her superficial behaviour; her rebellion and revolt, her degradation and her glory, did not want to shout and assert themselves; she felt no less than before, but without excitement. In spite of her agitation last night she had slept well, and on rising had spent nearly half an hour in her bath of green light, which had both soothed and braced her.

She was shown up at once to the drawing-room, and after a few moments the servant appeared again, and, saying that Lord Arthur would receive her, led the way to his sitting-room. But even before she saw him her heart sank, for her nostrils caught the crisp scent of a cigarette. He well knew her feeling on the subject of men smoking, and that he should receive her thus she felt to be horribly ominous; but, making a great call on her resolution, she entered.

He was sitting in a long chair by the window, and got up when she entered. They shook hands in silence, and the door closed behind the maid who had admitted her. Then he pointed to a chair, and they both sat down again. Never in her life had Beatrice felt so utterly resourceless. At last she spoke.

'Lord Arthur,' she said, 'why were you so unkind to me last night? I came, of course, on purpose to see you. Why did you make a stranger of me, oh – it was worse than that; why did you make an enemy of me?'

He did not look at her, but answered slowly, weighing his words.

'I made a stranger, if you will, of you,' he said, 'in order that you should not ask for this interview. I wished to spare yourself and me.'

'Then why did you grant it me?' she asked.

'Because I was weak; because I found myself unable to say no, because –' and he stopped.

A sudden light sprang into Beatrice's eyes.

'Because?' she said.

'Because I love you,' he said.

Miss Chevening was not considered conventional even by an unconventional age, yet some busy automatic cell in her brain surprised her by making it known to her that she was not shocked. Then a huge soft flood of joy came up and drowned all other consciousness, and from the depths there came her answer, calm with the calmness that comes in all great moments, either of joy or sorrow.

'And I am here to ask you to marry me, Arthur,' it said.

'And this is why I wished to spare yourself and me,' he answered.

Then, for the first time, he looked at her.

'So go,' he said, hoarsely. 'Go at once.'

He asked an impossible thing; and even while the words were being spoken, he knew it to be so.

'Yet that would not be fair to either of us,' he added almost immediately.

'No,' she answered. 'For I have asked you to marry me, and you have said you loved me. Yet you tell me to go.'

Again he looked at her.

'Ah, why did you do this thing?' he cried. 'There are plenty of women whom you might have left to introduce the bill, and very likely carried it, and I should not have cared. But that you should! You have said publicly and authoritatively that you despise men, that you consider them unworthy to have a voice in any matter that concerns the public good. Yet you can ask me to marry you. What do you mean? You are making a fool of me or of the nation, and I do not know which, and I cannot believe either. Yet one it must be.'

'Oh, you are wrong!' she cried, 'utterly, grossly wrong. It is true that I do not think men should have any voice in political matters, but not because I despise them, but because it is not their sphere.'

He made an impatient sign of dissent.

'There is no explanation possible even to you,' he said. 'If we are worthy of respect, we are worthy of a share in the work of the government. You do not think so. You do not respect men, and I am a man. We should neither of us be true to ourselves if we married. A wife must respect her husband, a husband must feel that she does so. Love is not enough without esteem.'

She rose, throwing her hands apart with a hopeless gesture.

'Then you have never loved,' she said. 'If you had loved, you would know there is nothing else in the world.'

'Then I have never loved,' he replied.

'Ah, your voice rang false there,' she said, with a sudden flash of exultation.

'It did. And your voice will ring false, my poor Beatrice, when you make a great speech which all the world will applaud about depriving men of the franchise because they are unworthy of a voice in national affairs; however strongly you may speak, you will not really feel quite sure about it. And you will know it, perhaps then, perhaps afterwards, and the applause of the world will be like hoots of derision in your ears.'

He stood up also, and grasped her roughly by the wrists.

'For I am not going to lose you,' he said, 'do not think that for a moment. You think I am weak except in mere muscles, perhaps, that I care only for games when you hit a silly ball from bush to bunker. It is true that up till now I have cared for little else. Then I met you and soon I loved you, and that has awakenend me. But I do not regret the time I have wasted with the silly ball. That will be the instrument with which I shall fight you. Yes, because we love each other we are going to fight, fight hard for all we are worth, loving each other all the time. And you are going to be beaten, my dearest, and I am going to be your master and your abject slave. Ah, you trembled then; you are frightened.'

She wrested her wrists free, and stood before him with flashing angry eyes.

'Frightened!' she said. 'Indeed, you do not know me.'

'Indeed I do, but up till this moment you did not know me. You will learn. You were frightened, I tell you, but only for a moment. Come, Beatrice, we love each other, and there must be no paltry falsehoods like that between us. So confess it, you were frightened.'

She met his eyes in silence, and looked away, then met them again with a pleading look.

'Yes, I was frightened for a moment,' she said, 'you were so violent.'

'Not so violent,' he said, 'but I was stronger than you thought. Now sit down again.'

'So there is our programme,' he went on. 'A fight not to death, but to life. The world has gone strangely topsy-turvey in the last hundred years, and for my own small part I do not acquiesce in it. Just for once a man is going to win a woman, and I am he. I am going to fight you, and the prize is you. I said, by the way, last night that I was not going to the Derby. That was because I was deeply offended with you, and because I did not see what I must do. Since then I have thought it all out, and I will come with you. Many thanks.'

She laughed.

'Quite impossible, I am afraid,' she said. 'I have just asked Mrs. Torrington. I wrote to her before coming here.'

'Then you will have to put her off,' he said.

She laughed again.

'Oh, you are irresistible,' she cried, with an extraordinarily frank gaiety.

'I intend that you shall find me so in many things. Now you must go, I have a hundred things to do.'

Beatrice got up, feeling hugely exhilarated. His statement, 'for I am not going to lose you,' had brought her life and energy. Utterly different as he had shown himself from what she had imagined him to be, the reality was what she had loved, though hitherto it been but potential. Already, for one moment, he had frightened her, and though she was disposed to tell herself that this had been but a superficial tremor, she knew that it was not so, and was half ashamed of it, half gloried in it. Then, in obedience to his dismissal, she rose and held out her hand.

'So it is to be war,' she said. 'Shake hands on it.'

He took her hand in his, then suddenly threw his arms round her and kissed her.

'War,' he said, 'and then love.'

She resisted but for a moment, then without a word, but with the banner of her love for him flying red in her face, she turned and left him.

The door closed behind her, but Lord Arthur still stood where he was in the centre of the room, flushing deeply, like her, under the brown tan of his skin, his blue eyes bright and dancing with great excitement. Then, after giving her time to get clear of the house, he crossed the hall and went into his father's room.

The Duke was sitting in a very comfortable chair, doing, as was his custom, absolutely nothing. This habit was due, so he considered, not to laziness of disposition, but to excessive and self-supporting activity of mind. Folk of more indolent brain could not behave thus; their sluggishness required a spur in the way of employment of some kind. In support of his theory he adduced the evidence that he never fell asleep while sitting with vacant hands; a less active mind, on the other hand, would have found it impossible to keep awake. Certainly he was awake now, and he looked up eagerly when his son entered.

'Well?' he asked.

'I was right,' said Arthur. 'It all happened as I told you it would, and at the end I just caught and kissed her. Lord, I love that girl!'

'And she?'

'She behaved like a girl, as she is, not like a man in skirts. Father, it's the most wonderful thing! She and I have hopped back a hundred years.'

'So it appears. I wish, by the way, it had been compatible with the demands of honour to secure a complete cinematograph of your interview. It would have been a most useful thing for you in your coming campaign.'

'I know it would, but of course it was impossible. Here again I have gone back a hundred years. Ninety-nine men out of a hundred would have done it.'

'A hundred-and-one,' observed his father.

'True, I forgot you. Also, I am going to the Derby,' said he.

'I thought you said you had refused.'

'I had refused,' said Arthur, 'and I made her throw over Mrs. Torrington and take me instead.'

'I still don't quite understand your attitude.'

'It is perfectly simple,' said Arthur, lighting another cigarette. 'I don't care one stroke about the franchise, as you know, but I very much care that the woman whom I intend to marry, should publicly, like this, declare her belief in the unworthiness of men to govern. If any other woman had introduced it, I should not mind. Oh, it is only a sentiment, perhaps, but surely a perfectly intelligible one. Then, again, I intend to marry her; it is to be that way round, because I am old-fashioned, and if I fight her over this, and beat her, as I propose to do, it will put us in our proper positions. And after that I will lay myself down for her to trample on, if she wishes, for then she will understand that I do it, not because I am a man and her inferior, but because I am a man, and I will do anything for her. But I can't talk of it, even to you. Come, let us get to work.'

Lord Arthur had been elected only a few months ago to be president of the Central Athletic Committee, and an hour later telegrams were twitching and winking over all the wires in England, to the presidents of all country athletic clubs, bidding them attend an extraordinary presidential meeting next day in London. If they were absolutely unable to attend themselves, they were ordered to furnish some member of their local committee who should in all things represent them. This meeting, so ran the message, was thus hurriedly convened, to deliberate and take steps upon a matter of the very first importance, which admitted of no delay. Noon was the hour for the meeting, and it was particularly requested that all gentlemen would be punctual, as it would be followed at two o'clock by another meeting of the Central Committee of Men's Rights, at which the attendance of certain members of the athletic committee would be required.

It was not many hours before faint rumours and shortly afterwards confirmation of this news began to spread through London, and by three o'clock that afternoon the athletic clubs were full and buzzing with conjecture. Grosvenor Square, where the Duke of Ireland's house stood, was a seething mass of reporters and interviewers all clamouring to see Lord Arthur, who denied himself to everybody; but who, if the truth had been known, had disguised himself with a long adhesive moustache and large green goggle spectacles, and was even now mingling with the crowd at his father's door, and was hearing what London in general had to say about the matter. Once or twice as he shouldered his way about he exchanged the ghost of a smile with a feeble old gentleman of bowed shoulder and white-bearded chin, who in point of fact was none other than the Duke himself, who, thus travestied, was also gleaning information as to the reception of the news.

Beyond these two there was that afternoon in London perhaps only one person who even suspected what would be the matter which was to be laid before the meeting of athletic presidents next day. As soon as she had seen the notice of the meeting cast on to her own private news-board in her room in the House, Beatrice remembered in a flash those words of Lord Arthur, 'I do not regret the time I have wasted with the silly ball. That is the instrument with which I shall fight you.' The connection between the two seemed to her vital, incomprehensible, and irresistible. For a few moments she sat puzzling and pondering, then the whistle from the news-board, warning her of a fresh message, made her look up. The Central Council of Men's Rights, it said, would meet at two o'clock next afternoon.

Those of our readers who know the history of the turf will remember that the new Derby track was used for the first time this year. For several years previously the Motor Club had been freely criticised in the Press for not running this historic race over a track which provided a better test of climbing and staying powers, and, as always happens, when in the year 2000 they yielded to the pressure, and laid down the present track starting from Epsom, then going over Box Hill to Forest Row and East Grinstead, and back through Godstone and Reigate, they were again subjected to much vituperation and criticism for setting so hilly a course. The fact was that many owners thinking that there was no real chance of the course being changed, had built the motors which they entered for this year of a type suitable to the old and much flatter course, but altogether unsuitable for the new race, where staying and climbing power was as necessary as sprinting. Beatrice, wise woman as she was, had entered two cars, one very light and without a chance of success if the course was changed, the other built with this change in view.

The scene of bustle and confusion in the paddock, to use the name which has so strangely survived to our day, had died down – the last oilings had been done, the last mast hoisted with its sail reefed closely round the yard, gears had been tested, turbines spun, screws subjected to a final wrench of the driver, and everyone was waiting for the signal to go down to the starting-post. Lord Arthur had arrived some ten minutes ago, and, still standing by the Juno, where Beatrice had taken her place, seemed the very picture of serene nonchalance.

'Yes, decidedly you are going to win,' he said; 'it can't be otherwise. It would spoil' – and he looked at her as he spoke low – 'it would spoil the subsequent completeness.'

A little colour showed in her cheeks, and she smiled at him.

'There is a truce, then, between us for the next hour,' she said.

'No – alliance,' said he. 'By the way, what did you make of our athletic meeting?'

'Ah, let us drop that for the present,' she said. 'I want to think of nothing just now but the race. Get up, Lord Arthur; they are opening the paddock gates.'

'Let us go down last,' said he. 'Indeed, we must; look how they are all jostling to get out. It is so *chic* to go down last to the starting-post and get back again first. There goes Blue Bacillus; that's right, the driver is nervous – do you see? What a woman! She nearly took the kerbstone. I like to see other drivers nervous.'

'You won't see this one,' remarked Beatrice.

'I know I shan't. There, let us go.'

From outside shouts and roars had gone up from the stands as the various cars rushed down the course to the starting-post, Blue Bacillus in especial being greeted with a tremendous ovation. But the popular enthusiasm, particularly when it was known who occupied Beatrice's box-seat, was reserved for the Juno, and the beautiful Prime Minister, idol as she was of the heart of London, met with an unparalleled welcome. The stands loaded with megaphones went by them in a flash, and running some hundred yards beyond the starting post, she turned the machine in little more than its own length, and slid up to her place. Then, she with the starting lever in her hand, he with the rope ready to unfurl and set the sail on the moment, they waited in tense silence for the fall of the flag.

Down it went, and from a million waiting throats rose the great roar that year by year goes up on the start for the Derby. Simultaneously Beatrice pressed over the starting lever, and the transparent oil silk sail flew out full-bellied across the front of the car. The track was as dry as a bone, thanks to the sun and wind, and in the space of a couple of hundred yards the Juno's turbines were at full speed, with hardly the loss of a single revolution through skidding. But rapidly as she approached racing pace, the lighter cars, Blue Bacillus already taking the lead, were making the most of this following wind and before they were two miles from the grand stand had established a lead of a couple of hundred yards. But faulty steering on the part of Mrs. Theodosa and Lithia gave a place for the Juno on the inside of the track which should make her a present of nearly a quarter of a mile before they come to Boxhill, and put them in a more favourable position, and Beatrice gave a sigh of relief.

'Not bad,' she said, 'but we shall want it all. The lighter cars are feeling the wind. It's just a sailing match at present. How's the water gauge?'

Lord Arthur leaned forward.

'Steady. Can you give us any more speed?'

'Not a revolution. There's the five-mile post. What's the time?'

'Six and a half minutes. Quickest start I ever saw. Blue Bacillus must be doing her miles nearly level. We've just got to wait for the hills.'

Mrs. Theodosia had by this time recovered her lost ground, and was drawing up to Blue Bacillus and Gold. They had all three got inside berths, a couple of hundred yards between each. Then came Lithia a quarter of a mile behind the last of these, and another half mile behind them Flying Fish and

Juno. The light cars had certainly made the most of the wind, and such a lead before the foot of Boxhill was a long one. But on the rise of the ground the qualities of Juno, Quinine and Capsule, all of better climbing capacity, began to tell, and these three nearly abreast were within three-quarters of a mile of the leaders when half the ascent was done. Flying Fish was going badly, and the rattle of her pump as the Juno overhauled and passed her promised ill for her negotiation of the East Grinstead hill, if ever she came to it. Quinine and Capsule, on the other hand, did not yield a yard to the Juno on the long ascent, and it was evident that she had at least three dangerous rivals. The wind, which had been steady from the same quarter up till now, shifted a point to the east, and each car, as the road turned eastwards at the top, took in its sail which would not be needed again unless the wind went quite round. Here a little bungling on the part of Capsule gave the Juno a slight advantage for Lord Arthur had taken in sail with the speed of a conjuring trick. This done, he again examined the water gauge.

'Lost a quarter of an inch,' he said. 'I should cut off power down the steepest part of this hill and let the pump catch up.'

Beatrice strained her eyes forward.

'Can't afford it,' she said. 'Look at Bacillus.'

'It will be false economy,' said Lord Arthur, 'but as you please.'

She frowned.

'I am sure you are wrong,' she said, as they whirled down the descent. But he saw her pull the lever over, and laughed.

'So you are not quite sure,' he said.

Suddenly he pointed forward to the sharp corner at the bottom of the hill, a quarter of a mile only ahead of them

'Go wide,' he yelled. There had been an accident on the inside of the track. 'Gently, that's enough. Lord! Here's this Capsule nearly on us.'

For a moment it was doubtful whether the two cars would foul. The Capsule was going straight for the inside of the track, the Juno crossing her path for the outside, in obedience to Lord Arthur's shout. He had seen a small jet of steam rising from behind the trees by the corner, and instantly the possibility that someone was overturned occurred to him. Then, as they cleared the Capsule with only some ten yards to spare, they shot round the outside of the track, and saw he was right. Overturned in the scrub on the inside of the course was Mrs. Theodosia, her driving wheels spinning furiously in the air. Forty yards off sat her driver in a clump of bushes, looking extremely dazed. From the Capsule came a wild yell and the heavy grind of the brakes, and Lord Arthur, looking round, saw she had just avoided a collision, but had, of course, lost all her speed.

'Sharp curve in the middle of the hill, isn't there?' asked Beatrice, as they gathered pace.

'Yes, very sharp,' said he. 'But we must take it as hard as we can lick.'

'Of course. Sorry if I upset you.'

Trees, gardens, houses went by in blurred lines of green and white as the pace grew wilder and more reckless.

The motor had acquired an uncomfortable oscillating motion, and once, Beatrice looked uneasily at her companion.

'Shall I put the brake on?' she asked. 'For if we upset we shall not win the race.'

'Nor shall we if you put the brake on,' said he. 'It is certain that Bacillus hasn't taken this hill at full tilt, she has not enough stability, and she will have begun the East Grinstead Hill slow. We, on the other hand, if we get there, will begin it very fast. Sit more this way.'

They had entered on the curve at frightful speed, and the oscillation had increased till from moment to moment, the outer wheels of the motor left the ground in horrible lengthening pulsations. Once Lord Arthur thought they were over. 'For God's sake, don't hold on, Beatrice,' he said, 'let it throw you clear. Two more like that and we are done . . . Ah, we are round instead. And there are the other two.'

From this point they could see across the intervening valley on to the side of East Grinstead Hill, and there sure enough, going very slowly at the beginning of the steep ascent, were the two others, still neck to neck. And Beatrice laughed aloud.

'Why, this pace will carry us half a mile up,' she said. 'We catch them and pass them a mile before the top.'

Lord Arthur did not answer, but kept an anxious eye on the water gauge, which he saw, somewhat to his dismay, had sunk nearly an inch since they left Epsom, and it was clear that either the pump was not good enough for this racing work, or that there was some imperfect action going on in the recomposition of the water back from its resolved gases. But he said nothing of his discovery to his companion, for it was essential to their success that they should use every ounce of power at their command during the next eight miles of hilly ground, for the two other cars, both light, would have to be completely outdistanced before they came to the level on which it was evident that they were the faster travellers. So, since the knowledge could only discompose Beatrice, and it was fatal to try to economise over these hills, he kept the matter to himself.

'Blue Bacillus is coming up rapidly,' he said. 'Are we running at full speed?'

'Yes. How far have we to go? And how is the water?'

'About four miles more; you can see the grand stand. We are losing water rapidly.'

The moving speck came nearer with agonising rapidity. Already Lord Arthur could see clearly the face of the woman who drove it, and it annoyed him to observe that she wore a broad smile. For another mile they bowled along in silence.

'We did that in sixty-four seconds,' remarked Beatrice. 'Please take down the wind screen, Lord Arthur. It checks us a little.'

'You will have the hair blown off your head,' said he.

'Then I shall be bald. Be quick!'

He undid the catches that held the glass plate which protected their faces, and laid it down at their feet, staggering for a moment with the blast of air that met them. Then, looking behind, he saw to his intense annoyance that Blue Bacillus had followed his example.

'Two miles more,' he said. 'They are a hundred yards behind.'

Thirty seconds saw the two cars level, thirty-five seconds saw Bacillus a length ahead. Suddenly Lord Arthur reached across Beatrice, and shut down the power that controlled the pump.

'It's our only chance,' he said, 'and pray God they don't do the same. The pump uses five-horse power at least.'

A slight smile stole around Beatrice's mouth, and with one hand she drew her rug over the lever, so that the others could not see its unusual position. There was still rather more than a mile to go. It was pure toss-up whether or no the water in the reservoir was sufficient to last. But with the power thus added to the turbines, the Juno bounded forwards, and not more than half a mile from home drew level again. Already the track on each side was thick with faces, for never had there been so close a finish. But slowly and very surely the Juno drew ahead, slowly and very surely the water in the gauge sank and sank, then it disappeared completely; at any second their speed might diminish, but they had four lengths in hand.

Suddenly the end came; the hissing of the gases on to the turbine ceased entirely . . . there was a white post a little ahead; a little behind was a racing motor. A roar of human voices surged and swelled round them, the racing motor drew alongside, the white post also drew alongside. The white post passed, the racing motor also passed, and Beatrice's voice in a whisper said to Lord Arthur:

'Look at the number board; I can see nothing.'

'Juno, Blue Bacillus,' said Lord Arthur, and suddenly his exultation burst all bounds.

'O, you were lucky to have a man with you,' he cried. 'Mrs. Torrington would never have thought of cutting off the pump. Even you didn't think of it, you peerless woman. My congratulations!'

CHAPTER V

Beatrice was sitting by the open window in her room in the house overlooking the Thames, vainly trying to concentrate her mind on the speech which she would have to make next day on the bill for the disenfranchisement of men. But her mind steadily refused to be concentrated, and little bits of it ran in all directions like spilt quicksilver. A large globule of it, so to speak, was flying along the Derby track again, recalling and reviewing every mile of the race of the day before, now, with exulting pride, now in a sort of ecstasy of degradation. The pride was natural enough; she had won the blue ribbon of the turf after a closer contest and in quicker time than it had ever been run before. And no less natural, perhaps, was the ecstatic degradation, for her own honesty told her that it was not she who had won the race at all, but he who had sat beside her. Here was the degradation, the race had not been hers, for if she had run it her own way, without economy of power on the down grades, the Juno would never have lasted out. And that spendid reckless stroke of cutting off the pumpage in the last mile! That alone had saved the race, and it was not she who had done it. When Blue Bacillus passed them she was beaten, and she had known it. Then came the brown lean hand across her, and the Juno had sprung forward again. Twice had Lord Arthur saved her. Yet because it was he, there was ecstasy in the humiliation.

She got up, and began to pace up and down the room, hoping that by moving about she might calm the turmoil and scurry of her disobedient brain, but off it started on a fresh hare. This time it was the athletic meeting of two days before, about which nothing more had become known. The presidents had met and gone home again, and the subject of their meeting still was secret. That some counter-stroke to the Disenfranchisement Bill was planned or in consideration she had no doubt, and whatever it was, it was certain to be successful as far as it went, for the athletic club committees were still in the hands of men and Lord Arthur had told her that there was complete unanimity at the meeting, though he had refused to answer any further questions. The matter would be made public on the evening before the Disenfranchisement Bill came on; that and no more had he told her. It might, in fact, appear on the news-board at any moment.

Suddenly her door was thrown open, and Mrs. Torrington hurried in.

'Ah! have you heard, have you heard?' she cried. 'My dear Beatrice, we are done, we are absolutely done. Oh, the incredible meanness of men!'

Never had the calm and judicial state-historian displayed so pitiful a display of agitation, and Beatrice for the moment was quite alarmed.

'My dear Alice,' she said, 'what is the matter? Have a glass of bromide.'

'Bromide!' howled the excited historian. 'A pint of chloroform would not have the slightest effect on me. No more golf, no more croquet, no more cricket, no more tennis for any of us, except at South Shields.'

Beatrice sat down.

'This has something to do with the athletic meeting last Monday?' she asked.

'Yes, indeed it has something to do with it. And your dear friend Lord Arthur is at the bottom of it, the top of it rather. You must go to him at once and insist on his dropping it. You must tell him you will not marry him otherwise.'

'Unfortunately he has already said that he will not marry me,' said Beatrice with a strange and unaccountable feeling of exhilaration again. 'But you haven't yet told me what has happened. My news-board, as you see, has gone to be mended. I have heard nothing.'

'Well, it is short and simple enough,' said Mrs. Torrington. 'At the same hour at which the House meets upon the Disenfranchisement Bill every athletic club throughout the country also meets and also the Men's Rights Society. And the moment that the bill is passed, if it is passed, the president of each club will propose the expulsion of all women from the club. Oh, it is hideous! The only club in the country which has a majority of women on the committee is the club at South Shields. We shall all have to become members of the South Shields Club. Have you ever seen their golf course? It is one bunker from the first tee to the last hole. The worst bunkers are the greens, and the worst green is rather more level than their croquet lawns and tennis courts. Give me a season ticket to South Shields,' she cried desperately.

'But it is unheard of,' said Beatrice.

'Quite; you will hear of it now, though. Grosvenor Square is a mob of women all trying to storm Ireland House. The lower floor is barricaded, but they were putting up a fire-escape in order to get into the drawing-room windows. Lord Arthur was on the balcony directing a garden hose down it.'

Mrs. Torrington laughed in a shrill, unkind manner.

'Oh, you are a splendid champion of women,' she said. 'I only hope your order may be too late. Lord Arthur is the ringleader. If the women can only get hold of him the movement may be quenched. The man refused you, too. Have you no pride?'

'Plenty, but I do not happen to desire to be a murderess.'

'Murder, who talks of murder?' said Mrs. Torrington.

'Do they want to catch him just in order to take care of him and keep him safe?' said Beatrice. 'Alice, I must go there: I cannot stop. I may be able to do something.'

'You are a love-sick schoolgirl,' said Mrs. Torrington.

For a moment a white anger surged up in Beatrice's mind, and the other thought she would have struck her.

'Anyhow, you may thank your stars I have a decent control over myself,' she said.

Mrs. Torrington rose too.

'I am sorry,' she said. 'I should not have said or thought that. Forgive me, Beatrice. The other news is that the whole of the unmarrried portion of the Men's Rights Society have taken vows of celibacy if this bill is carried.'

Beatrice smiled.

'I do not think they will keep them long,' she said.

In five minutes she was at Grosvenor Square, and despite the real seriousness of the position she could for a moment have laughed aloud at the comedy of it. A large mob of yelling women surged round Ireland House, the lower windows of which were all shuttered. On the balcony above the front door stood a very familiar figure in shirt sleeves. He was smoking a pipe, in the public eye of London, and in his hands he held a large-nozzled garden hose, with which he played on the mob of women who were trying to effect a landing with the fire-escape. Seen at this distance Beatrice could see that he wore a broad smile, and his father, who was standing by him, was convulsed with laughter. His efforts were chiefly directed against three hard, stern-featured women, who made the most heroical efforts to mount, but every now and then, after driving them off, he would sweep the mob with cheerful impartiality. Evidently he was safe as long as the water held out, and apparently in the wild excitement it had occurred to nobody except Beatrice that they had only to cut off Ireland House from the main to reduce it to submission.

She was soon recognised, and a way was opened for her to the foot of the fire escape. Here she mounted the motor which had drawn the escape, and by degrees the tumult grew less, and she held a hurried colloquy with the leader of the mob.

Lord Arthur had also seen her, and he put his pipe in his pocket, and directed the water in a fantastic waving arch to the outlying portions of the mob, away from the centre where she stood.

But her arguments were of no avail: the three hard-natured women, all well-known athletes, demanded an unconditional surrender. It was in vain that Beatrice threatened them with the Riot Act, and warned them of the coming of the police, and, shaking their grim heads, they again advanced to the fire-escape. Suddenly a thought struck her, and, jumping down, she pushed in front of them, and before any could stop her had mounted the rounds of the ladder.

'Now, come on,' she cried. 'Here's the Derby winner waiting for you. Squirt over my head, Lord Arthur,' she called up to the balcony.

At that the riot broke out afresh, but with the screams and groans were mingled cheers. Her sudden plucky action, above all the allusion to the race, had divided the sympathies of the mob, and here once more were the two who had received that tremendous ovation fighting together against the whole world. Women, ever keen-sighted for the picturesque, saw here a captivating coincidence. Even the grim ringleaders wavered: to try to pull a Prime Minister off a fire-escape was an adventure which demanded consideration.

Suddenly with a rush the police poured into the square, taking advantage of this indecision of the mob to push their way round the pavement in front of the house. The manoeuvre was so quickly accomplished that the news of their arrival had not yet reached the further parts of the mob before the cordon was completely formed.

'And now,' said Beatrice to the more warlike part of the crowd who swarmed round the bottom of the ladder, 'I will get down if you will allow me.'

Then suddenly indignation and chivalry rose high in her.

'Oh, you are a plucky lot,' she cried, 'a thousand women against two men, and one's a duke! What odds do you require?'

Later that evening the Cabinet met, and found but long faces for each other. A fatal mistake, everyone felt, had been made in not sounding, and, if neccessary, conciliating the athletocracy. It had been taken for granted that the franchise was a subject on which they took no interest, but now, to the general consternation, it was found to be a subject with regard to which their interest took a disagreeably aggressive form. None but Beatrice and Mrs. Torrington knew the true inception of the movement, and that all women should be expelled from athletic clubs was a prospect impossible to contemplate. It was in vain that Mrs. Chambers, a bold and original politician, urged a firm front. They had been threatened, in itself an indignity. It was below the proper status of women to notice it. At this point Beatrice interrupted.

'But it has been noticed,' she said. 'I do not know if you were in Grosvenor Square this afternoon, but if you were you would agree that it has not been passed over.'

'And the Prime Minister, I am told, took the side of this Lord Arthur,' said Mrs. Chambers virulently. 'May I ask if she did so from sympathy with his principles or regard for his person?'

Beatrice drew herself up; she knew that none present could mistake the meaning of this.

'From neither,' she said, 'but because rioting and violent crime are not officially permitted. May I ask what the Home Secretary would have done under the circumstances?'

'I should not have defied the Misses Rayner from the rungs of the fire-escape,' she said bitterly. 'But to return to the main point, it is, I repeat, impossible that we should yield to threats. Are women so utterly without the power of organisation that they cannot start athletic clubs for themselves?'

'And marry each other?' asked Mrs. Torrington very suavely, 'for the Men's Rights Society are sworn to celibacy.'

Mrs. Chambers's jaw distinctly dropped. She was a widow of some personal attractions, and was known to be matrimonially disposed towards one of the handsomest and richest heirs in London.

'I had not heard of that,' she said. 'Is there any reason to suppose it is true?'

'There is no possibility of supposing anything else,' said Mrs. Torrington.

Beatrice struck her bell.

'We must first find out whether we are all of one mind about introducing the bill at all,' she said. 'I will ask you, therefore, to vote by ballot on the subject. A black ball signifies that the depositor is against introducing the bill, a white one that she is in favour of it.'

The votes were handed in in silence. Beatrice counted them openly.

'The bill will be introduced to-morrow,' she said, 'by the narrow majority of two votes. The meeting is adjourned.'

Twenty-four hours later the athletic committees in a hundred club houses were watching the news-boards. For more than an hour they had breathlessly followed the Prime Minister's speech in favour of the disenfranchisement, and, despite their sex, rounds of applause had burst from a hundred throats in the committee rooms, so masterly and agile was her attack. It was impossible not to admire her wonderful skill in the arrangement of damaging facts against men, and not the least marvellous part of the performance was her bravery in attempting thus magnificently to lead this forlorn and desperate hope. His action had had exactly the effect Lord Arthur had anticipated, and after the first wild burst of indignation, thousands of women had realised the uselessness of the attempt to carry the bill through. And in the House itself, not only from the Opposition but from the party in power, Beatrice had been fiercely assailed, and was fighting, as it were, with her back to the wall. Even the redoubtable Mrs. Chambers had been silenced by the bitterness of the leader of the Opposition, and Mrs. Torrington had been reduced to tears, so said the news-board. Thus in silence all waited for the reading of the vote, and in tense expectation watched the ticking of the figures on the board. The Government had been defeated by an overwhelming majority.

Lord Arthur, in the presidential chair of the central committee, sprang to his feet.

'Gentlemen,' he said, 'we shall not have to resort to these extreme measures, which none would have deplored more than I. The meeting is adjourned.'

Late that night a solitary woman's figure was pacing up and down Grosvenor Square. Every now and then she paused, wrestling with her pride, yet unable to subdue it. But by degrees the extent of her walk grew shorter, till at last she took turns of not more than twenty yards, ten on each side of Ireland House.

The windows were mostly dark, but above the porch two were flung wide, and a pale oblong of electric light was thrown on to the soft dark of the air outside. From moment to moment she looked up at that window, and now and then she half opened her mouth as if to call. Then suddenly the lights were extinguished, and a dark figure stepped on to the balcony, and Beatrice drew back into the shadow cast by the porch.

He leaned there for a minute or two, whistling softly to himself some old and simple melody with a very great sweetness and truth of tone, but stopped in the middle, and from below she heard a quick impatient sigh. He was leaning much over the balcony, and she dared not move for fear he should catch sight of her. Then he seemed to bend over even more, and suddenly she heard her own name gently called.

'Beatrice,' he said. 'Is it you? Can it be you?'

At that her pride, now more than half conquered by the events of the day, more than half soothed into torpor by the coolness and greatness of night, sprang up again, forbidding her to speak, wrestling desperately with her love which had driven her here. But for the moment pride was predominant. He had humbled her, wounded her; and though her whole soul cried out for the comfort he alone could give, the false feeling made a hard, though, if she had known it, but a brittle crust over her love. So she stood there still and silent.

'I know it is you,' said the voice again. 'I am coming down.'

At that she turned and ran swiftly across the Square; but it would seem that he had seen her, for in half a minute she heard steps running behind her. Never since men had been assigned their proper place had a man behaved in so unmanly a way. Then realising that running only made matters worse, she stopped and faced round.

'Ah, it is you,' she said. 'I congratulate you on your day's work. And you finish it well. Is it your custom to run after women like this?'

'I have never done it before,' he said. 'And in turn is it your custom to run away from men?'

Then suddenly something within her broke and fell in fragments.

'Oh, Arthur, Arthur,' she cried. 'You have beaten me, you have humiliated me. I can never hold up my head again.'

For answer he caught her to him.

'Lay it there, lay it on my breast,' he said. 'Was there not to be war between us? And what did I tell you should follow after? Answer me, Beatrice.'

She clung closer to him, sobbing.

'Answer me, answer me,' he repeated.

'L – love,' she answered.

* * * * *

EDITOR'S NOTE

When I suggested to Mr. E.F. Benson the idea of writing the GENTLEWOMAN Xmas Number as in the year 2000, he thus expressed himself in a letter:

'It is not so long ago that the world was startled into loud laughter by the movement known as "The New Woman." To some it appeared merely humorous, to most merely futile, to a few it held the germs of something neither futile nor ridiculous, but huge and tragical. The eventual supremacy of woman over man was this germ, and if it was destined to come to fruition neither woman nor man could afford to laugh. Since, then, a Xmas Number is not the fit field for tragedy, some other view had to be taken of it; it had to be considered in some of its less weighty and appalling aspects. It was in fact, too serious to be treated otherwise than lightly. By degrees, too, a dim, unformulated hope began to dawn; it might be that man would still have a word to say on certain matters, that there would still be a province of human life where a woman would be unable to compete successfully with them. Here, perhaps, they might make a stand, the last, it might be, but in a fortress hard to carry.'

I wonder, does the ascent of women mean the descent of men? Women's upward flight progresses with terrifying velocity, though, with delightful feminine perverseness, she is getting less like the Angels the higher her flight – perhaps because she gets more like man. Where in the world, will women be a century hence? She will not know herself. The fair feminine of the year 2000 will deny that one of Miss Lillian Young's exquisite fashion pictures (then having an honoured place in the British Museum) could possibly represent her great-grandmother. She will discredit the records of our time in all that they tell of women's present tastes: and emotions, dress and amusements.

To help the historians, and interest the present generation, this Christmas Number is devised as having been written in the year 2000. For months past writers and artists have been living a hundred years hence, when all the strange forces of living and locomotion, now but dimly recognised, shall be moving the people mentally and physically in perfected daily use. In one thing only will there be no change – 'All Gentlewomen will read the GENTLEWOMAN.

3

RETROSPECTS

During the 1890s the cult of labelling things as 'new' became a trend in popular culture, in which the 'new woman' and the 'new journalism' were major elements. But as the nineteenth century closed an important feature of transition was in bidding farewell to the 'old'. As the editor of the *Lady's Pictorial* (5 January 1901) stated:

Our old century has served us well. It has given us some of the greatest men that England has ever rocked on her bosom; it has given our best beloved and greatest Sovereign; it has yielded to us some of the greatest scientific treasures the world has ever known, and so we cry *Vale* with sincere regret.

Many of the retrospectives were light-hearted: 'The History of the Corset' appeared in the *Lady's Realm* in July 1901, and *Queen* printed 'A Century of Puddings' listed alphabetically during December 1900 and January 1901. The recipes included 'Railway Pudding' and 'Vice-Chancellor's Pudding' amongst the more obvious 'Queen', 'Quince' and 'Summer' puddings. Others were more serious: the American *Cosmopolitan* published 'The First Lady of Our Land' in February 1901, recalling the Presidents' wives since the office was first held; the popular British *Girl's Own Paper* offered 'Girls of Fifty Years Ago And Now' in January 1901 to mark the new century.

This chapter contains a selection of appraisals about nineteenth-century change which particularly affected women. Only a few of the articles from the compendious *Gentlewoman, Old and New Century Number* are included. Helen Blackburn's *Dates for the Century* from the last issue of the *Woman's Suffrage Calendar* is just one example of several such publications both in Britain and America. In 1899 the *Woman's Century Calendar*, edited by Carrie Chapman Catt, published by the National American Woman Suffrage Association, New York, focussed on dates of significance for American women, but like its British counterpart encompassed also world events; the *Gentlewoman* printed a detailed table of dates on 12 January 1901.

'A Nineteenth Century Valedictory,' H.B.B., *Woman's Journal*
(Boston), 29 December 1900, p. 412

With this issue of the WOMAN'S JOURNAL we bid farewell to the Nineteenth Century. It seems natural and timely to compare the past and the present condition of women, and to review the results so far attained by the advocates of their enfranchisement.

At the opening of the century the status of women all over the world was discouraging in the extreme. The French Revolution had collapsed into military despotism. The nations of Christendom were discordant and belligerent. Racial antipathies, ancestral superstitions, and theological bigotry reigned supreme. Kingcraft, priestcraft, and aristocracy dominated the bodies and souls of men and women. The reformation had spent its force, and Protestantism had settled back into various forms of spiritual bondage. Science was dreaded and proscribed. Asia was steeped in oriental apathy, Africa was a tropical jungle, Australia was a desert. In Mexico and South America Spain had engrafted medieval despotism upon Indian savagery. Only in England and the United States existed a measure of free thought and representative government, and our own democratic institutions were poisoned by the virus of negro slavery. The rights of women were not even a subject of discussion. In every country women remained legally and politically enslaved. The Roman and the Common Law alike held them as subjects. In the Christian family, as in the Mohammedan harem, they were physically, mentally, and morally in fetters.

Suddenly, in 1790, this world-wide and age-long night of woman's subjection was illuminated by a ray of light. Mary Wollstonecraft published in London her plea for emancipation, entitled 'The Rights of Women.' For the first time in the world's history a woman pleaded the cause of her sex, and demanded social and political equality with men. Her book was ridiculed, denounced, and ignored. But it was the germ which has grown and developed, until to-day the movement is recognized and respected throughout the civilized world.

The American Revolution had resulted in a partial emancipation of thought. In 1776 the Quaker colonists of New Jersey struck out the words 'male freeholder' from the suffrage clause of their province charter, and substituted the words 'all inhabitants worth £50.' Then and there, for the first time, a few women of property voted. But when, in 1807, the property qualifications were swept away, this exceptional right was extinguished by an arbitrary and unconstitutional legal enactment.

It was not until 1837 that the woman's battle fairly began. Naturally, it first took place inside the ranks of the Abolitionists, and its earliest opponents were the New England clergy. The first demand was for freedom of speech. In 1837 Sarah and Angelina Grimké, South Carolina women, having freed their slaves, began to lecture in Massachusetts against negro slavery. A Pastoral

Letter was immediately issued by the General Association of orthodox Congregational Churches, at its convention in West Brookfield, denouncing those 'who encourage females to bear an obtrusive and ostentatious part in measure of reform,' or who 'countenance any of that sex who so far forget themselves as to itinerate in the character of public lecturers and teachers.' Young Lucy Stone sat in the gallery of the church where this Letter was read, and heard it with indignation. Then and there she consecrated herself to the mission of securing equal rights for women. From that day it became a burning and dividing question; first among the Abolitionists themselves, and soon throughout the country at large. Naturally, with the movement of women for freedom came the remonstrance from among the women themselves, in Catherine Beecher's essay on 'The Duty of American Females,' addressed to Angelina Grimké, and refuted by the latter in the columns of the *Liberator*. The controversy rent the Anti-Slavery Society in twain, and has continued with ever-increasing activity to the present hour.

The battle has taken various forms. First it was for free speech, then for the right of women to take part in public movements, then for the removal of social, industrial, educational, legal, political, and religious disabilities. The work was so all pervading that now, after 63 years, people do not comprehend the radical changes already affected by it in the position of women. The most conservative women to-day exercise without question social, educational, industrial, legal, and religious privileges and activities which were regarded with horror half a century ago. Even political rights are accepted when once conferred. Within a month the most reactionary and exclusive coteries of Boston feminine conservatism have worked with enthusiasm to enlist women as voters for Boston school committees, while deprecating with amusing inconsistency the cooperation of 'women suffragists.' In four States this very year more than 200,000 women have voted in the election of president. In twenty other States they have the right of school suffrage, and in one other full municipal suffrage. Even in states where as yet they have no votes they are elected to important political offices, and exert a growing influence in public affairs.

All honor to the brave pioneers! Frances Wright led the way in 1820. In 1837 came Sarah and Angelina Grimké, Abby Kelly, Luretia Mott, Ernestine L. Rose, and Margaret Fuller. A few years later followed Lucy Stone, Elizabeth Dana Gage, Paulina Wright, Harriot K. Hunt, Antoinette L. Brown, Elizabeth Cady Stanton, Sarah Otis Ernst, and Susan B. Anthony. Soon after came Clarissa H. Nichols of Vermont, Elizabeth B. Chace of Rhode Island, Caroline M. Severance and Josephine Griffing of Ohio, Jane G. Swisshelm and Mary Grew of Pennsylvania, Mary F. Thomas and Amanda Way of Indiana. In the sixties came Julia Ward Howe, Edna D. Cheney, Abby W. May, Elizabeth K. Churchell, Sarah Shaw Russell, Mary A. Livermore, and Hannah Tracy Cutler; in the seventies, Frances Willard, and Clara Barton, and Margaret Campbell, and a host of other women equally worthy, noble, intellectual, exemplary, and refined. It has been a glorious company, of whom the world was not worthy. Modest and unassuming, thoughtful and considerate, most of them married women, faithful to their husbands and devoted to their homes, it has been a privilege to have known them, and to be able to recall those (alas, the great majority) who have gone before us 'to that bourne whence no traveller returns.' Their unselfish labors have transformed social usages, revolutionized legal codes, purified literature, opened colleges and professional schools, established coeducation, secured admission to varied forms of industry, and converted hostility and contempt into toleration, sympathy, and respect.

In this beneficent work these women have had the continuous sympathy and cooperation of just and generous men. As early as 1836 Abraham Lincoln, as a candidate for the Illinois Legislature, in a published statement of his political views, avowed himself in favor of woman suffrage. In 1833 Rev. J.J. Shipperd, the father and founder of Oberlin College, announced as among its objects equal educational advantages for 'the hitherto misjudged and neglected sex.' In 1840, in England, Wendell Phillips and William Lloyd Garrison championed the right of women to be members of the World's Anti-Slavery Convention. In 1850 Robert Dale Owen, in the Indiana Constitutional Convention, secured independent property rights for married women. Gerrit Smith, Theodore D. Weld, Joshua R. Giddings, Charles C. Burleigh, Oliver Johnson, Elizur Wright, Stephen Foster, George William Curtis, Ralph Waldo Emerson, Theodore Parker, George W. Julian, Salmon P. Chase, Thomas Wentworth Higginson, Samuel E. Sewall, James Freeman Clarke, William I. Bowditch, William Dudley Foulke, George F. Hoar, Thomas B. Reed, Gilbert Haven, the Brothers Garrison, John K. Wildman, and many more came to the aid of aspiring womanhood in its early struggle for legal and political equality. Such supporters were a guarantee of victory.

'The Closing Century – Its Losses and Its Gains,' editorial,
Englishwoman's Review (London), 15 October 1900, pp. 221–5

Before another issue of this Review appears, Mankind will have set up another of the landmarks by which they note the roads of History – a century will have closed, memorable in many aspects, but so far as these pages are concerned, memorable as one of those turning points in the affairs of women which have appeared at long intervals in the march of all civilised races.

Such a turning point came once in dim ages for the Hellenic women, when the freedom that had marked all early Aryan families disappeared for the women of Greece, so that the light of its intellectual sunshine never penetrated the secluded dwelling-places of its daughters.

Such a turning point came to the women of India when free Vedic life was shadowed over by the Mahommedan invasion, and women had to shelter in the shadow of the zenana.

The crippled feet of China, the veiled faces of Turkey, reveal similar turning points where the balance of interdependence between men and women was disturbed.

These overbalancings came not in a moment; they were the results of many interacting influences which slowly worked together towards a climax. It would be a wondrous chapter of history to ravel out all those slow developments; but more to the purpose for us now if we can unravel the workings that have brought the Anglo-Saxon race to a similar turning point. History repeats itself; and at this very day it is repeating itself in bringing a long series of interacting causes to such another turning point in the age of steam, as befell in the age of bronze, and perchance, too, of stone.

In the century about to touch its last hour industrial changes have forced the work of a thousand homes to one giant factory, turning picturesque villages into murky towns, while accumulating political changes have brought the united wills of the ruled to influence the ruler, where once the will of the ruler stood self-proclaimed alone. Thus civic and economic forces have combined to set the balance wavering – whether (in Anglo-Saxon phrase) the 'loaf-giver' shall be free in her goings and comings in the busy haunts of industry, whether the 'peace-weaver' shall have any part in the representative voice of the nation.

Truly, history repeats itself – but then it is with a difference. There is a difference between the turning point of the Anglo-Saxon civilisation and those of China, or Turkey, or India, or Greece. Those were due to upheavals of war and conquest; ours is due to the incursions of science into the domain of history, and the leaven of a new idea in civil life; for what is constitutional representation but the translation into practical politics of the Christian ideal of the value of every single soul? The essence of popular representation is that each one shall be a potential citizen.

Again, while history is silent as to whether any efforts were made by the women of the old civilisation, any protest raised by them against the encroachments on the light and liberty of their lives, we know that in our day women have made vigorous efforts to preserve and broaden the foothold of co-operation and interdependence between men and women in the duties and responsibilities of life. It has been the privilege of this Review to chronicle those efforts, with their attendant gains and losses, through the greater part of the period during which those efforts have taken visible and tangible form.

And now, at the arrival at this new landmark in the journey, it will perhaps repay to pause and count up the measure of loss and gain. For we must reckon our losses along with our gains.

First and most prominent of these must be reckoned the closing up of the avenues to direct representation, and that at a time when those avenues were in the act of being broadened and made smooth for men. Each of our Reform Acts of 1832, 1867 and 1884 has widened the circle of direct influence on the sovereign power of Parliament for men, and has in corresponding degree forced women further back from influence on that sovereign power; in other words, has made the opinion of women of less and less value in proportion as the increased attention paid to the opinions of all classes of men has given an impetus to legislation, and especially to legislation affecting domestic and industrial interests.

So it has come to pass that now when women most need to maintain their industrial independence, they find that access to the only protection worthy of the name is denied them, and they are classed with, and treated as if they were, children. What though it is called by the illusory name of protection? By its results shall it be judged – incessant lamentations over miserable pay, and down-trodden sweated toilers, followed by a constant cry for more protection as the fruits of previous 'protection' ripen to their bitter end. So they go on from weakness to weakness, and as men and women cannot be treated apart without injury to both, so men, too, have taken up the notion that protection comes not by strength that makes for self-reliance, but by the tinkerings of law, and year by year their ideas of duty and responsibility to themselves, their wives, their children, their parents, their employers, become more lax and more vague. They cry out for law to do all their thinking for them, and so Nemesis creeps along. To spell well is treated as a more important thing in the conduct of life than to bear oneself courteously. A knowledge of the alphabet is held a better start in life than a persevering spirit, and for a child to be useful to its mother is made well nigh a sin by the fetish of education, *i.e.*, education as understood by the School Board.

Such would be our losses – were Acts of Parliament the only forces at work. But there is another force which brings some counteracting gain. Let us look, then, at our gains, and we shall perceive some gleams of better things.

The first and greatest gain is an equal standard of knowledge for men and women, with the result that the achievements of women in literature, science, and art, once treated as abnormal and exceptional, are now quite normal and usual; and the liberal learning, once confined to the very few in favoured circumstances, is within reach of numbers. And it has been recognised as a corollary to this that women's occupations also deserve systematic training, with the result that when once the training was given, the resourcefulness of women has enabled them to follow out new lines, and a new independence has dawned upon them. Married women have asserted and obtained the right to their own earnings and their own property, which the changing conditions of wealth had well-nigh destroyed. Mothers have gained some of those rights over their children which had been forgotten in the changing conditions of society.

All these changes have promoted the sense of personal responsibility which comes of independence, and have made many more women apprehend that they have a duty to the community. The Crown, since the advent of the Stuart dynasty, has ceased to appoint women to public offices of trust, like the women sheriffs and custodians of castles in olden times; but the Sovereign People have placed them by popular vote on many Boards of local administration, and some Government Departments have discovered that they can be useful as inspectors, and occasionally on departmental committees.

To compare these losses and gains reveals, on the one side an effort to repress and restrain; on the other an effort to draw out and strengthen. Which shall win?

It depends on the answer to the question – which is greatest, the Human Being or the woman? It is the persistent consideration of the woman in the Human Being, instead of the Human Being in the woman, that has lowered the chivalry of modern knights.

Chivalry dies not; it is everywhere, where the strong help the weak. But there is a selfish order of chivalry and a sympathetic order. The selfish order rejoices in encircling the weak with its strong arm, but it glories more in the strength of its arm than in the help to the sufferer, and heeds not that the very strength of its grasp may destroy the vigour of the life to be protected.

The sympathetic order thinks only how it shall put a staff of strength into the hands of the weak, leading them on from strength to strength.

Both kinds are at work amongst us to-day; but it is the selfish order that has predominated hitherto in our man-represented legislature, ready to enact restrictions and regulations to 'protect,' but hesitates, Parliament after Parliament, to give the staff that supports and makes for the only protection that is secure.

Verily when one considers the disease, the slums of vice and crime that stain the world's greatest centres, and when, too, one sees the oasis of order and cleanliness that spreads round the work of some one or more women workers here and there, one is ready to ask: Are these miseries a retribution for the one-sided economy that has shut the mother element out of all public places, and denied women their status as citizens?

'American Women as Inventors', Elizabeth L. Banks,
Cassell's Magazine (London), June 1901, pp. 47–51

'John, where's the baby-jumper?'
'Out in the front yard, hanging on the apple-tree!'
'Well, bring it to the kitchen, so I can get dinner!'

The American farmer, who has wandered from the field to the pump for a drink of water, being thus enjoined by his wife, gets the apparatus from the apple-tree, takes it to the kitchen, and hangs it on a hook. Master Willie, aged nine months, is placed therein, and the farmer's wife proceeds to make preparations for the mid-day dinner. Not a bit of rush and worry about it. The dinner is on time, it is well cooked, and the farmer's wife, without the sign of a 'hired-girl' to help her, is able to sit smiling, rosy, and happy at the table, dishing out the spring peas while her husband carves the leg of lamb.

And it's all on account of the 'baby-jumper'!

Everybody who knows anything at all about the human infant knows that during its early years, or, rather, I should say its early months, it has a predilection for being carried about and jumped up and down in its nurse's or mother's arms. It follows that the American mother who not only has no nurse for her baby, but has no servant to do her housework, must provide herself with a patent baby-jumper; so she goes to the furniture store and buys one, and, as I said before, it is the secret of her happy home!

Now, this admirable time- and labour-saving machine was invented by an American woman, Mrs. Adele Wilson, of Chicago. I do not know anything about this lady's financial circumstances at the present time. Let it be hoped that she has grown as rich as she is famous from the boon she conferred on tired American mothers; but I fancy that when she first gave her attention to the invention of the automatic baby-jumper she must have been engaged in rolling out pie-crust with her right hand, while with her left hand and arm she held a baby, and jumped it up and down, and that then, necessity being the mother of invention, she got her idea for a self-acting baby-jumper. The invention is a swing-like arrangement, made of straps and cloth and wood and wire, constituting a sort of round harness, with braces for the arms if the baby wants to stand and be jumped, and with an adjustable saddle if the baby prefers to be jumped sitting. At the top is a coiled wire spring, by which it is fastened to a tree in the yard or a hook in the house. Then the child, fastened in, is perfectly safe, the spring is set in motion, and the baby is jumped to its heart's content.

Since the first American woman inventor, Mrs. Mary Kies, of Connecticut, took out a patent for a process of weaving straw with silk in 1809, the list of women inventors at the Patent Office in Washington has become a very large one. During recent years, so great has become the number of women inventors, and so interesting their inventions, that a particular and conspicuous space is now given to the models of their inventions, so that to investigate the subject of the American woman's mechanical genius and originality one has but to ask at the Patent Office to be shown the Woman's Department.

The study of these women's inventions is also a study of the development of woman during the past ninety years, for the specifications of the patents are arranged in chronological order. In the early years of the century one notes that most of the inventions had to do with weaving, spinning, sewing, and woman's wearing apparel. After Mrs. Kies invented her straw and silk weaving apparatus, she was followed by a Mrs. Brush with a new and improved corset. Then came a process for whitening leghorn straw, and a new work-table. The years flew on and brought curious devices in the way of hoop-skirts, muffs, and methods for cutting and fitting dresses. Afterwards came devices for amusing children, then time- and labour-saving inventions for the busy house-wife and mother. With the advent of the sewing machine there came suggestions and improvements that only a woman could have thought of, and when, about a quarter of a century ago, women began to take posts as clerks, stenographers, typists, etc., there rushed into the Patent Office strange and original pens and pencils and automatic erasers. During the past ten years American women do not seem to have been devoting themselves to any one particular line of inventions, which means that their lives and their minds have broadened, and there is hardly a line or pursuit which, in the last decade, the American woman has not considered when she has gone forth inventing. She has not only taken into consideration the peculiar wants of her own sex, or of both sexes. She has gone a generous step further, and given her attention to patenting ideas designed to benefit mankind exclusively, as witness the invention of a moustache guard to enable a man to drink tea and coffee comfortably and neatly; the pantaloon tree, a continual blessing in a man's wardrobe; a machine for making cigarettes; a neck-tie clasp and holder, and shirt-front protector.

It is in the matter of 'combining' that the inventive genius of the American woman seems most to exhibit itself. The United States is the land of the folding-bed, the folding wash-stand, and the 'combined hair-curler, comber, and brusher,' along with various other combinations, and in the designing and perfecting of these combinations the American woman has had no small share. What to the traveller could be more convenient, for instance, than the 'combined bath-tub and travelling bag,' the model of which is to be found among the women's inventions at the Washington Patent Office? You leave home, satchel in hand, all your things neatly packed in it. You arrive at an inn situated in a foreign country where bath-tubs are unknown, or perhaps there is a public bath-tub which you do not like the idea of using. You unpack your satchel, made of india-rubber, painted leather-colour on the outside, press a button, adjust a few springs, and lo! you have a bath-tub, life-size!

Then there is the combined trunk, bureau, and writing desk, which also appeals to the traveller, and was, too, invented by an American woman; the folding umbrella or parasol, which you may fold up till it measures but a few inches, and is easily packed in your hand-bag; there is the combined kitchen and ironing table; the combined child's carriage and cradle; the combined horse-detacher and brake; the combined chair and sewing-machine top; the combined baby-charmer, protector, and dental cutter; the combined trunk and couch, by means of which one may always be provided with a comfortable bed while travelling by simply unlocking one's trunk. All these comforts and luxuries are the result of the American woman's cunning brain-work.

It is an American woman also who has invented the life-preserving corset, now so popular among women who cross from New York to Liverpool.

But of all the clever combinations invented by my countrywomen, it seems to me that the 'combined washing-machine and see-saw' is the most ingenious and useful. It was Mrs. Sarah Sewell, of President McKinley's state, Ohio, who devised this clever means of making the children of the household do the family washing. Monday, instead of the day of all days in the week to be dreaded, has now become the happiest day of all days in American families where the washing is done at home, while the large laundry establishments that make use of this simple contrivance for washing linen are paying little boys and girls high wages to sit in the teeter seats and see-saw joyously all day long.

'Jimmy and Mary, you may come in and do the washing!' calls the mother to her eight- or ten-year old hopefuls, who anxiously await her summons. Into the kitchen they go – or, if the weather is fine, the machine may be set up in the back yard – Jimmy seats himself on a sort of swing-board arrangement at one end of a round tub, and Mary makes a place for herself in the other swing. The machine is a hollow receiver, with a rotary clothes-holder supported on axles. By means of a crank and rods and levers it is made to go round and round by the children who sit on the teeter to which the machine is attached.

'See-saw, see-saw, now we're up, and now we're down,
See-saw, see-saw, now we're off for London town!'

shout the merry youngsters. The only drawback is that the washing is done so soon, and the teeter is not allowed to be played with except when linen is in the tub. Those persons who have no children of their own borrow their neighbours' on wash-days, or even pay them a nickel or a dime for their services. It is indeed a wonderful invention, and one calculated to mark an era in American workaday life. . . .

Dish-washing, that bugbear of house-wife and servant, the thing one must always be doing and yet can never get done, has, of course, been the subject of grave consideration and attention by the American women inventors. They have devised no less than thirty or forty different dish-washing machines, but, as yet, none of them has become popular, or perhaps I should say perfected for ordinary use. The dish pan of hot, soapy water with the dish-cloth and towel remains still the only recognised method of dish-washing.

Nearly all the modern appliances for making housekeeping easy have been the inventions of American women. A clothes-wringer, now known all over the world, was the invention of a negro charwoman in Washington. Not knowing the value of it, though she found it a useful adjunct to her own washing-day, she sold the idea to a man for eighteen dollars – less than four pounds. Had she kept it she and all her descendants would have been immensely wealthy. A self-closing bread-bin is one of the latest of the American woman's inventions, and one from which the inventor will doubtless make a fortune. It is only a cylindrical bin that closes itself the instant bread is put into it. It is also used for cake and biscuits. Then there is the pea-shelling machine, the cabbage-cutter, the various vegetable-slicing machines, the self-acting knife-washer, which keeps the handles from being put into the hot water and loosened, the egg-breaker, the fruit and vegetable peeling-machines, the raisin seeders. Patents for all these household necessities have been issued by the American Patent Office to women. . . .

Everyone has heard the phrase 'Yankee ingenuity,' and the English people are apt, in hearing it, to give the word 'Yankee' the broad meaning of American. This, however, is not the way the term is used in the United States. 'Yankee ingenuity' comes only from the New England States, where the true Yankees live. The New England women are quite as ingenious and inventive as the New England men. What is known as 'Yankee land' has produced a far greater number of women as inventors than any other section of its size in the world. After New England come the Western States, where, by the way, many of the Yankee women have emigrated. In the sunny Southern States there seem to be born very few women as inventors, although it was a Southern woman who invented the hand cotton picker a number of years ago.

'Woman: Some Phases and Crazes,' Lady Jeune,
Gentlewoman: Old and New Century Number
(London), 5 January 1901, p. 10

In every community at varying periods there have been curious and un-accountable fashions and fancies, either in amusements, occupation, dress, or religion, and in England we have been no exception to the rule. . . . Dress and amusement are generally the crazes we have followed most wildly, and though many of them are of later years, the pages of *Punch* remind us of some which are unknown or forgotten by this generation. The pictures of the time when Bloomerism was the fashion, when the strong-minded women of England threatened to follow their transatlantic sisters by adopting an emasculated form of dress, is well known to those who study the back numbers of the *Punch* of the time. Then it was to be all the fashion for a woman in putting on 'bloomers' to take up all the pursuits of a man. She was to shoot, ride, drink, and as much as possible shape her life on the same lines as her lord and master, and generally be as clever an imitation of him in his life, faults, and virtues as she could be. Some of us remember the horror and surprise the half trouser and half petticoat which was the garb the bloomer adopted [*sic*]. The bloomer was, however, a healthy woman. She was of flesh and blood, with no desire to escape the obligations of her sex. Nor was she ashamed of or unwilling to admit the superiority of man. She only wanted to copy him as closely as might be, her object being to prove that he was not a much 'better fellow' than her self. Some decades later saw the birth of another female development, but the New Woman took herself much more seriously. Not only was she physically prepared to take her stand with man, but morally and intellectually she would take no lower place in the world. Her mission was a complete reversal of the law of the sexes, and in no way was she satisfied to be on the same level as men;

hers was a higher, a more exalted aspiration; the old-fashioned career of the wife and mother was to be thrown aside, and in the neurotic atmosphere of a *fin de siècle* society, the lives of women were to be entirely changed. The New Woman made a great deal of noise and attracted much attention. We were told the whole structure of society was to be shaken to its foundations, and that the lives of men and women were to be placed on a higher, freer, nobler basis, and that the obligations of maternity and wifehood might be left to those women who were content to follow the old-fashioned, aimless career of their ancestors. The New Woman has, however, had her day, and has disappeared.

Can one talk of fashions as a craze? If so, we have lived through crinoline, which, judging by the outcry its threatened adoption produced a few years ago, was as much dreaded as the small-pox. That was a glorious instance of the want of vanity in the Englishwoman's nature, for nothing could have been more inconvenient, ugly and unbecoming than the crinoline, and we loved it and gloried in it. No door was too small, no carriage too circumscribed, no marital protest too strong to make us give it up. Larger and larger it grew, more unwieldy, more uncomfortable, but because it was the fashion English women bore it, and wore it, with the greatest heroism; and when the craze abated they abandoned it with real regret. It is perhaps hardly just to cite the crinoline epoch as a 'phase or a craze,' and yet it went perilously near it. One cannot call to mind many amusements which merit so true a title save one. Bicycling has come to stay; lawn tennis has held its own; croquet has re-appeared in invigorated power; but there was in the sixties a mad craze after 'rinking.' Everybody rinked – before breakfast, after dinner, all day long. A lucky inventor made skates on wheels which could be used on asphalt, and everyone bought them, and learnt to rink. Every disused barn, crystal palace, empty building of any size or shape, was made into a rink, and in London all classes rubbed shoulders at Olympia, Prince's, and elsewhere. There surely was never in the memory of man such a furore for any amusement for so short a time; but, alas! the fickleness of the goddess of pleasure and the fact that the existing places became also the happy hunting grounds of the frailer sisterhoods struck the note of their doom; they disappeared as rapidly as they came. Even the sacred cause of charity has had its *moment délire*, for we can nearly all of us remember the delights of 'slumming.' For our own credit let it be said, it grew out of a genuine feeling of sympathy and sorrow for the poor in London and the big towns; but the well-to-do and kind-hearted could not resist the excitement of seeing how half the world lived, and so for a time 'slumming' was all the fashion, and smart women and men, eager to probe the mysteries and horrors of the East-End, gave up time and legitimate amusement to dwell on pictures of suffering, vice, and wickedness. *Punch* held our humanitarian craze up to scorn and ridicule in his picture of parties of well-dressed people going down in the evening to Whitechapel and Seven Dials. Everyone talked of nothing else, and every class was engaged in the thought of the blackness of the picture. A great many men and women went in search of the truth, and out of that phase of English curiosity much good has come. There is a delightful story told, which shows to what an extent the feeling existed that something terrible must be shown to observers by the purveyors of these horrors. An exalted personage went to see one of the worst dens in the worst slums of London, accompanied by some friends and the local sanitory inspector, who did not know the rank of his visitor. As the party reached a place where sin, poverty, and wickedness abounded on every side, the cicerone slapped the August person on the back, exclaiming, 'What do you think of that, old pal?' But surely the most curious of all the phases and crazes which have come over English society was the wave of aestheticism which for many years held sway, when all with a true conception of art worshipped in ecstasy before works that had no ideal of outline, no grace of imagination, no beauty of colour, when everything was *en couleur degradée*, and the votaries of culture and art were swathed in clinging robes of dirty-looking green, yellow, and blue material. When the male apostle of the gospel of art endeavoured to adapt his dress, appearance, and ways of life to suit the fashionable craze, Postlwaithe was the embodiment of the 'greeny-yallery' (sic) fancy of the hour. Dress was ugly, decoration was cold and dirty-looking, furniture was uncomfortable, and there was a meagre starved look over all that was considered the gospel of art. Mercifully, aestheticism died of inanition, and the ridicule of the world sounded its knell. A few faithful souls still cling to the memory of its ruined temples, but the reaction is one of colour in decoration and dress, which is the more brilliant in contrast to its sombre predecessor. What the next fancy that arises will be one cannot say; there are so many sources from which amusement and originality can be evolved. Electricity is still in its infancy, and there are endless developments which it may produce. Whatever it is, it must be something within the range of people of moderate incomes, because in this country pleasure and amusement are no longer the monopoly of the rich, for the phases and crazes of modern life, with all their attendant follies, must be those in which every class can participate.

'Woman in Science,' Miss Agnes M. Clerke, *Gentlewoman:*
Old and New Century Number (London), 5 January 1901, p. 12

Although no higher summits in science have been reached by women during the nineteenth century than in earlier times, their average performance has amazingly improved. Indeed, until lately, there was no 'average performance' on their part to be recorded. Individuals of powerful genius emerged now and again from domestic or cloistered obscurity, and did what it was given to them to do amid acclamations. But their course was too peculiar to excite emulation. It lay at a hopeless distance from ordinary female experience. Hence, they had no disciples of their own sex. The auditors of their discourses, the readers of their treatises, were men. And the first was perhaps the brightest of these apparitions. Here, as elsewhere, Greek intellect claimed supremacy. Hypatia, the Muse of Alexandria, has not, so far, been outshone. Nor can any later mathematical work by a woman vie with the 'Analytical Institutions' of Maria Agnesi, printed upwards of a century and a half ago. The future, however, depends much more upon the capacity of many than upon the inspiration of a few. And a distinctive note of the recent age is the display of a widely diffused feminine capacity for high and sustained mental toil. We have touched the shore of a New Atlantis, where the 'compilers' and 'deprecators' of Solomon's House – to say nothing of stray 'merchants of light' and occasional 'interpreters of nature' – are 'ladies and pale-visaged maids.' Of this coming aid to the advancement of knowledge, Bacon's glowing visions gave him no hint; yet it doubles the reserves of humanity, and must tend effectually to quicken the pace of the torch-bearers in the millennial race.

Caroline Herschel does not fit easily into the Baconian framework of classification. She was much more than a mere 'hand' in a scientific factory; yet she made no pretence to rank as an accredited emissary to the Unknown. Far different from Bacon's *savante* –

> Un astrolabe en main, qui a, dans sa gouttière,
> A suivre Jupiter passe la nuit entière,

she was led skyward by her heart rather than by her head, and along a path of self-sacrifice. Her personal ambition as a vocalist had to give way to the demands of duty and affection. The struggle was interior, but severe. She allowed none to know what it cost her to exchange the concert-stage for the observatory. It was dreary work at first. Night after night, and all night long, she sat, rigid with cold, or worn with fatigue, yet invariably alert, by her brother's telescope. Her devotion made his achievements possible. No hired assistant could have coped with his unsparing energy. But she was, in her way, as indomitable as he. She had his rapidity, too. No lagging brain directed the movements of her small person; eye, ear, and hand acted like lightening. Finally, her enthusiasm was kindled, and 'consolation prizes,' in the shape of eight comet discoveries, fell to her share. Her catalogues of stars and nebulae, although works of simple computation, testified, by the judgement with which they were planned and the perfection with which they were executed, to her possession of faculties of no common order.

Mary Somerville, on the contrary, was born what she became. She was a mathematician of the 'inevitable' type. A simple Roxburghshire lassie, she taught herself algebra and geometry by stealth, in the intervals of learning Johnson's Dictionary by heart, the form of education prescribed for her at school. In 1831 she published an abridged translation of Lapace's 'Mécanique Céleste,' which drew from its author the remark that she was the only woman who correctly apprehended the abstruse trains of reasoning therein embodied.

This noteworthy performance excited the applause of the learned, the awe-struck admiration of the ignorant. It was followed up, after three years, by a masterly treatise, 'On the Connexion of the Physical Sciences,' the more general scope of which obtained for it a wider circulation. It passed through many editions, and is still read. Six editions of her 'Physical Geography' were issued from 1848 onward, and the book was stamped with authoritative approval by the bestowal, in 1869, of the Royal Geographical Society's Victoria gold medal. A volume on 'Molecular and Microscopic Science,' published in 1869, was an astonishing production for a lady nearly ninety years of age, who, more-over, took a keen interest in the 'Mediterranean' eclipse of the sun, visible December 22, 1870. She died at Naples, November 29, 1872, in the full possession of her faculties. Her sunny and serene existence was one prolonged contradiction of Beauchene's sour apothegm, 'La science rend les hommes rare-ment aimables, les femmes jamais.' Time respected even her external graces. She looked young when dates and registers declared her to be old. A foe to pedantry, she cultivated the ornamental and useful arts of life – music, drawing, needlework, housewifery. The offer of 'a penny for her thoughts,' once evoked the laughing avowal that they were concerned with a 'new bonnet.'

Mrs. Somerville cultivated the traditional astronomy; Lady Huggins is a modern astrophysicist. Spontaneously she was groping her way, on one side of St. George's Channel, towards the science which Sir William Huggins, on the other, was establishing on a secure basis. The coalescence of their lines of endeavour ensued in 1875, with noteworthy results. Margaret Lindsay Huggins has thus aided, on equal terms, in the fulfilment of a great career, possibly at some cost and sacrifice, for originative instincts are obstinate; they can only be brought under the co-operative yoke by purposeful restraint and sustained enthusiasm. Just a year ago Sir William and Lady Huggins issued jointly, as the first volume of 'Tulse Hill Publications,' an 'Atlas of Representative Stellar Spectra.' This sumptuous folio, distinguished by the managers of the Royal Institution with the Actonian prize of one hundred guineas, includes an extensive set of plates portraying the spectral varieties of the stars from photographs taken at Tulse Hill, accompanied by profound discussions of their significance as regards cosmic life-history. It is adorned with original drawings of great interest by Lady Huggins. It may be added that she is the first Irishwoman who has attained scientific eminence.

Miss Elizabeth Brown took an active part in the foundation of the British Astronomical Association, and was for nine years director of its solar section. A skilful and assiduous solar artist, she travelled indefatigably, on occasions of total eclipse, to such parts of the globe as were crossed by the moon's shadow. The misdoings of the elements, however, largely frustrated her exertions. At Trinidad, in 1886, she saw something, but not much, of the glorious phenomena revealed by obscurations; absolutely nothing at Moscow and in Lapland in 1887 and 1896. Her disappointments are gaily chronicled in the booklets entitled, 'Caught in the Tropics' and 'In Pursuit of a Shadow.' While preparing for a fourth expedition to view the 'Spanish' eclipse of last May she was overtaken by sudden death, March 5, 1900.

Mrs. Walter Maunder has been more fortunate. Her first eclipse, the track of which bisected the Indian Peninsula, January 22, 1898, afforded a magnificent opportunity, amply availed of. With a tint lens one and a-half inches in diameter, she succeeded in photographing coronal streamers far exceeding in length any previously recorded by chemical means; and her repetition of the experiment at Algiers, May 28, 1900, had a less striking outcome only because of the shortness of totality inconveniently limited the time allowable for exposures. Her start in the astronomical course dates from 1891, when, as Miss Dill Russell, she accepted the post of computer in the Royal Observatory, Greenwich. Four years later she married the distinguished physical assistant in the establishment.

Miss Alice Everett was a member of the same staff for about five years. In 1895 she transferred her services to the Potsdam Observatory, and there, until July 1899, devoted herself with extreme diligence to the measurement of stars on photographic chart-plates. For this kind of work women show a marked aptitude. Their patience, rapidity of perception, delicacy of sight and touch, are invaluable in micro metrical research. They are, hence, extensively employed in the various forms of celestial survey now progressing all over the world, and can claim many discoveries in connection with them.

Two *virtual* Senior Wranglers have issued from ladies' colleges – Miss Charlotte Scott and Miss Philippa Fawcett. Miss Scott was appointed in 1888, Professor of Mathematics at Bryn Mawr College, Pennsylvania, and became, in 1899, one of the co-editors of the *American Journal of Mathematics*. Miss Fawcett has preferred to turn her abstract powers to account in physical inquiries. To physics also Miss Dorothy Marshall, Lecturer on Natural Science at Girton College, has made meritorious contributions; while electrical investigations have been carried out by Mrs. Ayrton.

Miss Eleanor Ormerod is a fellow of the Entomological and of the Royal Meteorological Societies. Her 'Manual of Injurious Insects' is of standard and permanent utility; she is the leading authority on the pests of the farm and the orchard. For many years she acted as Examiner in Agriculture at the University of Edinburgh; and the Société Nationale d'Acclimatation de France awarded her a silver medal in 1899. Her unique position is due, not only to the persistent minuteness of her inquiries, but to the sagacity with which she has co-ordinated their results. Nothing is more remarkable in the recent development of female scientific ability than the variety in its mode of display. In geology, for instance, Miss Caroline Raisin is an acknowledged expert; Miss A.W. Buckland takes high rank as an ethnologist; Mrs. Percy Frankland labours effectively in the wonderland of bacteriology; Miss Alice Lee is a well-known biologist; and many more names might be cited.

The popularisation of science, in particular, falls within the scope of our sex. Women have usually an instinct for teaching. They can divine by sympathy and disentangle by deft thought, perplexities which they do not share. Even Mrs. Marcet's old-world 'Conversations on Chemistry' deserved, by their homely sincerity, the vogue which they enjoyed, and they determined Faraday's vocation. Better things were indeed to come. Beginners in biology can have no safer or more delightful guide than Mrs. Fisher (Arabella Buckley), whose 'Life and Her Children,' 'Winners in Life's Race,' and 'Fairyland of Science' have charmed thousands of readers. Miss Agnes Giberne has written admirable elementary books on astronomy entitled, 'Sun, Moon, and Stars,' and 'Radiant Suns'; she has treated geology in a corresponding style in 'The World's Foundations,' and meteorological physics in 'The Ocean of Air.' Finally the present writer has published 'A Popular History of Astronomy during the Nineteenth Century,' 'The System of the Stars,' 'The Herschels and Modern Astronomy,' and is part-author of a volume on astronomy in the 'Concise Knowledge Library.'

'Woman and the Law,' Dr J.G. Shipman, LL.D, MP,
Gentlewoman: Old and New Century Number (London),
5 January 1901, p. 16

During the century which has just closed woman in more directions than one has taken a long step forward. She has come more and more in the light, and the dawn of the New Century reveals her personality with more clearness than was possible a hundred years ago. I am, of course, speaking of woman in the eye of the law.

Within the region of private law, woman, as woman, does not seem, in modern times, to have suffered from the disqualification of sex to any very appreciable extent. She has been able to hold property, to make contracts and break them, to commit torts and pay for them, with practically as much facility and freedom as her inferior colleague man. In one important department of the law, however, woman has suffered, and is still suffering, from a gross injustice. Her right to succeed to real property, where no will has been made, is not a right which she enjoys equally with man. By the law of primogeniture, which to the shame of our democratic age still exists, the real estate of any person dying without a will descends to the eldest son, if there are more sons than one, and it only descends to a daughter if there are not sons at all. I admit there is an injustice to the younger sons, but the injustice is greater to an elder daughter. If there are several daughters they all share equally. That, at any rate, is a rule of common sense, but not of primogeniture. The reason given for preferring the male to the female is called a feudal one. I might make it plainer by calling it a fighting one. In the case of the now extinguished tenure by knight service there was some sort of justification for preferring a tenant who could render knight service. But this rule of descent held good, or rather bad, even in the gentler tenure of free socage, where no knight service was required, and the fact that it reigns supreme to-day shows that behind the feudal reason there is another, and one which is not working in the interests of women.

When we consider woman as wife then we see that the disqualification of coverture, or marriage, has been greater than that of mere sex.

By the common law of England a wife's personality is merged in that of her husband. They are said to be one, a position very much to the advantage of the legal one – the husband. By the fact of the marriage alone the property of the woman became practically the man's. The husband's power, however, was not quite so great over his wife's land as it was over her goods. It was practically absolute in the latter case. With respect to land he had very large rights during the marriage, but if his wife outlived him she came to her own again. If he survived her, then descendible property went to her heir, subject under certain conditions to a right which he might have to enjoy it for the remainder of his life.

The wife's power over her land was practically nothing. She could neither sell nor will; but husband and wife, acting in blessed unity and observing certain forms, could dispose of her property to their heart's delight.

A long time before the beginning of the last century the Courts of Equity, exercising a jurisdiction independent of that of the Common Law, had begun the pleasing process of disentangling the personality of the wife from that of the husband. The object in view was to separate the property intended for the benefit of the wife and keep it from the interfering hand of her spouse. This they did with the most complete success. Perhaps the most important case tending to that result was one which, in 1865, declared that a 'femme covert (married woman), where not restrained from alienation, has incident to her separate estate, and without any express power, a complete right of alienation by instrument inter vivos, or will.' The work which equity has done on behalf of the separate estate of a married woman culminated in the Married Women's Property Act of 1882. By that Act a woman, married after it came into force, has absolute power over all the property which was her own at the time of her marriage, or which she, in any way, has acquired after. Even women married before the 1st of January, 1883, have a similar power over any property which comes to them after that date.

Until the interesting case of Mr. Jackson in 1891 it was thought by many that a husband could compel his wife to live with him. That idea is now exploded, and although he may have obtained an order entitling him to a restitution of conjugal rights, there is really no power to give it practical effect, since an Act has been passed abolishing imprisonment for the contempt with which it was often received.

Want of space forbids me to touch upon that kindly course of legislation protecting women from many of the hardships incident to certain trades and unwomanly forms of labour. It will be found in the Factory Acts of the latter half of the last century.

Within the reign of public law, woman, as woman, has suffered a disqualification of sex. The late Lord Esher, in a case touching upon the electoral rights of woman, said: 'By the common law of England women are not in general deemed capable of exercising public functions, though there are certain exceptional cases where a well-recognised custom to the contrary has become established, as in the case of overseers of the poor; and, of course, if women are especially mentioned in an Act of Parliament they will be qualified.'

In another case (Charlton v. Lings, L.R.4, C.P.374) there is some very instructive reading upon this branch of our subject. I refer to it because in that case a celebrated judge (the late Mr. Justice Willes) said, with reference to the exclusion of woman from public functions, 'What was the cause of it it is not necessary to go into; but admitting that fickleness of judgement and liability to influence have sometimes been suggested as the ground of exclusion, I must protest against its being supposed to arise in this country . . . from any underrating of the sex, either in point of intellect or worth. That would be quite inconsistent with one of the glories of our civilisation – the respect and honour in which women are held. This is not a mere fancy of my own, but will be found in Selden, in the discussion of the origin of the exclusion of women from judicial and like public functions, where the author gives preference to this reason, that the exemption was founded upon motives of decorum, and was a privilege of the sex. Selden's Works, Vol. I, pp. 1083–5.'

It is, however, within the domain of public law that woman, as woman and not as wife, has made a very perceptible advance during the last Century. Within that period she obtained the right to vote at a municipal election, whether in the provinces or the new London municipal areas, but she failed to win the right to be elected to sit as mayor, alderman, or councillor. Similarly with reference to the county council elections. The right to sit on the County Council was, however, tested in the case of the late Lady Sandhurst, who, it will be remembered, had been elected as one of the two councillors for the Brixton Division in 1889. There was little hope of a successful result. In fact the hope, both nominal and real, was all on the other side, and the victory of Mr. Beresford-Hope had the ungallant effect of preventing an excellent woman from devoting her experience and ability where it could best be utilised. It may be noticed as a comforting concession to woman, even though she be a wife, that she is allowed not only to vote for, but to sit as, a parish or district councillor; but it is carefully provided that if she should be selected as chairman of a district council, she must forego the honour of a justiceship of the peace.

These concessions may be regarded as crumbs of comfort – or shall we say as tubs, thrown out to the lady whale to play with, in the hope that the ship of State may be spared her attacks? For, after all, the Parliamentary vote is the blue riband of their enfranchising efforts. Yet it is strange that women are not wholly united upon this question. Many of them are still content with the tubs – I don't necessarily mean the washing-tubs. We of the opposite sex who demand the complete enfranchisement of woman in the eye of the law are cheered by the fact that the history of reform shows that not necessarily to those who are to receive its blessings come the energy and hope of winning them. When the present century shall have reached its close, the fair chronicler of that distant day, writing from the seats of the mighty and not from the humble one I am permitted to occupy, will be able to show that the comparatively few legal and political inequalities, momentous though they be, have long since ceased to exist. May it also be within her power to justify their removal by glorying in the many instances of woman holding the highest offices of State with a dignity and decorum worthy of that great Queen-sovereign whose name alone would seem to have called forth and consecrated the very period so largely reserved to the victory of woman.

'Woman and the Stage,' Mrs Kendal, *Gentlewoman: Old and New Century Number* (London), 5 January 1901, p. 26

It has been a century of progress in stage matters, taking all in all. No second Mrs. Siddons has arisen in the nineteenth century (I am speaking of the English stage only, and of actresses in particular), for though Mrs. Siddons lived till 1831 her dramatic triumphs belonged essentially to the close of the previous century, as did those of Mrs. Jordan, Miss Farren, and Miss Pope.

But there is a goodly list of names, great if not so great, belonging to the last hundred years. Those of Louisa Brunton, Miss Duncan, Mrs. Glover, Mrs. Charles Kemble are among the earliest; of more recent date, among many others, I call to mind Miss O'Neill, Frances Ann Kemble, Helen Faucit, Adelaide Neilson, Kate Terry.

It is commonly asked whether the great actors and actresses of years ago were to reappear before us now we should delight in them as keenly as did our forefathers, or whether we would not rather find them stilted, affected, unnatural. I fancy we are secretly inclined to suspect them of ranting, of bombastic speech and gesture.

This is scarcely fair. Certainly 'realism' as we understand the term today was undreamt of a hundred (even fifty) years ago. I think, however, we may safely accept the testimony of such men as Lamb, Hazlitt, and Leigh Hunt. The man who wrote of Bensley, 'He was totally destitute of trick and artifice; he seemed to come upon the stage to do the poet's message simply; . . . he let the passion or the sentiment do its own work without prop or bolstering,' would no more have tolerated gross affectation than we should to-day.

When we remember that even Mrs. Siddons once played *Portia*, and 'with vast success,' dressed in a 'salmon-coloured sack and coat,' and Mrs. Crouch one of the witches in 'Macbeth' in a 'killing fancy hat, her hair superbly powdered, rouge laid on with delicate effect, and her whole exquisite person enveloped in a cloud of point lace and fine linen,' we must either assume stupendous powers of imagination on the part of the audience, or else allow full measure of compelling genius to the artists.

Some of the incongruities and anachronisms in the old days are delicious to read about. One instance will better illustrate the enormous progress made between that time and our own than columns of formal comparison. It is recorded that one celebrated old actor in the part of *Falstaff*, just after the fight, when *Falstaff* is supposed to sit on the stump of a tree and philosophise, 'calmly sank down into a crimson velvet chair with gold claws and blue fringes, conveniently pitched on the field of battle'!

Another man played *Earl Percy* with 'pendant locks, profusely powdered, prettily tied up in a cluster of light blue streamers.' Kemble, it is well known, played *Hamlet* in powdered hair and the Order of the Garter beneath his knee. Those were simple days. But in the sense of being unburdened by details and unhampered by hair-splitting controversies, perhaps the art was purer, less subtle, but more direct.

Of modern times the most deplorable change from an artistic point of view is the supersession – the virtual supersession, that is – of the old-fashioned stock companies.

There can be no dispute over their incomparable excellence, as school and training ground for the young actor. Where else would he find such varied opportunities, such a field for downright practical experience? Where else would the young actress have the chance 'within a week to play everything from *Lady Macbeth* to *Papillonnetta*'? In these days of long runs when the beginner is given a tiny part how can he help 'indifference creeping o'er his soul' say at the 105th performance?

However, I said it has been a century of progress, and so, on the whole, I think it has. First (and in the eyes of some foremost) the conditions of our profession, material as well as social, have improved to an extent that would have been deemed impossible even in my own grandfather's time. No doubt hard times are still endured by hundreds of young beginners, men and women; but compare their struggles and sacrifices with those, for instance, of Edmund Kean and his wife in their early days. Once, for lack of means, husband and wife had to walk from Birmingham to Swansea, two hundred miles.

Consider the difference of the social atmosphere that the actor of today breathes and lives in. Much less than a century ago actors were outcasts and vagabonds, classed in public notices along with cattle and puppies.

The enormous importance the stage has latterly attained as a factor in public life and thought gives cause for satisfied reflection too. To quote Lamb again: 'We do not go to the theatre like our ancestors to escape from the pressures of reality, *so much as to confirm our experience of it*, to make assurance double and take a bond of fate.'

As an educator the theatre is at once popular and considerable. Viewed from its highest point, it might almost lay claim to be that famous royal road to learning denounced in our childish days as a phantom and miserable delusion. Its influence is unbounded, and spreads over every class of society.

The public taste has improved, and as a correlative, the standard of modern plays. As the moral (or immoral) trend of the modern problem play, it seems to me a vast amount of nonsense has been written about its deleterious effect; in my opinion in nine cases out of ten it has made unthinking people think, and in the tenth case it has probably been far less unpleasant than the broad buffoonery of the old farces and burlesques.

The stage of today ranks as high – and deservedly so – as any other profession, and offers a position to the right man and woman, honourable alike to artist and individual. The 'right' man and woman are those whose watchword is 'work.' (It was Betterton, I think, who at seventy years of age said he had only just mastered the rudiments of his art.) Incessant work, incessant observation, untiring application. 'We fall to rise, are baffled to fight better.'

'Woman and Fashion,' Juno, *Gentlewoman: Old and New Century Number* (London), 5 January 1901, p. 28

It is with the century, as it reveals itself in the ways of its womenfolk, that I want to talk in this column. A woman's tastes and temperament may express themselves in the poise of her head-gear or the twist of her cravat, so a period's fashion will portray its tendencies, positively mirror back its dominating spirit. We women of to-day perhaps have too great a 'conceit of ourselves,' but as we run our eye along the narrative of clothes from the beginning to the end of the 19th century, it seems to us that while history repeats itself continually, only to-day can it be said that grace and good common sense are found balancing each other. In the modes and manners of the moment we revive the particular elegancies but not the eccentricities of past phases. It is immensely interesting, peeping back, to regard simultaneously 'the daughters of Eve' in 1801 and 1900. They have many points in common. There is the same clinging silhouette, the evidence of the same love of the picturesque, indeed, almost the same bolero. There is the same delightful defiance of the weather, too, only in more reckless degree. It is for a winter walk she is rigged, that graceful sprite in the muslin cap. Fashion will have these flings, when the love of loveliness possesses her beyond reason. She is an irresponsible creature, and 'chassez le naturel et il revient en galop.' At the beginning of the century the modes of the First Empire completely dominated the English spirit, a phase which the Parisians founded on the reversion to classic simplicity under the Directory and the Consulate, these periods of the demolition of all inter-vening established order and tradition. One supposes that in England the phase could have meant nothing more than fascination. The Parisienne of the period was a picture; in fact, she was first a picture and afterwards a woman.

Muslins, and all soft, thin fabrics went from season to season, irrespective of the climate, which we suppose was no more ideal then than to-day. A feature that interests us just now was the wearing of big picturesque hats of satin or black velvet with evening dress, for dances, dinner, parties, the opera, the theatre, etc., along with which often appeared big muffs. The whim undoubtedly is immensely becoming, and as far as the hats are concerned, may be revived for all we know in our own day, indeed has already been hinted at. Of course, then as now, there were always those who rode hard and fast after fashion and those who followed her at a discreet distance, and many portraits exist to prove that the warm winter pelisse of velvet or silk clad in winter the shoulders of the more sensible.

Between the years of 1820 and 1850 a gradual revulsion from the antique set in, the waist removed itself from its quaint position under the arms, and settled down where nature ordained it was to be, from which, with unimportant changes, it has never since moved. The same movement produced also a tendency to widen and shorten the skirts and to employ materials which stood out. Embroiderings in bright colourings, gold braid, and fringes put in an appearance. But these years were distinctly unsettled – at least, the earlier part.

Early in the '30's was an interesting epoch in the manners of the mere man, for then he was settling down to the simplicity of his present-day attire and dispensing with his elegant knee-breeches – this, however, only after a struggle between the practical and the ornate that had lasted since the close of the eighteenth century. Despite some of its follies, it is a very attractive period, the early years of her Majesty's reign, when a beautiful girl-Queen led the van of fashion with a sweet and graceful simplicity. A fashionable maiden of '38 . . . airing her poke-bonneted demure charm . . . is going to church, I should imagine. Our artist has been studying the career of Her Royal Highness from several points of view, and whilst here we survey her in outdoor guise, [other pages] reveal her in the sporting garb . . . in her Court gowns, and . . . in the indoor gowns that have prevailed during the passing of a hundred years. The practical was not so important an element in sporting attire in those times, and the daughter of to-day will eye with derision that voluminous and romantic riding-gear. To come back to the poke-bonneted beauty, however. Though expansive as to petticoats, it was not yet the crinoline but petticoat that was to be held responsible for this feature of her attire. That was reserved for a later era. It is said that the skirts widened themselves to balance the width of the shoulders, all the bodices of this period being dominated by the pelerine idea. The pelerine was the most popular wrap of both London and Paris for a long time, and its inspiration was everywhere evident. *A la pelerine* was the leading idea. Sleeves, too, were larger both in obedience and of necessity. Hairdressing was often a little aggressive also, the hair standing in loops around the head. The waistline was becoming gradually longer and more pointed in front, and about the year 1840 to possess a small waist was the first of all feminine charms, and the fashion papers of the moment gave their readers wrinkles in the ways and means of its attainment. The habited damsel of this precise era is positively wasp-like in her slenderness, and so again is the ringleted and rose-adorned young thing with spreading skirts ready for the dance. By 1842 all frocks were trailing again, and a Parisian wag was suggesting in one of the journals that there was no reason in the city authorities employing scavengers when the ladies were so willing to give their services gratis. At this time, too, prevailed those dreadfully funny little parasols with long fringes and doubling-up handles, which must in those days with the big bonnets have looked extraordinarily quaint. This also was the age of the lace mitten as well as the ringlet and of the gorgeous waistcoats of the men to which Thackeray refers in *Vanity Fair*, when he relates how 'Joseph Sedley went to town in a waistcoat of crimson satin, embroidered with gold butterflies and a rich blue satin stock and gold pin.'

That the tall silk hat supplanted the beaver about 1840 was another notable fact, the new species coming from Paris and very rapidly becoming a permanent institution, though abused during all these intervening sixty years. A period of unredeemed ugliness, a period guilty of reviving the crinoline, occurred between the '50's and the '70's. Don't these balloon-like beings . . . condemn themselves, and, not only by reason of their crinolines, but by the gorgeousness of their fabrics, too ostentatious and heavy for grace, even were they not distended from the figure by the hooped petticoat. Indeed, it is protested that the gorgeous material was the cause and the hooped petticoat the result of all this wandering from sense and elegance. In 1850, even girls went to dinner parties in brocades, damasks, and moiré antiques. A silk frock was the hall mark of gentility, for then people possessed 'best clothes.' This, too, was the era of the Indian shawl and coalscuttle bonnet, filled in round the face with a bewitching arrangement of flowers and lace quillings and tied under the chin with broad expanding ribbons. That flounced and velvet pelissed lady . . . imagined herself very elegant we are convinced.

By 1860 the crinoline, revived in '54, was at its height. This revival, by the way, has been attributed to the Empress Eugenie. Even little girls were set up in crinolines, and some of the pictures of little girls in crinolines, and, terrible to relate, little boys arrayed in frilled trousers are too funny for words. There is attributed to the Empress Eugenie, also, a revival of the clear white muslin frock.

It is interesting to notice that the forerunner of our modern-day blouse – the Garibaldi – appeared in '65. By '68 the crinoline had ceased to exist, and the revulsion from width resulted by about 1876 in the peculiarly monstrous costume on the right. In the crinoline our grandmothers could scarcely sit down. In '76 their daughters could neither walk nor sit with any ease.

At the beginning of the '80's the great aesthetic movement, at first a colour cult and then a craze, was set afloat. Taste went back with a rush to soft clinging fabrics, and the colour sense, being immensely cultivated, resulted in a great advance in textile manufactures.

The features of our own day are too familiar to need comment; the tailor costume, the teagown, and special fashions for children are its absolutely new features. We were never at the same moment so luxurious and so practical, and Dame fashion would indeed have to be versatile to keep pace with the woman of 1901 – a creature who can lounge as effectually as she can take a fence, who is at once luxurious, practical, *feministe* and athletic, perhaps the most remarkable type of the womanhood a remarkable century has produced.

'Woman in Literature,' Mrs Wilfrid Meynell, *Gentlewoman: Old and New Century Number* (London), 5 January 1901, p. 30

The nineteenth century has produced women writers out of all proportion to women artists, and it is the novelists that swell the count. Women have worked in a multitude upon the other arts, but yet not in relation to their numbers. In the novel, on the other hand, they have done more than is proportionate. They have written the little novel, the story for children, in the following of Maria Edgeworth, the novel of humour and manners in the following of Jane Austen, the novel of emotion and will in the following of Charlotte Brontë, and the theological novel in the wake of George Eliot. But of these authors by far the most influential has been Charlotte Brontë. Her history, her work, her sorrows, took the imagination of man, woman, and child; and with the ambition, the day-dream, the self-consciousness, and the anger of women born to obscurity, her example wrought. To the unnumbered ranks of girls destined, most unjustly, to one inevitable career of teaching, the fame of the governess, poor, born in obscurity, and ill-favoured, but with a fiery heart, was a single message of hope and suggestion of glory. Many a woman out of reach of envy towards the fortunate and the brilliant, was touched to the quick by the renown of the unfortunate author of *Jane Eyre*. It seemed a possible, a not improbable, an accessible splendour; something golden lurking in the dullest of all dull worlds, and discoverable once again – haply, yet once again. *Jane Eyre* went far to make half a century of novelists, but the first half century had been made, more or less, by an eighteenth century example – that of Fanny Burney. The surprise of Dr. Burney and the success of *Evelina* tempted many a daughter, excited many a maid. The echo of that publication lasted long.

Needless to say, only the minor novelists, and those whose names can hardly take their place in the history of the century, subjected themselves thus to the suggestions of the example of genius. Great authors, on the contrary, were born, bred, and did their work singly. Apart from the two already named as the setters of examples, they have all, in their degree and place, stood alone; and singular, separate, the first of her kind, the first great author of the nineteenth century who was a woman, was one of these founders of dynasties – the satirist, Jane Austen. Her work is closely limited; it has nothing free, nothing spiritual, nothing remote. It deals with character as the discipline of the preceding century had left it amongst the educated, fairly rich, and entirely untravelled. All the persons of her little drama confess one doctrine of religion and acknowledge one law of morals; their differences are those slight ones that are so much more humourous than great ones – small disparities of rank and breeding, with the vulgarities a little below and the patronage or evasion a little above; and the more human diversities of temperament (yet these, too, small), wherewith man and women are born even into a world moulded and regulated by the passage of the eighteenth century. Never were novels more strictly novels of society than these records of narrow, easy, provincial life – that is, novels of the relative aspect of men to one another, rather than their aspect to Nature or to God. Never was an original genius so content amid such a world, or fine art more easily intent upon little things. Extravagant things have been said of Jane Austen – for instance, she has been coupled with Shakespeare by the very inspiration of blunder; but it is no extravagance to say of her that she is a faultless artist; nay, this is but negative praise to give to one who has exquisite excellences. Susan Ferrier obviously had ambitions in the direction of Miss Austen's somewhat derisive humour, but with a more girlish romance of invention in her plots. She was much read in the thirties. Tennyson, falling into her mood of gay costume-romance, took the central incident of one of her clever stories for the subject of his *Lady Clare*. She has humour, roughly ironical, and good humour as well, a farcical enjoyment of the ill-dressing, the solecisms, of her grotesque characters; as for the irreproachable persons of the company, they always speak 'with increasing agitation.' A few women – the Misses Porter, who wrote romances, Mrs. Gore, who wrote the fashionable novel down to the fifties, need not detain us. But Miss Edgeworth was another founder of a dynasty – as a novelist of Irish life spirited, as a writer for young girls full of invention, too prim in her work for children, and in every case insistent in respect of the moral.

In and about the forties there was a new outbreak of the literature of women. To name but a few authors then in the vigour of their working day: Miss Barret, Mrs. Norton, and Miss Procter; Miss Kavanagh, Mrs. Gaskell, Miss Mitford, Charlotte and Emily Brontë, Miss Martineau, Mrs. Jameson, Miss Strickland, and Mrs. Somerville were writing. Of the two last it may be said that their work, albeit conveyed in books, is not, strictly speaking, literary. Nevertheless, the work of both was important in its kind. A 'movement' cannot produce genius, but it may stimulate a great number of abilities. And there can be no doubt that what was called in those days the woman movement, or woman's rights, or what not, had much to do with this sudden affluence of literary production. Amongst the throng, some of whose names – nay, a few only – I have just cited as contemporaries, three only were great authors – Elizabeth Barrett, Charlotte Brontë, Emily Brontë; and one only

– Mrs. Gaskell – was an author of fine talent. Miss Martineau wrote one book – a Norwegian story – in which something spiritual, something poetic appears, or is suggested; but the rest – political economy, domestic economy, travel – her travels in the Holy Land, for instance, how contentedly and even proudly dull a work! – everything is the work of an essentially undistinguished mind, and her style is the English of Commerce, neither simple nor beautiful. Miss Mitford has good negative quality, and some, finding in her no corruption, no affectation, no vulgarity, have mistaken her for a good writer. Mrs. Gaskell wrote not only one of the classic biographies of our literature – I have named the Life of Charlotte Brontë; she drew with a keen pen the portraits of women in her novels; the men are the convention of a sensible woman's imagination in that day, but the satire of Mrs. Gibson in *Wives and Daughters* is nature and art.

Charlotte Brontë, then, is central. Her genius was sufficient to itself, and it needed all its power. The narrowing limits of her world and her social conditions have often been dwelt upon; not so the far more oppressive limitations of the instrument she had to use – the English of her time, artificial, stale, tired out, Latinised, not in the Johnsonian manner, but as the circulars of trade have it. And this modern English was made yet more dull by the conditions of the school teacher and the governess. Yet out of this she broke, from this she rose, this her passion and her imagination cast off. She wrote a noble language in her hours of inspiration, and of her few novels the *Professor* only seems to be without inspiration. It is most frequent in *Villette*, but the passion of Jane Eyre is more intelligible than that of Lucy Snowe, and the story of Thornfield Hall must keep the first place. Emily Brontë's one romance, *Wuthering Heights*, is perhaps the work of even a greater genius, if any comparison is to be made, the two sisters being entirely different in intellect, temperament, and quality of power. Emily's imagination is as great as it is sombre; and as to her style, some five passages of the life and death of Heathcliff, and the final sentence of the book, reach, – or even make – a highwater mark of modern prose. Another height of literature was reached by George Eliot. The agnostic philosopher, with her few but all-persistent ethical thoughts and close and conscious style, succeeded her who had never studied prose and who was, albeit orthodox in faith and a clergyman's daughter in all her principles, a woman of impulse and emotion. George Eliot worked for one end – to convince man of moral obligation. She glorified it with beauty, enforced it with the sanctions of suffering, and refused to remit anything whatever of the penalties of wrongdoing – that is, of egoism. Acknowledging none of the religious codes, she found it necessary to make of 'the claims of others' a whole body of morality; and as 'others' have sometimes conflicting claims, those to be preferred were to be a man's kin, and, next, his race. George Eliot's wisdom and her humour have had ample reverence – her wit, perhaps, not quite so much, but her wit is exquisitely fine. She is a phrase-maker on occasion, but her habitual narrative style is even and pure.

Adam Bede made an epoch in English fiction, and stirred the nation, as did *Jane Eyre*; and with the addition to each one to her published works (the poems and *Theophrastus Such* excepted), George Eliot's honours were multiplied. The negation of fundamental morality that has had its vogue since her time has eclipsed her name for a while.

The poetry of women has dashed (dashed is unfortunately a rather appropriate word) up from the schoolgirlish, romantic rhymes of Letitia Elizabeth Landon, and the hardly more important verse of Mrs. Norton, and that of Mrs. Hemans, fluent and feeling, to the impetuous poetry – the work of genius ungoverned – of Elizabeth Barrett Browning, a violent poet who is nearly perfect in one little score of quiet poems, the best of all her work. Twenty years later comes Christina Rossetti, in whom a slight strain of her brother's genius lives – slight but true; impassioned and spiritual she is at her best, and a true lyrist. Her contemporary in youth was the popular and pleasant versifier, Adelaide Proctor. Jean Ingelow ceased her charming work long before her death, towards the close of the century. She, too, was a lyrist, too diffuse, but at her best delicate and true.

It is difficult to speak of the women who lived into the nineteenth century as of those who are living into the twentieth. Fanny Burney, Mary Wollstonecraft, Anne Radcliffe, Elizabeth Inchbald, Joanna Baillie, Hannah More, Anna Seward, were virtually eighteenth-century women, and writers now living may choose to belong to the twentieth century. But there are, at any rate, five novelists whose work has been peculiarly nineteenth-century work. Two of these – Mrs. Wood and Mrs. Oliphant – are gone; the three others who were read by many thousands of young people in the fifties and sixties, are living, and of the living we need cite no names.

'Children in the Century,' Mrs Jack Johnson, *Gentlewoman: Old and New Century Number* (London), 5 January 1901, p. 32

The space at my disposal will not, I know, allow of my making any comparison between the children of this century and others, but probably no other century has witnessed so extraordinary an evolution in child life as the one we have just left behind. It has affected both the well-to-do and the poorer classes, and though while in the latter it has been nothing more nor less than a rescue from slavery, in the former it has been a very desirable deliverance from priggishness. Surely the 'good child' of the commencement of the century was a more unendurable creature than its prototype of any preceding period. I suppose they had their moments of enjoyment, but one almost sheds tears over these poor little creatures when one contrasts the 'good times' of our day with the hours of blackboard, of wearisome 'learning by rote,' of stitching silly things, of repression, and endurance of even ill health as it was not considered 'good breeding' to speak about, even to your mother. And how limited their thoughts must have been during the silences which were considered 'respectful' with hardly any books at their disposal. There was *Sandford and Merton* certainly – whose author was killed by being thrown by a young horse he was trying to train on a new system – and Dr. Watts and Mrs. Trimmer's Tales – Hannah More's would have been considered 'too advanced' with her openly-expressed opinion that 'the kind of knowledge they do commonly acquire is easily attained, they learn everything in a superficial question-and-answer way or through abridgements, beauties, and compendiums, instead of reading books that require thought and attention.' Miss Edgeworth also fell foul of 'female accomplishments,' and here she is interesting reading enough, but the children had to swallow her very slightly-gilded pills of instruction and find their entertainment in it as well. When one comes to consider that conduct was regulated by such writings and the funny little starched heroines, with their well-timed questions and moral remarks, actually existed, it seems incredible that the distance between them and ourselves is not greater. The fact is they were much worse off than the children of the century preceding them who had their ballades, and towards the close the wonderful *Adventures of Baron Munchausen*, a style of literature not encouraged at the commencement of the 19th century, when a rather dull period – domestically speaking – had set in, and an outward austerity gave birth to a vast amount of hypocrisy – always the death of all innocent fun. Boys were packed off to school early, and what these were like in two classes of life can be gleaned from *Nicholas Nickleby*, and the early friendship between Dobbin and George Osborne in *Vanity Fair*. The one kind has been swept away, and the changes in the others are chiefly in less bullying and a more modern side of education. But in girls 'show' was the great demand; in fact, all through this early part of the century the worship of what was 'lady *like*' tended to leave all the old, useful knowledge out of a girl's education, giving in its place a smattering of so-called 'accomplishments.' A great number of people made money and tried by a process of 'refining' to make their offspring that which they were not naturally. There is no time when the children of a nation are so objectionable as when a period of imitation has set in. It is odd to think that simultaneously with this repressive education in England the old philosopher Friederich Wilhelm Frobel [*sic*] was living in Germany, evolving his theories with regard to children which were eventually to have such influence with the world. What would not these have given for even a very small sort of Kindergarten!

Young people were not very much encouraged to read, but we must remember that not only were books less numerous and more expensive, but so were circulating libraries. Here is an advertisement issued by Messrs. Saunders and Otley, in 1831, '£10. 10s. a year for fifteen books in town or thirty in the country; £8. 8s. for twelve in town, or twenty-four in the country.' The selection of a book would be a matter of some importance under these circumstances.

Just think what the arrival of Thackeray's *Rose and the Ring* in 1863 must have meant. Surely Bulbul and Giglio must have been precious indeed to little mortals who had hitherto chiefly read of children whose slightest act of disobedience was instantly punished by at least being eaten by lions! What delight there must have been in the early stories told by Mrs. Gatty and Miss Yonge. Then the books came thick and fast, translations of Mme. D'Aulnoy, of Hans Christian Andersen, and illustrators such as Alfred Crowquill, Mulready, Sir John Gilbert, and so on to Miss Greenaway and Caldecott down to our own day. And these pictures were for children – children who had been repressed and frightened by everything on earth and heaven, and other places as well, who were told to be silent, and never taught to think for themselves. Oh, what a great time was coming now!

Is it too strong an indictment of the earlier part of the century? Numerous vigorous minds have sprung from such surroundings and have given us what we most greatly prize to-day. The survival of the fittest is the usual accompaniment of most forms of evolution, but they don't recommend what they have come out of. Froebel's youth was a bitterly unhappy time. The loneliness of Ruskin's childhood, the forced precocity of John Stuart Mill's, the dreary details which Harriet Martineau gives of her childhood are not experiments we should care to try on our own children, even if they resulted in such intellectual heights. And what of those who did not come to the top?

How would one of the happy-go-lucky 'Tom boys' of to-day like to be relegated to bread and water merely because she had been so unladylike as to step on to a lower bough of a tree to look at a bird's nest? And yet this actually happened in the forties.

History was taught through the medium of little stories and questions and answers, and that their ideas on art may well have been a little odd may be gathered from a book of instruction dated 1814, wherein it states: 'When the Roman Empire became prey to the Goths and other barbarians, architecture was lost, and in its place was substituted a fanciful disproportionate mode of building called Gothic. . . . In this style is built Westminster Abbey . . . a confusing and irregular mass loaded with mean and trifling ornament.' But while ridiculous things were being inculcated in the nurseries of the wealthy, a far worse state of things were going on amongst the poor children outside of them.

Our sympathy was with the abolition of slavery, but I doubt if any of the 'darkies' could bring worse incidents to light than those suffered by the children of England dying under the whips of their taskmasters, maimed, deformed for life, and often when useless cast out in a yard to die, afterwards to be hurriedly buried in a plantation. These are not casual statements; each one can be found in reports of parliamentary inquiries and proved to be true. What wonder Elizabeth Barrett Browning sang the Cry of the Children! The only wonder is that every mother in England did not rise to quell the awful evil. History will certainly have something very strong to say about it. And the only comfort which every Englishman can take is that the century which saw this crime also saw the passing of laws to render its continuance impossible. Much remains to be done, but in the Queen's reign alone have fifty-four Acts of Parliament been passed to ameliorate the conditions of children. We are no worse than our neighbours in all probability, but can any nation be called properly civilised that requires fifty-four Acts of Parliament to make it kind to its children?

Ah! The old century has seen much which, pray God, no other century shall see again. Tiny little girls and boys of five or six years old drafted off to the Lancashire factories, 'sold' to them by the Poor Law Guardians as 'apprentices,' to be divided into two gangs – night and day – twelve hours each, their food so noisome that a man with a cowhide thong beat them till they ate it. Children have dropped exhausted and their limbs have been crushed off; no questions were asked, and there was no need to answer them if they had been. 'Little creatures,' said Sir Robert Peel in a speech in the House, 1816, 'are compelled to work even at the age of six years a period of perhaps fifteen or sixteen hours.' Mr. Oastler in 1830 stated the same thing, adding, 'even eighteen hours a day in some mills, without a single minute being set apart for meals, and that implements of cruelty were used to goad them on to this excessive labour.' It is difficult to believe that bills to repeal such an awful state of affairs should have received opposition, but they did, agreeing perhaps with Lord Beaumont, who in 1853 spoke of Lord Shaftesbury's bill to prohibit the wretched little children being forced up chimneys to sweep as 'a pitiful cant of pseudo-philanthropy.' And the evidence before the Children's Employment Commission in 1863 shows that the tender limbs of both boys and girls were treated with salt so as to harden them, that they suffered from 'sooty cancer,' that straw was lit under their bare feet when they hesitated to go up, and hundreds of other cruelties were practised. In the West Riding of Yorkshire children of five went daily to the coal-pits and worked with the adults. A sub-commissioner said he saw boys of seven who were down the pit all day long, and who never saw daylight except on Sundays; many of them grew up half imbecile. The flogging and ill-treatment that went on was very great. But it was not only in mines, not only in factories; the farmer worked his wretched gangs of children in the same brutal manner – knocked down, kicked, and this not the worst by any means. There are things to-day in the matter of training children as acrobats which may well be improved. But a great deal has been done.

I am tempted to talk of the wretched child-life on canal boats, of the miseries they endured in brickfields. My subject is too large to be well compressed. Perhaps the help that children are trying to give each other is one of the most hopeful signs, for what is begun in seedtime will be finished in harvest, and the man or woman who began as a child to think about such things is likely to accomplish some of them when they grow older.

'Woman and Education,' Miss Mabel Hawtrey, *Gentlewoman: Old and New Century Number* (London), 5 January 1901, p. xxiv

At the beginning of a new century it is interesting to look back and note what an advance has been made in this country during the last hundred years, and how women, by the great influence they have brought to bear on the educational movement, have entirely altered their status in society.

Not only has 'public elementary education been created, secondary education completely changed, technical education established, and University education remodelled and enlarged,' but these advantages are now extended to both sexes, whereas hitherto educational privileges had been reserved almost exclusively for males. In former days the education of girls of the upper and middle classes was entirely for show; it was the age when 'accomplishments reigned supreme,' and the tuition received in two years at a finishing boarding-school was all that was considered necessary. Miss Cobbe, in her description of the school to which she was sent, tells us that 'everything was taught in the inverse ration of its importance – at the bottom of the scale were morals and religion, and at the top were music and dancing.' Girls were to be educated for the marriage market, and men generally abhorred all learning in women. Those who in 1780 were members of the Blue Stocking Club fully realised with what odium they were regarded, for Mrs. Chapone advised her niece to avoid the study of classics and science for fear of exciting envy in one sex and jealousy in another, while Lady Wortley Montagu asserted that 'there is hardly a creature in the world more despicable and more liable to universal ridicule than that of a learned woman, but folly is reckoned so much our proper sphere, we are sooner pardoned any excesses of that than the least pretensions to reading and good sense.' There were, however, at this time practical reformers, one of these being Hannah More, who protested against the accomplishment craze and bravely asserted that 'a young lady might excel in French, Italian, and music, and yet be very badly educated if her mind remains untrained.' She met with great opposition in her work, and was openly ridiculed when, with her friend Miss Harrison, she began to teach the poor in back kitchens and barns. She was told that she would ruin agriculture, that if servants learned to read they would read their mistresses' letters, and if they learnt to write they would forge.

Maria Edgeworth was another who tried to raise the tone in her day, and by her writings did much to mould the thought and quicken the perception of those who came after.

It is customary to assert that the advance in education has been accomplished in the last fifty years, but it should be remembered that though the greatest pioneers in the work did not come into notice before this time, they themselves were the outcome of the movement which made itself felt in the early part of the century. Although schools were most defective, we find many instances of families where a high intellectual standard existed. Miss

Buss, who was one of the greatest educational pioneers, may be said to have been singularly fortunate in her home surroundings. Her father was a man of great literary and scientific tastes, and by his work as an artist and engraver was closely associated with the most famous authors and publishers of his day, so that his daughter was brought up in a very cultured atmosphere. She tells us herself that she had access to all his books, including the proofs of those he illustrated.

Miss Reid was another who owed much to the early home training, and after her husband's death in 1821 she devoted herself to furthering the education of her own sex. In course of time she formulated a scheme which was to 'embody a thoroughly liberal education, including all the higher branches of study in various departments, so that such intellectual privileges should be open to every woman seeking for truth and knowledge.' The practical result of this was that in 1849 she founded Bedford College, and utilised a house in Bedford Square for the purpose.

This was a marked time in the annals of woman's education, for a few months previously Queen's College, in Harley Street, had been opened by the Governesses' Benevolent Institution, the object of the society being to provide such instruction as would raise the status of the governess by improving her qualifications. Miss Buss was one of the first to attend the classes at Queen's College, and amongst other students we find Miss Beal, the present Principal of the Cheltenham Ladies' College, Dr. Sophia Jex-Blake (who was one of the first women to matriculate in medicine at Edinburgh University), and Miss Bishop (afterwards Principal of the Royal Holloway College).

The next step was in 1863, when the Cambridge local examinations were opened to girls, and though at the present time examinations are deprecated, it must be remembered that they have served their use in the past by raising the standard in schools. Miss Emily Davies, the founder of Girton College, took an active part in obtaining this concession, but she did not relax her efforts until the privileges of a University education were secured to women. Now eight of the ten Universities of Great Britain teach their students without distinction of sex, while two others allow women to attend lectures and examinations. Newnham College, which achieved such a reputation under Miss Clough, was originally instituted as a house of residence for women students who attended lectures at Cambridge.

The Royal Commission of 1864, appointed to survey secondary schools, would only have inquired into those for boys had not a petition signed by leading educational women been presented to them, asking that girls' schools might be included. When, however, the next Commission was appointed in 1894, women were included among the Commissioners, one of these being Mrs. Bryant, the first woman who took a Doctor's degree in Moral Science.

Money was of course needed for the schools and colleges, and Lady Stanley of Alderley, a great supporter of education, was one who gave financial help, for she contributed to Queen's College, and, with Madame Bodichon, George

Eliot, and others, raised funds to erect the present buildings of Girton College. She helped Mrs. William Grey to start the Girls' Public Day School Company, and was Vice-President of the Maria Grey Training College, founded by Miss Grey (after whom it was named), and her sister, Miss Shirreff, who was so instrumental in introducing the Kindergarten system into this country.

Physical development has received great attention from the reformers, so that the advantages of gymnastics and games are now fully recognised.

The inauguration of the Public Girls' Schools and Colleges has had a most beneficial effect in raising the standard in private schools, and amongst the latter there are many which have attained a high state of efficiency.

Compendium of Dates for the Century, from *Woman's Suffrage Calendar for 1899*, ed. Helen Blackburn
(Bristol: J. W. Arrowsmith – London: Simpkin, Marshall, Hamilton, Kent, and Co Ltd., 1898)

'Whatsoever things are good, whatsoever things are wise, whatsoever things are holy, must be accomplished by communion between brave men and brave women'.

(Anna Jameson)

COMPENDIUM OF DATES FOR THE CENTURY

1800 to 1809

These dates have nearly all appeared in former issues of the Calendar in their months. Arranged here by their years they mark the growth of the Women's movement, beginning with the birthdays of those whose lives have helped to make its history.

1801	Aug 17	–	Frederika Bremer born.
1802	July 12	–	Harriet Martineau born.
1803	Aug 7	–	Margaret Gillies born.
1805	Nov 14	–	Fanny Mendelssohn born.
1807	April 3	–	Mary Carpenter born.
1809	March 6	–	Mrs Barrett Browning born.
1809	July 5	–	George Sand born.

1810 to 1819

As to persons of this sex, the sex in which the half, more or less, of the whole species is contained – usually, if not constantly, have they on this occasion been passed over without notice: an omission which under a Mahommendan Government might have place with rather less prejudice to consistency than under a Christian one.

(Jeremy Bentham, *Plan of Parliamentary Reform*, 1817)

1810	May 22	–	Margaret Fuller born.
1812	July 2	–	Madame Grisi born.
1816	March 7	–	Mrs William Grey born.
1816	April 21	–	Charlotte Brontë born.
1817	July 15	–	Madame de Stael died.
1817	July 23	–	Jane Austen died.
1819	May 24	–	Queen Victoria born.
1819	Nov 22	–	George Eliot born.

1820 to 1829

Everywhere have females possessed the whole power of a despot, everywhere but in France, without objection. Talk of giving them as here the smallest fraction of a fraction of such a power, scorn without reason is all the answer you receive. From custom comes prejudice. No gnat too minute to be strained by it; no camel too great to be swallowed.

(*Radical Reform Bill*, December, 1819)

1820	Oct 6	–	Jenny Lind born.
1821	March 24	–	Madame Rachel born.
1821	June 24	–	Lady Duff Gordon born.
1821	Aug 1	–	Mrs Inchbald (dramatist) died.
1822	Dec 4	–	Miss F. Power Cobb born.
1823	Feb 7	–	Mrs Radcliffe (novelist) died.
1825	Oct 30	–	Adelaide Proctor born.
1827	Feb 27	–	Miss Lydia Becker born.
1828	Feb 8	–	Gold Medal, Royal Astron. Society, awarded to Miss Herschell.
1828	March 9	–	Mrs Barbauld died, aged 82.
1818	May 28	–	Mrs Somerville and Miss Herschell elected members of Royal Astron Society.

1830 to 1839

By our glorious Constitution, the wonder and envy of the world, the crown of these realms, being hereditary, has repeatedly graced, or been graced by, the brows of a female; and such an event is, as everybody knows, likely to recur again. . . . We may advert to the fact for the sake of showing with how much of political authority a woman may safely be entrusted; how much she may be invested with according to, not the wild theories of some modern speculator, but the wisdom of our ancestors and the perfection of our institutions. It is a fearful amount. . . . In the common opinion of common statesmen the fitness of a woman to vote for an individual's elevation to the temporary dignity of a legislator in the House of Commons is a mere joke: yet her naming scores of persons legislators for life, and all their heirs legislators too through all generations, is an essential portion of that ancestral wisdom under which we live. She is invested with the highest power of the State, or not entrusted with its meanest franchise. In truth this mystery is hard to swallow, and warily must a loyal subject steer his course, so as neither to be convicted of constructive treason by the Tories, nor ridiculed, even by Radicals for the extravagance of his theories.

(W. J. Fox, MP for Oldham, in the *Monthly Repository* for 1832)

1830	Dec 30	–	Madame de Genlis died.
1832	June 21	–	Miss Porter (novelist) died.
1832	June 21	–	The Reform Act, *from which women are excluded.*
1832	Nov 29	–	Louisa Alcott born.
1833	Aug 29	–	*Act destroying widows' right to dower.*
1833	Sept 4	–	Hannah More died, Age 88.
1835	Aug 31	–	Act to alter law as to voidable marriages.
1835	Sept 9	–	*Municipal Corporations Act deprived women of the Municipal vote.*
1836	Sept 22	–	Mrs Sherwood died.
1836	Dec 14	–	Miss F. R. Havergal born.
1837	June 20	–	Accession of Queen Victoria.
1838	Sept 7	–	Grace Darling saved passengers of Forfarshire.
1839	June 23	–	Lady Hester Stanhope died.

1840 to 1849

There are many ladies, I am happy to say, present; now it is a very anomalous and singular fact, that they cannot vote themselves, and yet that they have power of conferring votes upon other people. I wish they had the Franchise, they would often make a much better use of it than their husbands.

(Speech on Free Trade by Mr Cobden at Covent Garden Theatre, January 15, 1845)

1840	June 12	–	*Women's delegates refused admission to Anti-Slavery Convention.*
1842	Sept 21	–	Lady Sale released from captivity in Afghanistan.
1843	April 25	–	Princess Alice born.

1845	May 8	–	Anti-Corn Law Bazaar, Covent Garden.
1848	March 29	–	Lecture by Rev. F Denison Maurice on 'Queen's College: its object and methods.'
1848	May 1	–	Queen's College, Harley Street, opened.
1849	Jan 23	–	Elizabeth Blackwell, M.D. received diploma USA.
1849	May 21	–	Miss Edgeworth died.

1850 to 1855

There exists at the core of our social condition a great mistake to be corrected, and a great want supplied, that men and women must learn to understand each other, and work together for the common good, before any amount of permanent moral and religious progress can be effected: and that in the most comprehensive sense of the word we need SISTERS OF CHARITY everywhere.

(Mrs Jameson, Preface to *Sisters of Charity*)

1850	Oct 23	–	First Woman's Rights Convention, Masschusetts, USA.
1851	Feb 28	–	Joanna Baillie died, aged 89.
1851	Nov 2	–	Queen's College, London, incorporated.
1853	Dec 17	–	Prof. Sophia Kowalewski born.
1854	Nov 5	–	Miss Nightingale landed at Constantinople.
1855	Feb 14	–	Mrs Jameson's lecture on 'Sisters of Charity'.
1855	March 31	–	Charlotte Brontë died.

1856 to 1859

Every one must have observed the new influence which has not been asserted or sought, but is falling to the lot of women, in swaying the destinies of the world. It is not a share in directing the patronage of ministers and sharing in the councils of kings, but a portion in the formation and moulding of public opinion. . . . It seems to me – and I am confirmed in this by the bright examples of heroic benevolence – that if the younger generation are to be an improvement on their fathers, if sin is to have less dominion and religion more power, if vice is to be abashed and virtue to honoured, it is to woman we must look for such a generation.

(Lord John Russell, Presidential Address at Social Science Congress, 1858)

| 1856 | March | – | Petitions in favour of Married Women's Property. One with 3000 signatures of women. |

		–	Miss Meriton White (Madam Mario) refused admission to degree at London University.
1856	June 28	–	Mrs Jameson's lecture on Communion of Labour.
		–	Bible Women started by Mrs Ranyard.
1857	Jan 25	–	Princess Royal married.
1858	Mar 2	–	*Englishwoman's Journal*, now *Englishwoman's Review*, started.
1858	June 28	–	Mrs Marcet died, aged 90.
1858	July 14	–	First Ladies' Swimming Bath, London.
1858	Nov 12	–	Miss Hosmer went to Rome.
1858	Nov 16	–	George Eliot's *Adam Bede* finished.
1859	April 1	–	Amelia Sieveking died.
1859	June 22	–	Society for Employment of Women established.
1859	July 21	–	First Annual Meeting of Ladies' Sanitary Association.

1860 to 1865

'Woman's work' means nothing very honourable or conscientious now.
Alter its significance till it indicates the best work in the world.
(Caroline Dall, in *Woman's Right to Labour*, Boston USA 1890)

1860	Jan 18	–	Women admitted to Exams in Surgery, Sweden.
1860	March 17	–	Mrs Jameson died aged 75.
1861	March 26	–	*Victoria Press* established.
1863		–	Edinburgh Local Exams opened to Women.
1863	March 7	–	Princess Alexandra landed.
1864		–	Cambridge admitted girls formally to its Local Exams.
1865		–	Women's Union, Leipzig formed.
1865	Nov 13	–	Mrs Gaskell died.

1866

I say that in a country governed by a woman – where you allow women
to form part of the other estate of the realm – peeresses in their own
right, for example – where you allow a woman not only to hold land,
but to be a lady of the manor and hold legal courts – where a woman
by law may be a churchwarden and overseer of the poor – I do not
see, where she has so much to do with the State and Church, on what
reasons, if you come to right, she has not a right to vote.
(Speech by Mr Disraeli in the House of Commons, April 27)

Jan 1	–	Frederika Bremer died.
April 27	–	Mr Disraeli spoke in favour of Women's Suffrage in the House of Commons.
May	–	Mr J.S. Mill presented a petition for Enfranchisement of Women, signed by 1,499 Women.
Sept 1	–	Miss Carpenter started on her first visit to India.
Oct 6	–	'Reasons for the Franchise' read at Social Science Congress by Mrs Bodichon.
Nov 18	–	New England Women's Suffrage Association formed.

1867

If the law denied a vote to all but the possessors of 5,000 pounds a year, the poorest man in the nation might – and now and then would – acquire the suffrage; but neither birth, nor fortune, nor merit, nor exertion, nor intellect, nor even that great disposer of human affairs – accident, can ever enable any woman to have her voice counted in those national affairs which touch her and hers as nearly as any other person in the nation.

(Mr J.S. Mill in House of Commons, May 20)

Jan 11	–	Manchester Committee for Enfranchisement of Women started.
April 5	–	Petition from 1,606 Women Householders presented by Right Hon Russell Gurney, M.P.
May 20	–	Mr J.S. Mill's motion on Women's Suffrage in House of Commons.
Aug 27	–	Supplemental Charter, admitting Women to Exams at London University.
Oct 29	–	Edinburgh Ladies' Educational Association constituted.
Nov 6	–	National Society for Women's Suffrage formed.
Nov 26	–	Miss Lillie Maxwell voted for Mr Jacob Bright.

1868

When we ask why women are to be disfranchised, men meet us with levity and sophistry. Not to dwell on mere bantering – they reply, as if gravely, by asking whether women are to be magistrates, members of Parliament, prime ministers, and preachers. Such a reply confounds private right with public office. The vote is a right recognised in private persons for *self-defence* against officials, and (in English law) especially for the defence of property, whether against Crown or Parliament. The opponent confounds this with the right of being an official person.

(Prof. F.W. Newman, Leaflet published by Bristol W. S. Society)

Jan 24	–	Women's Suffrage Committee formed in Bristol.
April 1	–	Accession of Queen Ranavalomanjaka II, first Christian Queen of Madagascar.
April 14	–	First Public Meeting for Women's Suffrage (Manchester).
Aug 25	–	Paper on 'Equality of Women' read before British Assoc., at Norwich, by Miss Becker.
Sept 24	–	Claim of Women Occupiers allowed in the Revision Court, Ormskirk.
Nov 9	–	*Women disfranchised by decision of Court of Common Pleas.*

1869

Any woman would be derided who refused to obey the law on the plea that man did not include woman, and that therefore, she was not personally liable for breaking any law so worded; but when women came to ask for votes they discovered that the words importing the masculine gender were considered to include women in the clauses imposing burdens, and to exclude them in the clauses conferring privileges, in one and the same Act of Parliament.

(Miss Becker, lecture at Leeds)

	–	Edinburgh Association for University Education of Women formed.
April 10	–	*Droit de Femmes* (Paris) started.
May 15	–	National Women's Suffrage Association, USA [started].
July 17	–	First Public Meeting held in London in support of Women's Suffrage.
Aug 2	–	Municipal Franchise Amendment Act, conferring votes on Women.
Aug 4	–	Miss Margaret Sinclair died, Aged 86.
Oct 16	–	Hitchin Temporary College opened.
Nov 25	–	American Women's Suffrage Association formed.
Dec 2	–	Ordinance admitting Women to Queen's College Exams, Ireland.

1870

It would have been little short of a miracle if women could have risen from a condition of political non-existence in one year to the acquisition of the Municipal and in the next to that of the Parliamentary vote. Such celerity would have savoured of the magical, and would have been totally at variance with the manner in which grave questions have been hitherto discussed and made their way in this country.

(*Women's Suffrage Journal*, June)

Jan 14   –   Elise Lemonnier Schools, Paris, incorporated.

Feb 15   –   Women's Law Copying Office opened.

Feb 16   –   Bill for Removing Electoral Disabilities of Women introduced first time.

March 1   –   *Women's Suffrage Journal* started.

May 4   –   Second reading of Women's Electoral Disabilities Bill carried.

May 12   –   The Bill thrown out in Committee.

June 3   –   Matriculation Exams, Sweden, opened to women.

Aug 9   –   Married Women's Property Act.

Nov 24   –   First woman (Miss Becker) elected on School Board, Manchester.

1871

If nature has established an ineradicable and insuperable difference in the capacities and qualifications of the two sexes, nature can take care of itself. What nature has decided can safely be left to nature, but when we find people making themselves uneasy, for fear that nature's purposes should be frustrated unless law comes to her assistance, we may be pretty certain it is not nature they are so careful about, but law pretending to be nature. To all such pretences the growing improvement of mankind is making them more and more averse.

(Speech of Mr J.S. Mill in the Music Hall, Edinburgh, Jan 13)

Jan 12   –   Great Meeting in Music Hall, Edinburgh, in favour of Women's Suffrage.

May 3   –   Debate in the House of Commons on Women's Electoral Disabilities Bill.

July 11   –   Baroness Burdett-Coutts admitted to Freedom of the City.

July   –   National Health Society formed by Dr Elizabeth Blackwell.

Oct 23   –   Durham College of Science opened to Women.

Oct 27   –   National Education Union established.

Nov 14   –   Vigilance Association formed.

Dec 5   –   *L'Esperance* started in Switzerland.

1872

The low condition of girls' education may perhaps be assumed to be proved. Here and there a good school, here and there a few good teachers . . . but no notion how to make any instruction educational, no method, no thoroughness, no purpose. . . . It is fortunate perhaps that external circumstances, over which we have no control, by forcing a much larger number of women than formerly to provide for themselves, have given a new stimulus to the desire for improvement; have made it evident to the most reluctant that women must be unfit for the work that is become so necessary for them, unless they are better instructed.

(Miss Emily Shirreff)

Jan 17	–	Central Committee of the National Society for Women's Suffrage constituted.
Jan 22	–	*Married Women ruled incapable of voting in Municipal Elections by Court of Queen's Bench.*
May 1	–	Debate on Women's Electoral Disabilities Bill.
July 20	–	Girton College incorporated.
Nov 26	–	First Annual Meeting of the National Union for Improving the Education of Women.
Dec 6	–	Women's Suffrage Conference in Birmingham.

1873

In the last session of Parliament we took great pains on the subject of illiterate voters. It was interesting to see the two Houses of Parliament spending I do not know how many hours in devising schemes by which men who were too stupid to vote without assistance, should, nevertheless be enabled to record a vote. Am I putting forward an unreasonable claim, or demanding anything very extravagant, when I ask the House of Commons, which has bestowed so much care in devising means to enable illiterate men to vote, not to continue to withhold the suffrage from women of education and property?

(Speech by Mr Jacob Bright, in the House of Commons, April 30)

Jan 15	–	Journal of Education Union begun.
April 24	–	Act to amend Law as to Custody of Infants.
April 30	–	Debate on Women's Disabilities Bill.
May 8	–	Mr J.S. Mill died.
July 16	–	The Clothworkers' Company bestow the Freedom of their Company on the Baroness Burdett-Coutts.
Oct 4	–	Mrs Alfred Gatty died.

1874

The question at issue between Mr Mill and Mr Stephen in this controversy is simply whether women are human beings, with the full rights and responsibilities of humanity, or whether they are a superior kind of inferior beings, whose personal rights and duties must be regarded as subordinate to those of man, whether in fact the ludicrous misapplication which is so commonly made, both in jest and earnest, of the phrase 'lords of creation,' by using it with reference to the male sex instead of to the human race, is to be the rule on which the relative political and social position of the two sexes of humanity is to be based.

(Miss Becker, in 'Liberty, Equality, Fraternity'
(a reply to Mr Stephen))

Jan 15	–	Freedom of the city of Edinbro' conferred on Baroness Burdett-Coutts.
Feb 18	–	Mrs Nassau Senior appointed inspector of Workhouse Schools.
April 22	–	Women's Peace Society formed.
July 3	–	Women employed as Clerks, Stockholm Bank.
July 8	–	Women's Protective and Provident League formed.
July 19	–	Protection Orders given to wives in Scotland.
July 30	–	Married Women's Property Act (1870) Amendment Act.
Oct 14	–	London School of Medicine for Women opened.

1875

The Bill (Women's Disabilities Removal Bill) enjoys the distinction of being the only question of practical reform which has appealed to the new Parliament with greater success than to the former one.

(*Women's Suffrage Journal*, May)

April 17	–	Debate on Women's Suffrage Bill in House of Commons.
April 17	–	First Woman Poor-Law Guardian.
Oct 1	–	Pharmaceutical Exams, Ireland, opened to Women.
Oct 18	–	Newnham Hall, Cambridge, opened.
Dec 15	–	Women's Suffrage adopted by National Reform Union.

1876

I believe whenever you enfranchise a class, the first result of that enfranchisement is to make those who are enfranchised take a keener and a deeper interest in all that concerns the public affairs of the country. It does not draw them from their homes, it does not draw them from their shops, it does not draw them from their daily labour; but I believe that all experience will show that those who are the best workmen, those who are the best traders, and those who are the best merchants are those who are the best citizens; and I believe this will hold equally true when that day shall arrive when women who are ratepayers shall be enfranchised.

(Mr Fawcett (Rt Hon Henry), Speech in the House of Commons,
April 26)

Jan 20	–	Women admitted to Manchester New College.
April 21	–	British Women's Temperance Association formed.
April 27	–	Debate [on women's suffrage] in House of Commons.
August 11	–	Medical Act (known as 'Russel Gurney Act') permitting Medical Degrees to Women.
August 15	–	Mrs Hill's Statue of Livingstone unveiled, Edinburgh.

1877

Not for the bright face we shall see no more,
Not for the sweet voice we no more shall hear,
Not for the heart with kindness brimming o'er,
Large charity and sympathy sincere.

These are not things that ask a public pen
To blazon its memorial o'er her name
But that in public work she wrought with men
And faced their frowns and over-lived their blame.'
(Anonymous Lines on Mrs Nassau Senior
(quoted in *Englishwoman's Review*))

March 24	–	Mrs Nassau Senior died.
March 25	–	Mrs Chisholm (the Emigrants' Friend) died.
June 6	–	Debate [on women's suffrage] in House of Commons, Bill introduced by Mr Courtney.
June 14	–	Miss Mary Carpenter died.
June 15	–	Hon. Mrs Norton (Lady Stirling Maxwell) died.
July 31	–	Miss Edgar received B.A. degree, New Zealand.
Oct 1	–	Royal Free Hospital, London, admitted Women students.

1878

What has been done in these examinations (Cambridge Higher Local) ought rather to be regarded as a stepping-stone to higher things, than as a permanent resting-place. . . . We need to be on our guard against attaching too high a value to Degrees and Certificates. But this applies to both men and women. All that I urge is that where it would be said, as in the case of Masterships in the great schools for boys, that anyone not a graduate could scarcely be thought of, we should at least look forward to say the same thing as to a Mistresship.
(Miss Emily Davies, *Home and the Higher Education*, 1878)

| Jan 1 | – | Order of Crown of India founded. |
| Feb 3 | – | Lady Anna Gore Langton dies. |

March 4	–	New Charter of London University, admitting Women to degrees.
May 27	–	Matrimonial Causes (Wives' Protection) Act.
June 11	–	First L.A. Exam for women, St Andrew's University.
June 19	–	Debate on Women's Disabilities Bill.
July 24	–	Congress du *Droit des Femmes*, Paris.
Aug 16	–	Intermediate Education Act, Ireland.
Aug 23	–	Debate on Women's Suffrage, New Zealand Parliament.
Sept 28	–	First lectures of Society for Superior Instruction of Women, St. Petersburg.
Nov 23	–	Judgement given on Agar-Ellis case.
Dec 27	–	Mrs Grote died, aged 86.

1879

During this period (1870 to 1879) there have been presented to the House of Commons in favour of the Bill petitions with upwards of 2,000,000 signatures, and upwards of 1,300 public meetings have been held, that is an average of two meetings a week for the last thirteen years.

(From a Paper on the 'Progress of the Women's Suffrage Movement,' read by Miss Becker at the Social Science Congress 1879)

March 7	–	Debate on Mr Courtney's resolution in House of Commons.
May 20	–	Albemarle Club (for men and women) opened.
July 24	–	Workhouse Infirmary Nursing Association formed.
Aug 15	–	Act founding the Royal University of Ireland.
Oct 13	–	Somerville Hall, Oxford, opened.

1880

This hall was built in the cause of freedom, and some of us have learned our political lessons within its walls, many years ago, with distinguished men for our teachers, and we have learned from them how persistent effort leads to success in getting grievances redressed. Victory in one moral flight always leads to new warfare in other fields. . . . Women are learning along with good men that politics in their true sense have to do with human interests at large.

(Mrs M' Laren, speech as President of the Demonstration of Women, Free Trade Hall, Manchester, Feb. 3 1880)

Feb 3	–	Demonstration of Women in Tree Trade Hall, Manchester.
May 6	–	Demonstration of Women, St James' Hall, London.

Sept 22	–	Miss Geraldine Jewsbury died.
Oct 18	–	Mrs Jellicoe, founder of Alexandra College, Dublin, died.
Oct 22	–	Salvatore Morelli, Champion of Women in Italy, died.
Nov 4	–	Demonstration of Women in Colston Hall, Bristol.
Nov 30	–	Demonstration of Women, Albert Hall, Nottingham.
Dec 21	–	Secondary Education of Girls decreed in France.
Dec 21	–	Women's Suffrage passed by Legislature of Isle of Man.

1881

My Recollection goes back to the time when women first learned to combine, and a crowd of memories throng upon me when I think of the stirring times that gave birth to knowledge of their power, and practically began the movement which has culminated in a meeting like this. I received my baptism of fire in Manchester when our beloved member, John Bright, and his illustrious colleague, Mr Richard Cobden, waged their brilliant crusade against the protectionist policy of the Corn Laws. Monster meetings were held in Manchester, largely composed of women, and much of the material help that brought about that struggle to a glorious issue was due to the exertions of women.

(Mrs Crosskey, speech as President of the Demonstration of Women
in the Town Hall, Birmingham, Feb 22)

Jan 5	–	Royal assent to Women's Suffrage in Isle of Man.
Jan 31	–	The new Electoral Law promulgated at the Tynwald Court.
Feb 21	–	Somerville Club opened.
Feb 22	–	Demonstration of Women in Town Hall, Birmingham.
Feb 24	–	Women admitted to Tripos Exams, Cambridge.
March 21	–	Women voted for first time in Isle of Man.
June 3	–	Municipal Franchise extended to women in Scotland.
July 18	–	Married Women's Property Act (Scotland).
Nov 28	–	Demonstration of Women in St George's Hall, Bradford.
Dec 10	–	Midwives' Institute inaugurated.

1882

This Act (the Married Women's Property Act), the Magna Charta for Women, most appropriately received the assent of a Woman Sovereign on a Friday, the woman's day of the week.

Freitag, or Friday, is dedicated to Freia, the Scandinavian divine woman. . . . Henceforward, Friday is the beginning of a new era for women, and should be held as an honoured and fortunate day for all time to come.

(*Women's Suffrage Journal*, Sept)

Jan 28	—	Association of Irish Schoolmistresses, Dublin, formed.
Feb 27	—	Demonstration of Women, Sheffield.
March 29	—	Dora Greenwell died.
May 12	—	Municipal Franchise extended to women in Iceland.
Aug 12	—	Consolidated Married Women's Property Act received Royal assent.
Sept 8	—	First lady matriculated, Univ. of Christiana.
Oct 1	—	College Hall, Byng Place, London, opened.
Oct 27	—	First lady M.D. at Madrid University.
Nov 3	—	Demonstration of Women, Albert Hall, Glasgow.
Nov 22	—	Miss Rhoda Garrett died.

1883

They should recollect that this was no new struggle. It was only a continuation of the struggle, in which Liberals had taken part for the last fifty years. Therefore she trusted they would be true to their principles.

With the result of the high political teaching they had, in the past, they would endeavour faithfully, intelligently, and with what ability was given to them to uphold those great principles of liberty and trust in the people, which she believed had made the great Liberal party what it was, and which alone was capable of lifting it to the highest triumphs in the future.

(Speeches of Miss Jane E. Cobden and Mrs Helen Bright Clack at the Reform Conference at Leeds, October 17)

March 9	—	First Meeting of Canadian Women's Suffrage Association.
March 10	—	Two Indian Ladies took B.A. degrees Calcutta University.
April 5	—	Women's Suffrage Association formed in Canada.
April 13	—	Women's Suffrage introduced by Canadian Government.
April 23	—	Order of the Royal Red Cross founded.
July 16	—	Debate in House of Commons on Mr Hugh Mason's (Woman's Suffrage) resolution.
Oct 17	—	Parliamentary Reform Conference (Leeds) carry resolution in favour of Woman's Suffrage by a large majority.
Oct 17	—	Women's Suffrage adopted by Conference of Liberal Associations, Leeds.
Nov 19	—	Women ruled eligible to State Board of Health and Charity, Mass., USA.

1884

We have been told that the tendency now is downwards towards something like manhood suffrage. If that is so it is time you should connect that with the enfranchisement of those who are representatives of a high type than the great multitudes of the people to whom you will have to give the franchise. . . . I have no doubt that there are numbers of gentlemen here who have canvassed boroughs. They will have seen, from time to time, that after going into two or three shops and asking for the votes of those who are the owners, they have come to one perhaps of the most important shops and have been told, 'Oh, it is no use going in; there is no vote there. The owner is a woman.' You are admitting masses of non-propertied classes and refusing the vote to these. That is the ground, the Conservative ground, upon which we stand. That is the ground upon which Lord Beaconsfield stood. We have adhered to that view for seventeen years, and that is the ground upon which we stand now.

(Speech of Rt. Hon. Sir Stafford Northcote (Lord Iddleseigh) in the House of Commons, June 12, 1884)

Jan 25	–	National Reform Union Conference in Manchester carried a resolution in favour of Women's Suffrage by a large majority.
Feb 28	–	The University of Oxford admitted Women to Exams.
March 14	–	Municipal Suffrage to Women in Ontario.
June 10	–	*Mr Woodall's Amendment to the Representation of the People Bill rejected.*
July 7	–	Dispensary for Women, Bombay, opened.
Oct 22	–	B.A. degree conferred on nine Ladies, Royal University, Ireland.

1885

Might he not say that that Exhibition with all its variety – all its beautiful and excellent objects – the work of women's hands – would at least have this result, a higher general appreciation of the skill, the talent and the genius of women. And if with increased appreciation there would naturally be some added energy to give rise to a movement for increased scholastic establishments that would have for their special object the technical training of women – then indeed that Exhibition would have accomplished a very great result.

(Sir Joseph Weston (Mayor of Bristol). Speech at opening of Exhibition of Women's Industries, Feb 26, 1885)

Feb 26	–	Exhibition of Women's Industries opened, Bristol.
March 8	–	Mrs Downing Shearer died.

March 11   —   Lady Dufferin laid stone of Hostel for Women Students, Calcutta Medical College.

April 10   —   Princess of Wales received degree, Dr of Music, Royal University, Ireland.

May 2   —   B.A. degree conferred on Women for first time, Sydney University.

July 22   —   Resolution in favour of Women's Suffrage adopted in South Australian Parliament.

Aug 12   —   Countess of Dufferin's Fund for Medical Aid to Women in India started.

Aug 14   —   Criminal Law Amendment Act.

Oct 5   —   Aberdare Hall, Cardiff, opened.

Oct 7   —   Meeting at Lahore on Infant Marriage and Enforced Widowhood.

Nov 27   —   Miss Helen Prideaux died.

1886

The present House of Commons consists of 670 Members. Of these, 349 have either already supported the Women's Franchise Bill by their votes, or have promised to do so; 165 are known opponents; and the views of 156 on the question are unknown. The friends of this movement therefore constitute an actual majority of 28 in the whole House over opponents and neutrals combined. The 156 whose views are unknown consist almost exclusively of New Members.

(Women's Suffrage Journal, April)

Feb 19   —   Women's Suffrage Bill passed Second Reading without a Division.

April 17   —   Women Voted for the first time in Municipal Election, New Brunswick.

April 8   —   Dispensary for Women in Calcutta opened.

April 16   —   C.D. Acts repealed.

June 25   —   Guardianship of Infants Act, and Married Women's Maintenance Act, became Law.

June 30   —   Royal Holloway College for Women opened by the Queen.

July 27   —   Women's Memorial to Mr Fawcett unveiled.

Aug 22   —   Jeannette G. Wilkinson died.

Oct 12   —   Statue to Sister Dora unveiled, Walsall.

Dec 2   —   Mrs Emma Patterson (founder of Women's Protective and Provident League) died.

1887

Fifty full years . . . since the accession of Queen Victoria to the throne of her ancestors. Never before in the history of our country has an equal period of time been marked by such stupendous changes in the material and social conditions of Society. . . . We have no hesitation in assuming that the improvement in the legal and social position of women has been largely influenced by the fact that a woman is at the head of the State.

(*Women's Suffrage Journal*, June)

Jan 11	–	First Meeting of Irish Home Industries Association.
March 29	–	Municipal Franchise for Women rejected by Danish Upper House.
March 31	–	Irish Home Industries Association constituted.
May 12	–	Women's Suffrage Bill passed Second Reading, New Zealand House of Commons.
May 17	–	Deputation of Pit-brow Women to Home Secretary.
June 18	–	Miss Ramsay first in Classical Tripos, Cambridge.
June 21	–	The Jubilee Celebration.
Oct 12	–	Mrs Craik (Miss Muloch) died.
Oct 27	–	National Conservative Association, Scotland, pass Resolution in favour of Women's Suffrage (Glasgow).
Nov 2	–	Jenny Lind died.
Nov 3	–	Woman Graduates first admitted to Victoria University, Manchester.
Nov 23	–	National Union of Conservative Associations pass Resolution in favour of Women's Suffrage (Oxford).

1888

On the occasion of the visit of Her Majesty to Queen Margaret's College, Glasgow, August, 1888, in reply to an address of welcome from the Council of the College, Her Majesty said: 'Every movement which serves to raise the position of Women and extend the sphere of their influence has my warm approval.'

Jan 29	–	Mrs Howitt died, aged 89.
March 26	–	International Council of Women, Washington, USA [formed].
May 16	–	County Electors Act.
Aug 13	–	Local Government Act establishing County Councils.
Aug	–	Visit of Her Majesty to Queen Margaret's College, Glasgow.

1889

The Protest in the *Nineteenth Century Review* may be regarded as a
testimony to the strength of the movement for the enfranchisement of
women, and as evidence of a belief that the measure is likely to become
Law. For upwards of twenty years Women distinguished by their
personal character and ability, and by their work in various ways for the
benefit of the community, have been labouring earnestly and faithfully
for that which they believe to be the keystone of the arch, whereon rests
the true basis of the social fabric: the recognition of Women as sharers
with men in the political rights, duties and responsibilities of the people.
During the whole of this period no dissentient voice amongst women
themselves has found public or official expression. . . . Now, at last, the
long silence is broken, and we find 104 ladies coming forward to stem
the tide of enfranchisement for their sex.

(Miss Becker, A Reply to the Protest which appeared in the
Nineteenth Century of June)

	–	The University of Wales placed Women on an equality from its start, this year.
March 24	–	Singhalese Ladies' Association for education of Women [formed].
June 1	–	Protest in the *Nineteenth Century* against Women's Suffrage, signed by 104 ladies.
July 1	–	Declaration in favour of Women's Suffrage, in *Fortnightly Review*, signed by 2000 ladies.
Aug 26	–	Local Government (Scotland) Act, creating County Councils in Scotland.
Aug 26	–	Prevention of Cruelty to Children Act.
Sept 4	–	Miss Caroline Ashurst Biggs died.
Sept 30	–	Freedom of the City of Dublin conferred on Lady Sandhurst.

1890

Since the report was printed, the Committee have been deeply grieved
to receive the news of the very great loss they have sustained in the death
of their friend and colleague, Miss Becker. Her long experience, her
intimate knowledge of all matters bearing on the claims of women to
representation, her sagacity and her devotion to her work of the Society,
make her loss one that is most keenly felt and deeply deplored. The best
tribute which all who respect and mourn her can pay to her memory will
be to work more zealously in bringing about the speedy accomplishment
of the object to which her life was devoted.

(*Annual Report of the Central Committee of the National Society for
Women's Suffrage*)

June	–	Miss Fawcett and Miss Alford at head of Mathematical and Classical Tripos Lists.
July 11	–	Wyoming, USA, constituted as a State, retains Women's Suffrage in its Constitution.
July 18	–	Miss Becker dies at Geneva.
Aug 5	–	Resolution in favour of Women's Suffrage carried, New Zealand House of Representatives.
Nov 12	–	Bill for Women's Suffrage passed South Australian Legislator; but without the absolute majority required by the law of that colony.
Nov 14	–	National Union of Conservative Associations, Scotland, passed a Woman's Suffrage Resolution by a large majority (Dundee).

1891

I am bound for the sake of record, and not to seem to have altered my opinion, to say that in my judgment whenever the question of the franchise is brought up, the question of relaxing the restrictions which are now imposed on the voting of women will have to be considered.

(Speech of Lord Salisbury, at the United Club, July 15)

March 19	–	Age of Consent Bill passed in India.
Mar 19	–	Decision on the Clitheroe case declared the right of a wife to personal liberty.
March 28	–	Custody of Children Act.
Nov 23	–	National Union of Conservative Associations carried resolution in favour of Women's Suffrage by a large majority (Birmingham).

1892

Depend upon it, if any further alteration of the franchise is brought forward as a practical measure, this question will again arise, menacing and ripe for solution, and it will not be possible for this House to set it aside as a mere speculative plan advocated by a body of faddists. Then you will have to deal with the problem of Women's Suffrage, and to deal with it in a complete fashion.

(The Rt. Hon. A.J. Balfour, speech in the House of Commons)

Jan 8	–	Women first elected on School Boards in Canada.
Feb 27	–	Miss A.J. Clough died.
March 4	–	First Woman Professor at Zurich University.
March 23	–	Women first voted in Parochial Associations, Guernsey.

April 15   –   Miss Amelia Blandford Edwards died.
April 27   –   Debate in House of Commons on Women's Suffrage (Bill introduced by Sir A.K. Rollit).
June 3   –   Miss Emily Sturge died.
July 28   –   British Medical Association admitted Women.

1893

That the possession and exercise of suffrage by the women in Wyoming for the past quarter of a century has wrought no harm, and has done great good in many ways; that it has largely aided in banishing crime, pauperism and vice from this State, and that without any violent or oppressive legislation; that it has secured peaceful and orderly elections, good government and a remarkable degree of civilisation and public order: and we point with pride to the facts that, after nearly twenty-five years of woman suffrage, not one county in Wyoming has a poor-house; that our jails are almost empty, and crime, except that committed by strangers in the State, is almost unknown; and as a result of experience, we urge every civilised community to enfranchise its women without delay.

(Resolution of the House of Representatives, Wyoming, Feb 20)

Feb 20   –   Resolution on good results of Women's Suffrage passed by the House of Representatives of Wyoming, USA.
April 14   –   Degrees given to Women in Scotland first time.
May 15   –   'World's Congress of Representative Women,' Chicago.
May 27   –   Municipal suffrage to Women, Michigan, receives the Governor's assent.
Sept 5   –   St. Mary's University College High School for Girls, Dublin, opened.
Sept 16   –   First Girls' University College (Germany) Karlsruhe.
Sept 19   –   Women's Suffrage received Governor's assent, New Zealand.
Oct 19   –   Mrs Lucy Stone died, Boston, USA.
Dec 2   –   Proclamation by the Governor of Colorado announcing Women's right to vote.

1894

If the women of Great Britain do attain this holy privilege, they will use their power in a way that will greatly benefit the country. They will bring about temperance and better laws, and their influence on their husbands and children will be greater than ever. This new species of modes of action will undoubtedly stir men up; and those who oppose women doing these things are enemies of their country, and not friends to the human race in whatever part of the world. Let an example be now given by women of patient long-suffering, and I feel sure success will come; a new epoch will dawn for mankind, and the world, in many respects, will be purer and better than it has ever been.

(Speech by the Right Hon. Sir George Grey, at Annual Meeting of Women's Suffrage Society Central Committee)

	–	First Women Factory Inspectors this year.
	–	Also Women placed for first time on a Royal Commission.
March 12	–	Local Government Act creating District and Parish Councils.
Sept 5	–	Mrs Augusta Webster died.
Dec 11	–	The University of Durham petitioned the Queen for a Charter to grant Degrees to Women.
Dec 18	–	Act admitting Women to the Parliamentary Franchise in South Australia.
Dec 24	–	Miss Buss, founder of North London Collegiate School, died, aged 67.
Dec 29	–	Miss Christina Rossetti died.

1895

Referring to the General Election of this year, the *Englishwoman's Review* for October says:

Taking those Members of the present House of Commons who voted on the last occasion (when Sir Albert Rollit introduced the Bill in April, 1892) we find that of 177 who voted against the Bill, 66 were returned again at the recent General Election; but of the 154 who voted in favour, 82 were again returned. Thus the old friends present a decided majority over the old opponents; while the new Members, about 130 are understood to be favourable, against about 10 who are understood to be unfavourable.

Feb 16	–	The Dowager Lady Stanley of Alderly died.
March 20	–	University of Aberdeen conferred Honorary Degree of LL.D on Miss Jane Harrison.
March 20	–	Miss Bilgrami passed with Honours at Madras University – the first Mahomedan lady.
May 31	–	Miss Emily Faithfull died.
July 5	–	Factory and Workshops Amendment Bill.
July 5	–	Summary Jurisdiction (Married Women) Act.
July 5	–	Danish Exhibition of Women's Industries, Copenhagen.
Aug 8	–	A Woman's Suffrage Bill passed third reading in the House of Assembly, Tasmania.

Oct 15	–	The new Aberdare Hall of Residence, Cardiff opened.
Nov 20	–	Women permitted to be nominated as administrators of the Bureaux de Bienfaisance in Paris.

1896

We have heard something about the working of the indirect action of women in politics. In mechanics, we find that the more indirect the action the greater the friction. It is the possession of direct influence that has made public life as pleasant as it is. If your audience have no votes, they will take measures – and often of a drastic character to make you do as they wish; but if they are voters, they have only to give their votes to your opponents.

When the franchise was restricted, the men who exercised it were sensible of the responsibility they owed to the nation. Now it is so wide that voters think they are the nation, and do not trouble to think that half the nation is deprived of political power.
(Speech by Mr George Wyndham, M.P. at the Annual Meeting of the Central Committee of National Society for Women's Suffrage)

Mar 28	–	Mrs Rundle Charles died.
March 31	–	Women Poor-Law Guardian Bill (Ireland).
April 12	–	The Senate of Cambridge University decided against giving Degrees to Women.
April 25	–	Women voted for first time in South Australia.
May 19	–	Women's Suffrage Appeal presented in Westminster Hall, containing 257,000 signatures of Women.
June 30	–	Harriet Beecher Stowe died, aged 85.
June 31	–	*New German Civil Code (narrowing the rights of Women) passed in the Reichstag.*
June 31	–	Miss Cornelia Sorabje, LL.B., pleaded before a British Judge at Poona.
Sept	–	University Hall, St. Andrews, opened for Women Students.
Sept 8	–	International Conference on the interests of Women at Geneva.
Sept 19	–	International Conference of Women at Berlin.
Oct 1	–	All Scholarships in the Queen's Colleges, Ireland, opened to Women.
Oct 1	–	Durham University B.A., Degree opened to Women.
Oct 16	–	Conference of Women's Suffrage Societies in Birmingham.
Nov 8	–	Miss Isabella S.M. Tod (Belfast) died, aged 60.
Dec	–	Full Suffrage granted to Women in Idaho, USA.

1897

Work, work, work – such is the moral of the memorable debate in the House of Commons on February 3, with its majority of 71 in favour of Women's Suffrage. That majority is an undeniable fact, but it is one to encourage to fresh exertion. It is a time to rejoice – but not to rest; a time for hopeful faith, but not for quiescence.

The evils men see in the admission of women to responsible power are at worst evils arising from the occasional individual mistakes or follies, such as apply in every movement. The evils we see are deep seated in the constitution of things. Until the law which is the moral standard of the unthinking multitudes, treats women with equal respect, the average mind will not regard them as worthy of respect, nor women respect themselves. It is respect for women that is wanted to come as a purifying breeze and drive away the miasmas generated by this doctrine of inferiority that are sapping our national morality.

(*Englishwoman's Review*, April)

Jan 28	–	Mrs Massingberd died, aged 50.
Feb 3	–	Parliamentary Franchise Extension to Women Bill passed second reading by a majority of 71.
March 2	–	Baroness Posaner first woman to take degree of M.D. in Vienna.
March 3	–	Mrs Pease Nicholl died, aged 91.
March 4	–	Miss Emily Shirreff died, aged 82.
May	–	Women admitted to vote for Church Synod in Australia.
May 21	–	Cambridge University rejected admission of Women to Degrees.
June 14	–	Statue to Mrs Siddons unveiled at Paddington Green.
June 22	–	The Diamond Jubilee of Her Majesty the Queen.
July	–	Miss Benjamin admitted to the Bar in New Zealand.
July 20	–	Jean Ingelow died, aged 70.
Aug 4	–	Belgian Women's Congress at Brussels.
Aug 6	–	Order of Local Government Board abolishing Pauper Nurses.
Aug 19	–	Lady Cadogan's Irish Textile Exhibition opened in Dublin.
Oct 4	–	Prof. F.W. Newman (first Hon. Sec. of Bristol Women's Suffrage Society) died, aged 92.
Dec 7	–	Women's Suffrage carried at Conference of Liberal Federation, Derby.
Dec 7	–	Law enabling women in France to act as witnesses received President's assent.

Dec 7	–	Dinner given by Chinese ladies to European ladies at Shanghai to consider plans for a School for Girls.
Dec 9	–	First issue of *La Fronde* (a woman's daily paper) in Paris.

1898

In South Australia the Electoral Act has become blind to the question of sex, and the conditions of registration and voting are the same for all adults. The refining influence of women has made itself felt in this sphere as in every other: they have elevated the whole realm of politics without themselves losing a jot of their innate purity. 'No poorer they, but richer we,' by their addition to the electoral roll.

(Speech of the Hon. A.J. Cockburn (Agent General for South Australia) Annual Meeting Women's Suffrage Central Committee)

Jan 12	–	Mrs Cowden Clarke died, aged 91.
Jan 30	–	Bill permitting women to vote for Tribunaux de Commerce, France, passed.
Feb 6	–	Mlle Maria Deraismes died in Paris.
Feb 18	–	Fiftieth Anniversary of the first Women's Suffrage Convention, USA, celebrated at Washington.
Feb 27	–	Miss Sarah Lewin died, aged 86.
Mar 14	–	First Conference of the Alexandra College Guild, Dublin.
Mar 14	–	Women admitted to partial Suffrage in Louisiana, USA
April 21	–	First German Women's Club opened in Berlin.
May 1	–	Jubilee of Queen's College, Harley Street.
May 30	–	The Order of Oddfellows permit the establishment of Female Branches.
June 24	–	Deputation of Women's Suffrage League to the Premier of New South Wales.
July 9	–	Exhibition of Women's Work at the Hague opened.
Aug 10	–	Women's Suffrage passed second reading in the Legislative Assembly, Victoria. (*Rejected by Legislative Council, Sept 10.*)
Sept 6	–	Coronation of Queen Wilhelmina of Holland.
Sept 10	–	Assassination of the Empress Elizabeth of Austria at Geneva.
Nov 16	–	First Annual Meeting of National Union of Women's Suffrage Societies, Manchester.

4

POLITICS

The boundaries of 'politics' are hard to draw, and have been drawn here artificially. Every utterance in every magazine and journal had and has political significance, from title and price, to advertising and the contents of news items and features. But the focus of this chapter is broadly on women's achievement of political independence. And the subject is addressed through a variety of genres, from magazine fiction to after-dinner speech, to indicate the diverse methods by which readers' views could be manipulated and their self-image shaped.

Annie Swan's story represents a trend in the popular fiction of the day, which often imagined ways in which women could earn their own livings; this story is emphatic in its rejection of social (and narrative) norms, denying a heterosexual 'happy end' and promoting an alternative community of women. Three articles about work are included, to suggest the range of employment open to women, from street cleaner to dramatist, and to indicate the social labelling meted out to working women. Louisa Lawson's piece on 'old women' also addresses the subject of name calling and offers an early example of the campaign to alter public perception of women by scrutinising discourse. The closing article about Queen Victoria preempts her obituaries but sets the tone for the way she would be transfigured in the press following her death in January 1901.

'An Independent Woman,' Annie S. Swan, *Woman at Home*
(London), December 1899, pp. 265–74

'I certainly think that there is nothing to hinder you going out to earn your own living. This place is far too expensive to keep; I shall let it as soon as possible.'

The speaker, a tall well-built young fellow about eight-and-twenty, with a somewhat hard though rather handsome face, uttered these words in a tone of decision, at the same time regarding his sister, to whom they were addressed, with a somewhat furtive glance, as if not quite certain how she would take it.

140

Beyond a slight tremor of the eyelids she betrayed no sign of how much the words had wounded her. It was not altogether the prospect which dismayed her, but rather the heartlessness with which the proposition was made. They had no other kindred in the world so far as they knew, and they ought to have been devoted one to the other, but somehow Walter and Netta Firth had never even been able to get on together. They were very different by nature. Netta was sympathetic, unselfish and perhaps a trifle unpractical, whereas her brother was one of those who are determined to succeed, no matter at what cost to others. Their widowed mother has just died, and it might have been thought that they have drawn more closely together in their sorrow, but it was not so. Walter Firth had not approved of his mother and sister living in the old home. It had always seemed to him a needless piece of extravagance, and now that it had come into his possession he had determined to make something out of it. It was only a roomy and comfortable cottage in a remote village in Buckinghamshire, but it was just such a place as would be sought after by the weary Londoner in search of change and rest. Already he had a tenant in his mind's eye, and he had though it better to let Netta understand his intentions at once.

'Mother thought,' she said somewhat timidly, 'that, if I could get a few paying guests to come here, I might make a good living. Won't you let me try that, Walter?'

He shook his head.

'You haven't got it in you, Netta. You couldn't make it pay; you would be swindled on every hand. It would be far better for you to take a situation. I heard of one this morning which I think would suit you very well.'

'I should not like to take a situation of your seeking, Walter,' she said with a sudden flash, 'and I don't think that you are treating me very well.'

At this, Firth looked annoyed. Perhaps he was not entirely comfortable in his own mind, but he was determined at all hazards to let his sister understand that she must depend now on her own resources.

'Besides, you forget that the furniture of the house is mine, and you can't really let it without my consent.'

'I can't let it as it stands, of course, unless you agree,' he said, a trifle sullenly; 'but I don't think that you will be so foolish. I have got a very good offer for the house, and of course whatever rent is paid you will receive the half of it, which I consider will be a very fair arrangement and an equivalent for the use of the furniture, which you are so careful to remind me belongs to you.'

Netta bit her lip; she was on the verge of tears, but at the same time her natural and justifiable indignation at his treatment made her determined not to show it. She knew him to be in receipt of a very fair income, and felt that he might have given her the house as a means of livelihood, but she would not even hint at it.

'Fortunately it is just the time of the year to let a place like this,' said Firth, as he looked somewhat complacently out of the window across the little lawn to the green masses of the shrubbery, for which the little place was famed in the neighbourhood. 'There is some people coming down to see it to-morrow, and if they like it they want to take possession on the first of July, which is next Thursday, as you know. I cannot be here, I must return to Manchester tonight; but I hope you will take the trouble to be civil to them, and to tell them all the good points of the house. It will be to your own advantage if you do.'

'Anne can do that, Walter,' said the girl, with a faint, dreary smile. 'I would rather not have anything to do with them. I shall probably leave in the morning before they arrive.'

He turned and looked at her curiously.

'Leave in the morning to go where, may I ask? Have you anything in view?'

'I am going to London. Winnie Bartram has asked me to stay with her until I find something to do.'

Firth was surprised; he had not expected that his sister would come to any decision so quickly. It was certainly an immense relief to him, and yet he could not help regarding her in a somewhat puzzled manner.

'What does she do, this friend of yours?' he asked.

'She is one of the sanitary inspectors,' replied Netta, 'and she lives at Battersea.'

'Oh! One of the advanced women, is she? Still, if she has a post like that, it is quite possible she may be able to get something for you to do – perhaps an assistant inspectorship, or something of that sort.'

'There isn't any such thing,' replied Netta. 'There are only three lady inspectors in London; besides, it needs very special training; but you needn't trouble about me, Walter, you can go your own way, as you have so plainly indicated. Don't imagine I want to be a burden on you; I would rather go out as a domestic servant, which is probably what I shall come to, sooner or later.'

Firth shifted uneasily from one foot to the other. The exceeding bitter note in his sister's voice indicated something to him of her inward feeling.

'Come now, Netta; don't be so savage at me. You know what a small income I have. I have a job to make ends meet. I always thought that mother coddled you up too much, and that you ought to have been earning something long ago. It only makes it harder now, as you see.'

'I would rather not discuss the matter further with you,' cried the girl rebelliously, and ran out of the room. That same evening Walter Firth returned to his occupation at Manchester, and Netta took care to be out of the house at the time of his departure. She was determined to have no further speech with him. Next morning she departed to London, taking the most of her belongings with her, feeling a forlorn, almost a desperate creature. All this feeling of loneliness vanished, however, when she reached Paddington and saw Winifred Bartram waiting for her on the platform. Anything more unlike the common idea of the advanced or the emancipated woman could not well be imagined. Winifred was very pretty, which perhaps partly accounted for her great success as an inspector. She had been known to melt the heart of the most obdurate manager of factory or workshop, and had a way of getting what she wanted without much trouble. She was always beautifully and fittingly dressed; in fact, she bestowed a great deal of attention upon her personal appearance. It was one of her pet ideas that a woman can be much more useful and influential in the world if she makes the most of herself.

'Well, there you are, you poor pale-faced little thing,' she said affectionately as she greeted her old friend, at the same time taking in every detail of her face and figure. The heavy mourning she wore seemed to accentuate the paleness of her face, and gave her a sad and pathetic look which touched Winnie's tender heart at once. 'I wish I could have come down to be with you at this time, but I don't think I have ever been so busy in my life. I shall be so glad to have your help, when you feel able for it, with my correspondence. I wish you saw my desk this morning; it's enough to make the bravest and the most energetic quail.'

Somehow it was impossible to be dull or hopeless in that strong, brave presence. In an incredibly short space of time she had all Netta's luggage safely stowed on the top of a four-wheeler, and then putting her inside gave the Battersea address.

'I have just time to go home and have lunch with you, then I shall be out all the afternoon while you unpack and put your things away. My flat is very small, but I daresay it will hold us, and we shan't quarrel. I rather expected to see your brother with you; where is he?'

'Oh, he went back to Manchester last night, Winnie,' said the girl, and Winnie observed that her mouth hardened a little. 'It was not a minute too soon. I think that, if he had stayed another day, probably we should have quarrelled.'

'Oh, is it so bad as that? What could you possibly have to quarrel about?' asked Winifred with interest.

'He has been so hard and unsympathetic to me at this time, Winnie. The whole object of his life has been to show me quite evidently that I must not depend on him for anything. It is a dreadful thing to say of one's brother, but I can't help thinking he is the most utterly selfish person I have ever met.'

'Oh, well, I shouldn't trouble my head about him. We'll show him what women can do nowadays. Once upon a time, you know, when a girl was left as you are, she felt as if the heavens had fallen, but it is different now. If you only show a little pluck, you'll get on, never fear.'

Under this genial influence Netta Firth began to improve wonderfully in every way. She seemed quite suddenly to have some object in life, although what that object was she could not exactly put into words. For the first week or two she was busily engaged helping her friend in the clerical part of her work, at which she proved herself such an adept that Winifred herself was amazed.

'Why, you're what the story books call a "perfect treasure"', she said laughingly one day. 'Now you've straightened me up, we must try and find you something to do. They're always talking about appointing some new inspectors. How I wish you had a chance!'

'Oh, but I don't think I should like that work,' cried Netta, almost in dismay, some of the more unpleasant details of Winnie's duties rising vividly up before her. 'I should never have the nerve or courage for it. I am certain, if a man spoke to me as that manager at the box-making place spoke to you yesterday, I should simply die.'

'Oh no, you wouldn't,' said Winnie cheerfully; 'you'd get used to it. I'll see what can be done to day. We've got to show that precious brother of yours that we are not the weaker sex any longer.'

At length, through the influence of her friend, Netta Firth obtained a situation as clerk in a business house. It was not anything very ambitious or lucrative; still, the money sufficed for her simple needs, and gave to her that feeling of independence for which she craved. They were very happy together. Though out all day at their respective occupations, they met in the evening, ready to enjoy each other's companionship; and so the months slipped away with surprising swiftness. As they passed, Netta heard from time to time of her brother, and, had she been less prejudiced against him, she might have detected in his letters a certain note of anxiety concerning her. Although he would scarcely have admitted it, he had many times regretted his treatment of his sister. He had tried to still the voice of his own conscience with the thought that he had his own way to make in the world, and that it was impossible for him to be hampered with a helpless girl. Netta herself did not write often, and then she said as little as possible about herself and her life, so he had really no idea how thoroughly happy and comfortable she was.

At Christmas time he had a few days' holiday, and determined to go to London to see for himself how she was getting on. He dropped no hint of his intention, preferring to pay a visit unawares, so that he might find out exactly the state of affairs. The address – Lambert Mansions, Battersea Park – did not convey any definite idea to his mind. He supposed that the girls were in lodgings together. Winifred Bartram he had never seen although she had paid frequent visits to Netta at the old home. He arrived in London about seven o'clock in the evening, and after much inquiry and some considerable trouble he at last arrived at the huge block of flats, which occupied a very pleasant position overlooking the open space of Battersea Park. He had left his luggage at the station hotel, as he had very little knowledge of London, although he was naturally determined to spend as little money as possible. He found the number of the door without any difficulty, and his knock was answered by Miss Bartram, who looked at him in some amazement, not recognising him. When he asked for Miss Firth, however, some idea of his identity dawned upon her, and she had just bidden him walk in when Netta, who heard his voice, came hurrying out into the little hall.

'Why, Walter!' she exclaimed in surprise, but without the least cordiality, 'whatever brings you here?'

'I came to see how you were getting on, that's all,' he answered, and somehow he felt a trifle uncomfortable, he could not have told why. 'Won't you ask me to come in?'

'Why, certainly,' said Miss Bartram. 'We are just having our evening meal. Perhaps it is not the description of a meal which commends itself to a man, but all the same you'd better come in and share it.'

'Yes, do,' said Netta. 'Why didn't you write and tell us you were coming?'

'Well, because I wanted to see for myself how you are living,' he answered, as he took off his overcoat and hung it on the stand. Then Netta, feeling decidedly uncomfortable, showed him into the little sitting room. It was very small, but had a homely and comfortable look, and the two girls themselves looked so bright and thoroughly contented that somehow he felt a vague sense of intrusion.

'You seem to have very comfortable lodgings here,' he observed lamely, as he sat down.

'It isn't lodgings, Walter,' said Netta reprovingly. 'This is Miss Bartram's house, and she kindly allows me to be here as a guest for a very small consideration.'

'Now, Netta, don't exaggerate things,' cried Miss Bartram quickly. 'I assure you Mr Firth, she pays full value for anything she gets, and at the same time takes her full share of responsibility. You look rather mystified. Have you never heard of two women workers living in a flat together?'

'Oh yes, I have heard of it,' he said confusedly; 'but I did not think it was like this.' He was very much interested in Winifred Bartram. He had heard a good deal about her in the old days, and had rather scoffed at her as one of the advanced sisterhood who have thrown all conventional trammels to the winds; but that the reality was very different was proved to him during the hour he spent in that happy little home. Miss Bartram did not at all approve of him or of his attitude towards his sister, but it was not in her nature to be disagreeable or uncourteous to anybody; and while Netta was silent and evidently ill at ease, she did her best to keep the conversation going, and talked with even more than her usual brilliancy and ease. All the time, however, Walter Firth felt himself distinctly out of it. He had an odd feeling that the atmosphere was antagonistic to him, and that he was only there on sufferance. Netta was quite pleasant and cordial to him, but there was a something about her which seemed to indicate that she intended to live her own life, and that she wished no interference from him. When she accompanied him to the door, he looked at her keenly.

'When can I see you alone? I want to have a talk over things, and to hear what you really are about.'

'Oh, I'm very busy, Walter. I only have a little leisure in the evenings, and then I am tired; besides, there isn't anything to talk about.'

'But I want to hear what you are doing, and all about your salary and everything,' he said, a trifle impatiently.

'Well, I don't think I want to talk about those things to you at all, Walter. I'm getting on very well, thank you. Winifred has been very kind to me, and that is all.'

'Well, but I'm your brother, and I have a sort of right, you know, to look after you.'

A faintly derisive smile dawned for a moment on the girl's lips.

'Oh that's all very fine, Walter,' she said, a trifle drily; 'but I cannot quite forget how you cast me off six months ago. It was then I wanted help, not now, when I am getting on quite comfortably, thanks to Winifred.'

'Now I call that bearing malice, Netta,' said Walter rather reproachfully; 'and I didn't think you'd treat me like that.'

'You can't feel it as much as I felt it when I left Oakhurst,' she said; 'but there, there's no use recriminating. Don't let us talk about these matters at all. How long are you to be in London?'

'About three days. Shall I be allowed to come and see you again?'

'Oh yes, you can come as often as you like; but we are only disengaged in the evenings, except on Sundays. You can come here to dinner with us on Sunday, if you like.'

It was not a very pressing invitation, but Firth grasped at it eagerly. He was more interested than he would have cared to own; besides, Netta's indifference nettled him, and made him all the more anxious to see her again. She was greatly changed. Necessity had developed her self-reliance, and made a woman of her.

When Winifred heard that her friend's brother was coming on Sunday, she naturally wished to leave them to enjoy one another's company without the presence of a stranger, but Netta so eagerly implored her not to leave her that she remained.

They had a very happy meal together, and Walter Firth admired Winifred more and more. Like many other ignorant persons, he had conceived a strong and unreasoning prejudice against women who have foresight and determination enough to carve out a career for themselves, and he was surprised to find that one who had succeeded so well should be at the same time such a very sweet and attractive person; and when he went back to Manchester, he carried her image in his heart.

For the first time in his selfish life he was lifted completely out of himself, and became interested with all his heart and soul in the welfare of another.

That was but the beginning of many visits to London, and before long Netta saw how matters were drifting. She dared not say a word to Winifred, however, and had no means of knowing how she was disposed towards her brother.

It was about twelve months before matters came to a crisis. Firth arrived in London one dreary evening in November, and when he got out to Battersea he was surprised and in no way displeased to find Winifred alone.

'Netta has gone out to dine with some people she knows at Bayswater. I think I am rather jealous of these new friends of hers; they take her away from me a good deal. She didn't know you were coming – at least, she said nothing to me.'

'No, I didn't write to her; in fact, I only knew this morning that I could come,' answered Firth. 'I am up on business connected with my firm. The unexpected happened to me this morning, Miss Bartram.'

'What was that?' she asked again, but her interest certainly was not of the vivid order.

'I got an unexpected rise, not only in my income, but in my prospects. I am likely to be made a junior partner in spring.'

'Oh! And will that be a good thing?' she asked, with a faintly provoking smile on her lips.

'Yes; it should bring me in an income of fifteen hundred or perhaps two thousand a year. Not many men of my age attain to such a position.'

'Do they not?' she asked. 'What a lot of money you will be able to save!'

She was poking fun at him, only he did not see it.

'Well, I hope I shall save some,' he answered; 'but that is not how I regard it just at present. When a man has an assured position, it gives him more confidence for other things. Don't you ever get tired of this kind of life, Miss Bartram?'

'Tired of it, no. Why should I? I am entirely happy in it. Of course we all get fagged at times, but a few days' holiday puts me straight again. I wouldn't change places with anyone.'

'And would you be quite happy to live like this all your life?'

'Oh, I don't look so far ahead as that, Mr. Firth. Sufficient unto the day is the evil thereof.'

'Have you ever thought that you might marry?' was his next question.

'I never have. I don't intend to marry,' she answered quietly, but with determination.

'You might meet some one who would make you change your mind.'

'Possibly, only I haven't done so yet,' she answered, and the next moment she saw what was coming.

He rose from his chair, and stood directly in front of her, looking very handsome and manly and in earnest.

'I know I am a poor sort of fellow to aspire to a woman like you,' he began quite humbly, 'but all the same I wish you would give me a chance to win you. You are the first woman I have ever cared for. Don't you think that after a time, at least, you might think of me in that way?'

She shook her head.

'No, Mr. Firth, never. I assure you there is not the slightest hope or possibility of such a thing.'

'But why,' he asked, 'if there is no one else and I would do my utmost to make you happy?'

'As I told you, I shall never marry. I am not the sort of woman to settle down to the domestic life. I know we should quarrel; that would be a fore-gone conclusion. Some day, when you find the sort of woman who would accommodate herself to the life you have to offer, you will thank me for my refusal.'

But Firth was too much in earnest to take his dismissal so lightly, and he did his utmost to plead his cause successfully, but it was without avail. Perhaps because she had started prejudiced against him, her heart where he was concerned was as hard as the nether millstone, and when he took his leave at length he felt that his dismissal was final.

He did not go back to the flat on that occasion, and when Netta heard that he had been there she surmised what had happened, but she did not say a word about it, nor did Winifred for some time.

'Walter hasn't been here for a long time, Winnie,' she said one day, about three months after. 'Would you think me very curious if I ask what you said to him the last time he was here?'

'No I shouldn't. He asked me to marry him, Netta, and I declined.'

'Did he really?' asked Netta. 'I thought he would some day, and I felt sure, too, that it was hopeless.'

'It is quite hopeless,' said Winifred with conviction. 'I have no intention of marrying, but if I had I shouldn't choose a man like your brother, Netta. I did not tell him, but I don't think I shall ever quite forgive him for his treatment of you. It will do him good to know that we can live independently of him and his kind.'

In course of time Walter Firth tried again to induce Winifred Bartram to change her mind, but without success. Contrary to her expectation, he has not married yet, and he is a very much humbler-minded and sympathetic man than he was before such an experience came to him. I am afraid his sister did not give him the sympathy which perhaps he deserved.

'If Winnie had accepted you, Walter,' she said quite calmly one day, 'I should never be able to believe in anything again. It would have shattered all the ideals I possess.'

'The Woman Suffrage Movement,' Miss Helene Reinherz,
Humanitarian (London), September 1900, pp. 190–5

There has perhaps never been a time in the annals of the Woman's Suffrage Movement when its supporters have felt so profoundly discouraged as within the last few years. In some cases discouragement has almost led to inaction, and after much enthusiastic devotion to the cause, after immense labour, after the patient endurance of much obloquy and ridicule, it sometimes appears to the champions as if their cause were likely to die of inanition.

The records of the movement are remarkable; in some particulars they are unique. There was a time when every keen woman suffragist had such a number of things to urge that the market was in danger of being glutted with suffrage literature. There were endless arguments to be brought before the public, endless objections to be refuted, endless facts to be collected and classified, endless conclusions to be drawn. Then the arguments had to be re-stated in more persuasive form, clothed in fresh language and strengthened by a multitude of new examples which cropped up day by day.

In the days when the exclusion of women from all share in the government first began to be questioned, their opponents had an apparently irrefutable argument in the man's superior physical force and woman's inability to bear arms. But it soon had to be admitted that physical force had little to do with the matter, and that it was the taxpayer, rather than the soldier, who bore the burdens of the State and so earned the privilege of a share in its government.[1]

When the physical force argument began to fall into discredit, men turned their attention to the mental inferiority of women. Whereupon the suffragists pointed to the undeniable intellectual successes of women, to their achievements in the universities, in literature, in the teaching and medical professions, in business – in short, wherever they had not been debarred by law or rigid custom from the exercise of their natural gifts and energies. But this was not all. Women had yet to learn that an intellectual standard existed, and a test of mental ability separated the male voters from the non-voters. Neither of these reasons could stand the light of day.

---

1 It is useful to note that the number of men fighting for their country in the greatest war we have waged since the beginning of the century, is only 200,000 in a total male population of over 18,000,000, and that it is precisely these men who would have no share in the election of the next Parliament in the case of an immediate general election.

But, it was urged, there was nothing that men had do dearly at heart as the interest of their womankind, and they could safely be trusted to look after them.

There was something so delicate and touching about this argument that it seemed almost rude to bring forward facts to discredit it. But to begin with, there are over a million women in the United Kingdom who are not anybody's 'womenkind,' and therefore do not come within the area of this protected class. And history, conclusive and inexorable on this point, shows that no class can safely leave its interests in the hands of any other class. In this peculiarity of human nature lies the need for representative institutions.

That the interests of women have not been protected is so obvious a commonplace that it hardly needs to be insisted on. Governments in old and new countries alike, have done something for the education of their boys, and hardly anything for that of the girls. The Married Women's Property Act is barely twenty years old, and there is still no such protection for the inheritance – and, worse still, for the earnings of women, in other countries. Even in the home, which is accounted so peculiarly woman's domain that for a long time she was excluded from any other, her interests are not protected, for, according to the law, the children of a married woman belong to their father, and she has no jurisdiction over them.

Then there is all the legislation relating to the sexes with regard to which women have never in any way been consulted. If men had refrained from suiting this to their own convenience, they would have been extraordinarily generous. To take quite another example, a new Factory Bill relating to the employment of women is before Parliament, and a Shop Hours Bill is being brought in which will affect the prospects of a very large number of women. Yet the views of women, both of those who are likely to be affected by the bills if they become law, and of those who have spent much time and labour in studying the subject in all its bearings, are completely ignored.

All these things, however, are so obvious that it is tedious to recapitulate them. The suffragists long ago exhausted the arguments at their disposal, and stopped for sheer want of further reasoning to do battle with. They had brought forward a number of irrefutable arguments, a wealth of undeniable evidence that would have proved the most desperate case in the world many times over. They had done it so well and so thoroughly that nothing remained to be added. At last the subject became hackneyed, and still nothing had been achieved.

The arguments were never refuted, the facts were never denied. The matter was simply shelved from day to day, as might safely be done, since no politician is accountable to women for what he does or leaves undone. Day after day, and year after year, we heard the same arguments, which had no bearing on the question at all, but sufficed to convince the electors – if, indeed, they needed convincing – that it would be a pity to interfere with a state of things which was perfectly comfortable for themselves. It would be interesting to construct a conversation *à la* Ollendorf, illustrating the approved methods for the instruction of young politicians.

The suffragists point out that the present system of government, which piques itself on being entirely representative, actually leaves out of account more than one-half of the population.

They are told that women's sphere is the home, and her first duty to please her husband and be beautiful.

They urge that their interests are not protected, and point to some of the anomalies and inequalities of the present law.

They are told that the cradle lies athwart the entrance to the polling booth, and more to the same purpose.

They point out that there is not a single valid reason for refusing women the common privileges of citizenship, while exposing them to all its burdens.

They are warned not to descend from the beautiful, exalted impotence, and they are besought not to deprive man of the scope necessary for the exercise of his chivalrous instincts.

So women have learnt to be patient. They wondered a little what had become of the first principles of logic, but in time they learnt never to be surprised.

There is another line of argument most difficult to contend with, which is practically the only one now adopted by the opponents of the enfranchisement of women. This is the line of lofty superiority, of lively indignation; its usual expression is a smile, an exclamation of 'What next, I wonder!' or a threadbare allusion to women's want of logic, and the safety of the Empire.

Some years ago the question was raised in the University of Cambridge of granting degrees to women on the result of the examinations, which they took on the same terms and conditions as the men. The events on this occasion are remarkably instructive to the students of women's progress.

The case was a peculiar one. The universities are closed bodies, and as such can grant or refuse their honours as they please. They compel none to come to them, and if they refused admittance to their examinations or their degrees to any particular class or society, the exclusion might be arbitrary, the excluded might feel aggrieved, but the excluders would be within their rights. An arbitrary distinction of this kind would provoke much censure, and public opinion, or something more powerful, would probably interfere on behalf of the sufferers, if these had been excluded on any other ground than that of sex.

Whatever, then, may have been the intrinsic value of the arguments brought forward, or the motives really at work, the legislators were at any rate within their rights. The women were 'honoured guests,' and might be treated as unjustly as their hosts desired. Not that the authorities plumed themselves on this indisputable right of theirs to arbitrary and unreasonable action. On the contrary, they brought forward their case with something in the shape of argument, or, at any rate, of assertion. Their trump card, as might have been expected, was the 'thin end of the wedge' argument, and some of them were inclined to yield a trifling point, if only the women would pledge themselves, and all posterity, never to ask for any further concessions. The women humbly pointed out that to pledge posterity had never been deemed a human privilege. Then the rulers of the University thought better of their generosity, and withdrew their offer.

The 'thin end of the wedge' has ever been a popular argument, and generally effective in inverse ratio to its appropriateness. The cry is raised at every turn. In Cambridge it won the day. If women were allowed to have degrees, they might be Senators; if Senators, we might have a woman Vice-Chancellor of the University. And then!

The 'then' was never further defined, but it sufficed to ruin the women's cause.

The same thing precisely occurred when the London Government Bill (1899) was before Parliament. If women were admitted to seats on the new Borough Councils, they might rise, through their services to the community, to be aldermen, and even mayors. We might be threatened with a woman Lord Mayor of London. And then!

The same objection is still the most potent of all against the enfranchise-ment of women. If women have the parliamentary vote, the next thing will be that they will sit in Parliament, and then we may be governed by a woman Prime Minister. At this point it is usual to follow up the trump card with a variety of playful allusions, such as those to be-wigged Portias, Joans of Arc in khaki, etc., which generally amuse the audience to which they are addressed, though their precise bearing on the point is a little difficult to discover.

In view of these sinister warnings, it is remarkable that nowhere else can we find this extraordinary need of legislation against the encroachments of the unfit. This unfortunate class of persons has always been considered, at any rate, in an age of enlightened self-government, sufficiently handicapped by its own unfitness. On the other hand, where men have succeeded in raising themselves by their own exertions to posts of honour in the public service, that fact alone has ever been held a sufficient test of their ability. There has never been any regulation in the University, so far as we are aware, to prevent men who have failed to obtain honours, and have remained satisfied with an ordinary degree, from sitting in the Senate, because the pollman might in this way insert the thin end of the wedge, which would only stop at the Vice-Chancellorship. There has never been any law to prohibit junior clerks from sitting in Parliament, or Board School masters from becoming Cabinet Ministers. Such appointments might be exceedingly disastrous, but, oddly enough, it has never occurred to our legislators to take the proper precautions to guard against them.

It seems somewhat extraordinary, then, that the unfitness of women should need special legislation to prevent it from encroaching on the domain of man's capacity. It would tempt one to suppose that there were some extraneous considerations which, if women were eligible, would lead to their preferential appointment to all posts of honour and responsibility. Such a supposition is, to say the least, at variance with experience. In other cases of competition between men and women, we have not noticed that the woman is preferred where the merits of the two are identical and considerations of sex do not apply. On the contrary, instances might be quoted by the score, where, everything else being equal, the man is chosen and the woman rejected. And even if things are not equal, and the woman's qualifications are better than the man's, in nine cases out of ten, he is still chosen and she is rejected on the ground of sex.

It may safely be assumed, then, that no woman, however eligible, is likely to be Prime Minister, Lord Mayor of London, or Vice-Chancellor of the University of Cambridge, unless she is so far superior in all respects to her male competitors, as to overcome the intensely deep-rooted masculine prejudice that she would have to contend with. In which case the calamity implied in the 'And then!' does not appear to be very clear.

The entrance of women into public life will make a change for the better, but only a small and gradual change. There will be a wider field for electors to choose from, and naturally the community will have a chance of being better served. Within the field we may take it for granted that competitors will still find their own level, and that the fittest will have as good a chance of being chosen as before.

The issue is clear and inevitable, and the opponents of women's emancipation will find that while they are trying to make the clock work backwards, progress sweeps on inexorably in spite of their efforts. While men are never tired of telling women that their proper sphere is the home, thousands of young women of all classes are earning their livelihood and gaining in self-reliance and independence every day. It may be that man is right and that Nature has made the blunder, but we can hardly be blamed for giving Nature credit for greater wisdom than man.

To the young woman who has to make her own way in life, the demand for equal civil and political rights comes as naturally as the air she breathes. In the classroom, the office, or the workshop, she has learnt to rate at its true value the chivalry for which she is expected to barter her birthright. In part she knows this chivalry is but the artificial product of bad social arrangements; the rest is no more than she herself will give cheerfully, without taking any credit or asking for an equivalent, to every older woman. And this without any enquiry into their relative mental capacities, into the possession or non-possession by either of municipal privileges, or other considerations of this nature, too subtle doubtless, for the feminine intellect to appreciate.

While this question of justice and necessity continues to be treated with so much levity, and in so unreasonable an attitude, women can only console themselves with the reflection that the training which they are undergoing

[The table on pp. 154–155 relates to the extract on p. 156: 'Why Women are Employed in Factories in the United States'.]

Reasons for the employment of women and girls

	Better adapted	Cheaper	More industrious	More reliable	Neater	Cleaner	More rapid	More easily controlled	Quieter
Alabama	5	..	..	2	..	..	..	..	..
Connecticut	8	11	3	5	6	..	7	4	..
Delaware	2	1	..	..	..	..	..	..	..
Florida	11	2	..	3	1	..	..	1	..
Georgia	35	5	4	14	5	..	8	8	..
Illinois	39	8	1	..	2	..	1	1	..
Indiana	3	..	3	..	..	..	1	1	..
Iowa	21	7	1	8	5	..	1	1	..
Kentucky	14	1	..	3	..	..	..	..	..
Louisiana	6	3	..	..	..	..	1	1	..
Maine	23	11	..	..	..	..	1	..	..
Maryland	29	9	..	2	4	..	3	..	..
Massachusetts	26	15	4	4	6	..	6	2	..
Michigan	52	32	..	1	..	..	..	..	..
Minnesota	6	..	6	..	..	..	..	..	..
Mississippi	1	..	1	..	..	..	..	..	..
Missouri	17	7	..	..	..	..	5	..	..
New Hants	26	2	9	..	..	..	3	..	..
New Jersey	65	21	8	8	9	2	14	1	2
New York	179	109	7	22	18	4	8	8	2
North Carolina	19	2	..	1	1	..	2	5	..
Ohio	24	3	1	4	6	..	2	3	..
Pennsylviania	102	28	5	37	21	1	20	17	..
Rhode Island	20	18	..	1	..	..	..	..	..
South Carolina	17	2	1	3	1	..	4	4	1
Tennessee	7	2	..	2	..	..	3	3	..
Vermont	3	..	3	..	..	2	..	..	..
Virginia	12	3	..	1	6	3	3	8	..
West Virginia	25	6	3	5	4	..	2	4	..
Wisconsin	8	..	..	..	2	..	4	1	..
Total	804	318	60	26	97	12	19	74	5

Don't drink	More careful	More skilful	More polite	Content to work at one branch	More easily procured	More patient	Less liable to strike	Good effect on male employees	Total of factories that replied in each state
..	..	..	..	..	..	..	..	..	5
3	..	..	..	..	4	..	..	..	22
..	..	..	..	..	1	..	..	..	3
..	..	..	..	..	..	..	..	..	14
..	2	..	..	..	..	..	..	..	50
1	1	1	..	..	..	..	..	..	40
..	..	..	..	..	..	..	..	..	3
..	..	..	..	..	..	..	..	..	28
..	..	..	3	..	..	..	..	..	16
..	1	..	..	..	1	..	2	..	10
..	..	..	..	..	..	..	3	..	26
..	1	..	..	..	..	..	..	..	38
2	2	..	..	1	4	..	..	..	48
..	..	..	..	1	..	..	..	..	54
..	..	..	..	..	..	..	..	..	6
..	..	..	..	..	..	..	..	..	1
..	1	..	..	..	..	..	..	..	22
..	..	..	..	..	..	..	..	..	27
1	1	..	..	..	..	3	..	..	57
..	..	..	..	..	1	..	2	1	170
..	..	..	..	..	1	..	..	..	20
1	..	..	..	..	..	..	..	..	35
2	2	..	..	3	2	..	2	2	147
..	1	..	..	..	..	..	..	..	26
..	1	..	..	..	..	..	..	..	20
..	..	..	..	..	..	..	1	..	9
..	..	..	..	..	..	..	..	..	3
..	2	..	..	..	..	..	..	..	18
1	2	..	..	..	..	..	..	..	33
..	..	..	..	..	..	..	..	..	13
11	17	1	3	5	14	3	10	3	964

is perhaps the best that could be devised for them. The average intelligent woman has long ceased to take the utterances on the question of her enfranchisement, both in or out of parliament, at all seriously. Many years ago they may have roused to indignation and stung to injudicious retorts, now they rarely do more than amuse. The agitation will be successful in the end, because a new generation will arise, with minds unspoilt by false ideals, to whom the injustice of the existing system will appear intolerable. In the meantime, the training in patience and self-control, together with the insight gained into standards of political morality that are susceptible of much improvement, are of great value to women, and through them to the race.

'Why Women are Employed in Factories in the United States,'
Englishwoman's Review (London), 17 April 1900, pp. 104-5

The following table [pp. 154–155], showing the results of an enquiry made by the Labour Department of the United States into the reasons why manufacturers prefer to employ women, will perhaps be a new light to some of those who grumble that women are employed because they are cheaper than men.

The returns are to be found at pages 583 to 610 of the Eleventh Annual Report of the Commissioners of Labour, 1895–96 (Work and Wages of Men, Women and Children), and summarise the replies of 964 different firms, in all branches of manufacture in thirty States, as to their reasons for the employment of women and girls. Some firms gave one reason only, many gave two, some three or four, making a total of 1,580 reasons, in which, as will be seen, 'cheaper' occurs in the proportion of one-fifth, 'better adapted' occurs in close upon half, the remainder being distributed amongst a variety of reasons, of which 'more reliable' is the preponderating feature.

'Unwomanly Employments,' Priscilla E. Moulder,
an ex-factory worker, *Womanhood*
(London), August 1901, pp. 169–70

A great deal has been heard of late years about so-called unwomanly employment. On inquiry, however, this turns out to be a very vague assertion, and also very misleading. No one can draw up a code of rules, arranged on hard and fast lines, and then make the statement that is or that is not woman's work. To a reasonable being everything is woman's work, provided she can undertake it without injury to herself or detriment to public morals. Some years ago a clever lady was asked to define women's work, and the answer rather startled some of her male friends. The definition was 'Whatever is menial and badly paid.' On the whole, no answer could have been truer. Was it not the late Miss Frances Willard who ventured to hold the opinion that if there had been any honour or glory attached to domestic duties the men would have usurped that particular sphere of women's labour ages ago? This, however, by the way. Among the many occupations of women said to be unwomanly may be classed the calling of the London dustyard women. Now, there is not the slightest doubt that these women have to work hard and continuously. Twelve hours a day they stand, or sit, or dive among the refuse of London. The dustmen collect from the bins of decent neighbourhoods, and from the roads and gutters where live the army of the great 'unwashed,' and it is their duty to take the rubbish to the large dustyards to be found in various parts of London. These dustyard women are a stalwart and motley company. They have healthy-looking faces, strong bodies, and mighty muscles; while their attire is more noted for comfort than elegance. Their earnings amount to about 12 s. weekly, with coal and wood as perquisites. As for the charge of unwomanliness which has been thrown over and over again at this particular occupation, well, most of these women have never known any other calling. And, after all, the fact deserves to be taken into consideration that, what would naturally strike a superfine lady as unwomanly would not so strike these women, who simply look upon their employment as a matter of course. Back in the good old days it was considered quite too unwomanly to be strong and active. The more languid and lackadaisical and affected a woman could appear the more womanly she was voted.

Look what an outcry was raised about women being employed in the nail and chain trade. But the facts are nothing like so alarming in reality as they appear on the surface. I have often asked myself the question why there need be anything particularly unwomanly in turning out small nails and chains, but could never come to a satisfactory conclusion. It has been estimated that there are at least 10,000 women at work in the nail and chain trade. These women have from time to time been accused of various sins, which are generally spoken of as though they were inseparable from, or the outcome of, women being employed in this particular trade. Now the charge of immorality is absurd on the face of it. It is quite true that the sexes do mingle in the nail and chain trade, but it is generally members of the same family who work together in the tiny smithies. And, surely, if there were any undue amount of immorality among these women clergymen, and those who work among them, would be able to testify to the fact. On the contrary, however, those who are the most likely to know, say that there is no more immorality practised among women in the nail and chain trade than among those in other industrial spheres. What a noise, too, was made some years ago about the pit-brow women. But it would puzzle a wise person to say why the employment of sorting and sifting coal at the mouth of a pit was more unwomanly than, say, stone-picking in fields, or gathering fagots in woods and forests, both of which employments are common enough for women in agricultural districts. It will be still fresh in the public mind how a certain writer in a popular monthly magazine enlarged on the evils of wool-combing for women. By way of illustrating his article this writer had a photo inserted showing a woman with no clothes on the upper part of her body, and it was explained that this primitive costume was necessary, owing to the intense heat in which wool-combers are obliged to work. As far as my personal experience goes, I have never seen or heard about anything of the kind being a common practice. [. . .]

'Famous Women Dramatists,' *Woman's Life* (London),
22 December 1900, p. 105

The alleged resemblance between Mr Sydney Grundy's play *A Debt of Honour*, now running at the St. James's with *The Likeness of the Night*, which Mrs W. K. Clifford had printed in the *Anglo-Saxon Review* a few months ago, and which was recently produced by Mr and Mrs Kendal, calls attention to the large number of literary women who are now using the stage for the expression of their views and the telling of their stories.

Mrs Clifford herself is a dramatist who, till recently, has not had a play produced, although she has had both the works to which her name has been attached accepted. The other play was called *A Supreme Moment* and was printed in the *Nineteenth Century* in the summer of last year, while it was shortly after announced for production at the Avenue Theatre with Mrs Bernard Beers in the chief part, but it was subsequently postponed. As a novelist and short story writer she has always had a remarkably successful career.

Another distinguished authoress, Mrs Craigie who still elects to be known as John Oliver Hobbes, has had two plays produced by Mr George Alexander, *The Ambassador* and *Repentance*; the former proving a great success, and the latter, which was in one act, a failure. Mrs Craigie, who has had several other plays accepted, may definitely be considered to belong to the ring of dramatists, although she will not in all probability cease writing novels.

Yet a third novelist–playwright is George Fleming, as Miss Constance Fletcher elects to be called, who will be remembered as the author of *Mrs Lessingham*, produced at the Garrick some few years ago by Mr John Hare, and of *The Canary*, which was a feature of Mrs Patrick Campbell's first venture in management in association with Mr Forbes Robertson at the Prince of Wales' Theatre.

Mrs Oscar Beringer, the clever mother of two clever actresses, has had several plays produced at West-end theatres, among them being *Tares* and *A Bit of Old Chelsea*, in the latter of which Miss Annie Hughes made such a distinguished success, while another new comedy is on the eve of presentation.

Nor must mention of Miss Clo Graves – who has shortened the baptismal Clotilda into the form in which her name is at present known to the public –

be omitted. A dozen years or more ago, when a mere girl, she had an Egyptian tragedy in five acts, *Nitocris*, produced at the Drury Lane Theatre, and great expectations were formed of her. Of late, however, she has dropped the 'Ercles' vein and gone in for writing farces among the most recent of which have been *Nurse*, produced at the Globe, *The Bishop's Eye* at the Vaudeville, and *The Mother of Three* at the Comedy. With Miss Graves, in this last play, Miss Gertrude Kingston, the popular actress, was associated as author.

Actresses may, indeed, not infrequently be found among the ranks of playwrights. Miss Janet Achurch, for instance, is known to be the author of a play . . . Miss Janette Steer has also written for the stage on which she acts, as has Lady Bancroft, whose work was produced at the Garrick Theatre a few years ago by Mr Hare, Mrs Lancaster-Wallis, and others. Sarah Bernhardt, the universal genius, has written at least one play which has seen the footlights, and so has Miss Rosina Filippi, whose *Idyll of Seven Dials* is regarded as a little masterpiece, and who has also written several other plays, one of which was produced at the Court Theatre some time ago.

'The Woman's International Conference,' Sarah A. Tooley,
Lady's Realm (London), May 1899, pp. 90–95

As the principle of federation is fast becoming the keystone of the Empire, so is it being made the link to bind together women of various nationalities for the common cause of humanity. The concrete expression of this union is the International Council of Women. Although it is eleven years since it first originated, there are still those who ask, 'What is it?' Doubt seems to exist in the minds of some as to its being a permanent association, so possibly a short history of the Council, with descriptions of its officers, will prove of interest to the readers of the LADY'S REALM on the eve of the Congress in connection with it, which meets in London in June. Its constitution is rather unique, as it is a Council from which no women's counsel is excluded. The basis of membership is the Golden Rule: 'Do unto others as ye would that they should do unto you'; and as every one, of whatsoever nationality, religion, colour, sect, or party, is disposed to emphasise the excellence of that rule to everybody else, a more universal basis of agreement could not have been arrived at.

The International Council of Women is a federation of National Councils or Unions of women formed in various countries for the promotion of unity and mutual understanding between all associations of women working for the common welfare of the community. The objects of the Council are to provide a means of communication between women's organisations in all countries, and to enable women from all parts of the world to meet together to confer upon questions relating to the welfare of the family and the commonwealth.

When I attempt to define all the ramifications of this federation of councils which forms the International, I confess to a feeling of bewilderment. I can only compare it to that ingenious mechanical curiosity, the ivory box, which, when it is opened, reveals innumerable other boxes fitting inside each other. You keep taking out box after box, box after box, and yet others still smaller reveal themselves, until at last one of infinitesimal proportions is reached. Which is the 'real original' out of these boxes? There is no 'real original' – it is one box in many parts. . . . To sum up the puzzle briefly: the International Council is formed of National Councils, each of which is composed of representatives of the various women's associations in each respective country. At present National Councils have been formed, in the United States, Canada, Germany, Sweden, Great Britain and Ireland, New Zealand, New South Wales, and Italy, while the movement is taking shape in France, Holland, Denmark, Belgium, Finland, Switzerland; and delegates from these countries will be at the June gathering.

Women's meetings are so suggestive to the minds of many people of purely advanced propaganda that it may be as well to explain that the International Council has not specially identified itself with any one movement. This was guarded against by the originators, who though all adherents of the Temperance and Women's Suffrage Movements, drew up a constitution which expressly provided against either the International or its component parts, the National Councils, specially espousing those or any other controversial questions. The first meeting of the International took place in Washington in 1888, when Mrs Fawcett was elected President. For the succeeding five years the progress was not rapid; but when, in 1893, it held its first quinquennial meeting in Chicago, in connection with the Women's Branch of the World's Fair, the International began to gather strength. At that memorable meeting there were representative women from over thirty different nationalities, and the majority of these returned to their own countries pledged to form National Councils of Women in harmony with the constitution of the International. At the Chicago meeting, the following officers were elected: The Countess of Aberdeen, President; Mrs May Wright Sewall, United States, Vice-President; the Baroness Alexandra Gripenberg, Finland, Treasurer; Mrs Eva McLaren, Corresponding Secretary; Madame Maria Martin, France, Recording Secretary. All these ladies retain office to day, excepting Mrs Eva McLaren, who resigned two years ago on account of ill-health; and her place is now filled by Miss Teresa Wilson.

[. . .]

The gathering will afford an opportunity for the expression of the entente cordiale between the United States and Great Britain from the feminine standpoint. We hope to have the inspiring presence of Mrs May Wright Sewall, of Indianapolis, in our midst. She is the Vice-President of the Council, and has long been known as one of the foremost leaders amongst the women of the States. Her enthusiasm has a double danger, for it is both infectious and contagious. She is a charming personality, an admirable and effective speaker, and her organising powers are immense. She has twice been chosen

President of the United States Council. Mrs May Wright Sewall is very specially interested in questions of Education. She will be supported by other distinguished women from the States, who will give that racy originality to the debates which is so refreshing to European minds.

[. . .]

The congress in connection with the International Council is to be held in London from June 26 to July 2. Some three hundred delegates and speakers are expected to attend from various European countries, and from the United States, Canada, and Australasia, in addition to those from Great Britain and Ireland. Papers on a variety of topics will be read and discussed in connection with the different sections at the day sessions, and monster public meetings are to be held in the Queen's Hall upon International Arbitration and upon Women's Suffrage on the evenings of June 27 and 29 respectively. Men will be invited to speak at these meetings. There are also to be a variety of festive gatherings. The Duchess of Sutherland, who is always so ready to give her help and patronage to women's work, has kindly lent Stafford House for the evening reception, which precedes the first day of the Congress. Stafford House was a centre of light and leading in the early years of the reign, when the Duchess Harriet gave her support to many humanitarian movements; and the American delegates will recall that it was at Stafford House that Harriet Beecher Stowe delivered her first anti-slavery address in London. The Bishop and Mrs Creighton give a garden-party to delegates at Lambeth Palace, and Lady Battersea will hold a reception at Surrey House during the Congress Week; and there are other London hostesses who have expressed their wish to entertain the delegates, if time can be found. The headquarters of the Congress are at Westminster Town Hall, where two halls will be in use morning and evening. But this is not enough; and the two halls of St Martin's Town Hall have been engaged for sectional committees, while the Convocation Hall of the Church House, Westminster, has been requisitioned for the social and philanthropic work of the Congress. Westminster, indeed, is going to suffer an invasion and it is thought that the Houses of Parliament will scarcely be proof against the delegates. Would it not be wise of Mr Balfour and Sir Henry Campbell-Bannerman to face the situation at once, and have tiers of seats erected over the gallery, where the Congress ladies can view the proceedings in Parliament with ease and comfort? What will the foreign delegates think if they are committed to the present ladies' cage?

'Old Women,' Louisa Lawson, leader article, *Dawn* (Sydney),
November 1891

There is no contemptuous epithet in more common use among men than this: 'An old woman! A regular old woman!' It is not a new simile invented by each man out of his practical experience of old women, it is an old phrase picked up by boys and men from one another. It has come down from an earlier generation. It is indeed a phrase which summarises the past history of womankind. It is not alone because the poor creature is 'old', but also because she is a woman, that her name serves as a derisive epithet, along with names of other types used in contumely, like 'goose' and 'donkey'. There is no need to search books for evidence, and there is no room for doubt, because the way men thought of women is confessed in this phrase. It is clear that whenever the loss of youth destroyed woman's attractiveness to men, no attempt was made to hide the prevailing belief in the littleness, triviality, and inferiority of women. That belief is diminishing now, for within the last thirty years women have made wonderful advance, they have taken their place in the medical, journalistic and other professions; they have carried off honours in the universities; and have demonstrated in a hundred ways that with equal opportunities they can stand where men must look up, not down, towards them. How then has this old term of scorn survived? For it has survived and women even have grown used to it. Only the other day, a speaker, who addressed a large audience of men and women, said, 'There are too many old women in parliament already.' The term was obviously used in disparagement, but though there were many old women present, and a great number of young and middle-aged women, they did not rise and walk out. It was a common place phrase and used in perfect good faith, for it has so long been tacitly understood that women may be looked down upon with impunity. It was unconsciously used too, for the man does not despise his mother, nor regard her as a type of feeble foolishness, obstinacy and unreason. Yet every man who speaks with a sneer of 'a regular old woman' defiles the memory, or besmirches the character, of his mother.

Most of the present adult generation, have living mothers who are old women. Are those mothers contemptible? Are they not rather the best of their time? Do we not wish the old men had records as clean and could die with such light hearts as most of our old women? With the gentleness and good temper which come of a life unsullied by excesses; with the wisdom which comes of training young lives and watching children change to men and women – watching their careers, how they become happy, or how they become heart-broken; with the patience which comes from all the work and pain which few women escape; with all these things – and thousands of old women have them all – the name of 'old woman' should be a badge of honour and a synonym of worth.

Some talk with a sneer of 'old women in parliament!' Well, if shrewd sense, clean characters, and kind hearts be virtues in a member of the House of Legislature, we could elect from our old women a House with such talents for work, and with such guarantees of unselfishness and justice as the country has never been blessed with yet. The sneer is as much out of place in connection with parliament and politics as it is in each and every other connection. Indeed, the good influence of women, young and old, is just what we need to make politics a stepping stone to a happier national life. The young women must be included with the old in everything which is said about the sex, for all the young women are steadily graduating for the same degree. Every day brings them nearer the 'old woman' stage; and the qualities which will characterise their old age, are the qualities which make up their individuality now. Those qualities are not contemptible, and since the world has learned of late to admit women to a little more liberty and a little more respect, it must alter its tone in harmony. It will soon do so if the women never hear the sneer, 'old woman', without demanding instant apology; and if the men think of the old women of their own circle when they thus unthinkingly belittle their womanly, yet equal fellow creatures.

'Sovran Woman,' Marie Corelli, *Lady's Realm* (London),
July 1901, pp. 265–7

Miss Marie Corelli was the guest of the evening at a recent gathering at the Whitefriars Club, and replied to the toast 'Sovran Woman.' Miss Corelli's speech on that occasion was not published in any of the papers, and we are privileged to give it verbatim here. This was the first time that the eminent authoress ever addressed a literary gathering in London, and she showed herself as great an orator as she is a writer. She spoke in a musical voice, with clear enunciation and graceful gesture; her delivery was faultless from first to last, her remarks being accompanied by loud and continued applause, which lasted for many minutes after she had resumed her seat. In short, Miss Corelli received an enthusiastic ovation. Miss Corelli has never allowed her portrait to appear in the illustrated papers, as she shrinks from publicity. The following 'word-picture' of her, therefore, as she appeared on this occasion, supplied by an eye-witness, will be read with interest: 'The beautiful authoress wore a lovely "picture-dress" of ivory satin, the train being embroidered by hand, with a design of lilies worked in gold thread and pearls. A knot of black velvet lilies with diamond centres fastened the bodice on the left shoulder with very original and becoming effect. This exquisite gown was admirably suited to Miss Corelli's *spirituelle* style of beauty. Her abundant hair is of a golden shade, and curls and waves naturally about her head. She has a clear complexion, regular features, and her eyes are a deep blue and full of soul. Her figure is petite and perfectly proportioned. She is altogether a most charming personality.' It may be mentioned that the bouquet presented to Miss Corelli by the Whitefriars Club was composed of Marechal Neil roses, white lilac and stephanotis.

Miss Marie Corelli spoke as follows:

I find myself placed to-night in a rather strange and unique position. It is the first time I have ever spoken at a public dinner. It is equally the first time I have ever had to thank a London club of literary men for any kindness or consideration! The experience is altogether new to me, and I need scarcely say it is as pleasant as it is new.

When I started to come here to-night I thought of Daniel in the lions' den. Daniel knew he was going among lions; so did I. He thought it possible that some of them might bite: so did I. He was agreeably disappointed: so am I. I stand here surrounded by lions, and gentler animals I never met. They have been purring round me softly on either side all the evening, and I find them very agreeable companions. One of them, Dr Watson, better known to fame as Ian Maclaren, has just 'roared an 'twere any nightingale' (sic) in proposing the health of 'Sovran Woman.' I am sure his eloquence has moved all here present, especially those of my sex, to the profoundest admiration. Speaking for myself personally, I may say that never until to-night have I heard the words, 'Sovran Woman' pronounced by 'Sovran Man.' I do not think it can be a very ordinary expression, because the inspired individual who does the book-shop column in the *Daily Express* doesn't know what it means. In alluding to the approach of our present festivities, he said 'Dr Watson will propose the toast of "Sovran Women," – whatever that may mean.' Evidently, therefore it is an obscure term, not in general use among men.

Myself, I consider it a very pretty phrase; but I should not like to take it too seriously. It seems to me rather like a ballroom compliment. All women are acquainted with the dear old ballroom compliment – the worn and threadbare thing which our partner in the dance whispers to us at the close of the evening, how he never, never, never will forget – which if we are wise, we know means that he forgets all about us the very next morning. Without wishing to be too sceptical, the phrase 'Sovran Woman' seems to me something like that – one of those delightful but ephemeral flatteries which 'Sovran Man' is prone to use when he wishes to make himself exceptionally agreeable. He says it to-night – but will it hold good tomorrow? Will Dr Watson, for example, when he is asked to pronounce an opinion on a woman's work, look as bland and amiable as he does now, and breathe forth a fervent 'Sovran Woman!' before proceeding to pass judgment? These are dark and dreadful questions! I will not dwell upon them. At any rate, for tonight our gallant and chivalrous hosts of the Whitefriars have of their own free will paid us those honours which are always our rightful due, and have set us on those thrones which are truly ours to occupy for all time. For 'Sovran Woman' is queen of the whole world around, and 'Sovran Man' knows it. He pretends he doesn't, but he does.

We hear a great deal nowadays of strife and competition between the sexes, but surely there should be no strife between two halves of a perfect whole. Man is king, as woman is queen, and to do good work in the world the two must rule harmoniously together. One is not greater or less than the other; each has the qualities necessary to make both happy. And men and women are never seen at better advantage than when their total unlikeness to each other is most apparent. An effeminate man is contemptible; a masculine woman is ridiculous. It is not by asserting herself as the equal of man that 'Sovran Woman' will best keep her sovereignty; it is rather by emphasising and insisting on the great difference there is between herself and him. Imitation is, we know, the sincerest form of flattery; but to flatter man so much as to try to make ourselves in any way like him is carrying the compliment somewhat too far. We women can be useful workers in the world without sacrificing our chief birthright – Womanliness. It is not by copying man's dress, his sports, or his customs, that we shall keep and hold our best influence over him. His costume – if the gentlemen will permit me to say so – is really not worth imitating. His sports and his customs are of his nature, – not of ours. No woman ever gains anything by asserting that she is as good as a man. She ought to be so much better that any assertion of the kind is totally unnecessary.

It is generally understood and considered that man objects to that particular movement which is called the 'advancement of woman'! If he does so object, the objection is perfectly reasonable and natural. For long centuries of tradition and history in all countries he has been accustomed to make his own laws for his own convenience; and those laws have kept woman in a subordinate position as more or less of a drudge or a toy. It is rather difficult for him now to understand that with better education woman has higher aims, and that instead of crouching at his feet she wishes to walk at his side, the free companion of his thoughts, the inspirer of all good things to him, the defender of his honour, and his most faithful friend on this side Heaven. Surely this is what woman, in the truest sense of womanhood, means when she clamors for her 'rights.' She wants the right to help in the work of the world, the right to have a voice in the affairs of life and that of society in which she is compelled to take so great a part; – the right to suggest ways out of difficulty, to bring light out of darkness, and, above all, the right to inspire and encourage man to noble efforts by her own steadfast and bright example. I take it that the sum and substance of woman's ambition when she talks of her advancement in life and work is simply to help 'Sovran Man,' – not to help herself so much or nearly so much, as to help the whole work of the world. In arts and letters this must be or should be her chief concern. Rosa Bonheur has filled a court in the palace of art; George Eliot has built a corner of the temple of English literature. Woman can be either a Rosa Bonheur or a George Eliot without challenging an Edwin Landseer or a Walter Scott. There should be no quarrel. Time is lost and temper wasted in discussing comparisons and equalities. The rewards of art are the same for both sexes. Failure means poverty and contempt; success means the envy of malignant minds. It has always been so, and always will be so to the end of time. No worker in art or literature ever gathered the roses of triumph without the thorns.

We women may be justly proud of the fact that our work in every branch of art and industry is beginning to be a recognised factor in the progress of civilisation, but I think we should be careful that while we gain so much, we do not lose anything. Dr Watson, in his admirable speech, has gone very much along the old lines concerning the mistakes of woman – for instance, how she 'tidies up' a man. May she long continue to do so, for, alas, he is by nature a most untidy mortal. He has also touched on her love of dress. Long may she continue to be better dressed than he is! He has also spoken of her love for gossip. I venture to say that I never endured such a babel of gossiping tongues as I once heard while being entertained to luncheon at a men's club, nor have I known many more reputations picked to pieces than on that occasion.

I admit that women are very good at that sort of work, but so are men. It is a case of six of one and half a dozen of the other. And as regards our love of dress, we really have to thank 'Sovran Man' for it. He does not like to see us dressed in his fashion – he complains and strongly disapproves, if anyone of his family should attempt to put on clothes in the least like his. Therefore we have to dress more prettily to please him, and we do it. We generally succeed in pleasing him too! So let us always please him, and try by what we call our 'advancement' not to repel him, but rather to doubly attract and fascinate him. We do not want to be his rivals or combatants; we seek to be his friends and helpers. I am sure that is what all the best women wish. They don't want to be lonely, independent creatures roaming about the world without a man to say a kind word for them. They want to be the friends, the companions of men, and help them in every good cause. And I repeat that we should be careful not to repel 'Sovran Man' by our so-called advancement. We should, on the contrary, show him an increased charm of manner, a greater kindness, a greater helpfulness – for every man is our naturally born admirer and worshipper and it rests entirely with ourselves to keep him so.

Ladies and Gentlemen, I have no more to say except to thank Dr Watson for the somewhat doubting manner in which he proposed 'Sovran Woman' – and also to thank our hosts of the Whitefriars for the cordiality with which they responded to that rather hesitatingly handled toast! I thank Dr Watson and the Whitefriars Club on my own behalf and on behalf of my sex here present for their amiability towards us. However much we women may be haled from our thrones to-morrow in the conflict of this work-a-day world, it is pleasant to remember that we have been so graciously acknowledged the queens of to-night!

'What We Women Owe Our Queen,' Hon. Mrs Henry
Chetwynd, *Lady's Realm* (London), July 1899, pp. 330–31

In May our gracious Queen celebrated her eightieth birthday, and in June she entered upon the sixty-third year of her long beneficent reign; and still she fills the first place in our hearts. Much has been said regarding the great advances made in the arts, in commerce, and in manufacture during Her

Majesty's rule, but not so much of the benefits to women. To-day, women have the right of possession; fifty years ago a woman's earnings belonged legally to her husband, who perhaps earned nothing, and spent her property in drink.

Besides all this improvement, there are many things we owe our Queen to which it is important to call attention. All high stations give an example, which, filtering down, affects millions out of sight; and the example given by our Queen has affected so many, and done so much good, that one reason for our loyalty and reverence for Her Majesty's character is the gratitude we owe her for showing what a daughter, a wife, and a mother, should be.

As a daughter the Queen was a pattern to all, especially to those who, in these latter days, are too apt to forget the reverence and devotion due to a mother. As a wife, everyone acknowledges that the highest example was given by the Queen of what wedded life should be; and this example was shown under many difficulties which, but for the great unselfishness and the intuition that two very noble natures had of their respective positions, might have been insurmountable. Love taught the lesson. On the one hand, there was the self-restraint which made it possible to work incessantly in the shadow, and, whilst conscious of intellectual power above the average, to go without open recognition, and to suffer misconceptions and want of appreciation in silence. On the other hand, there was the full recognition from the wife, who understood her husband and his position together with a whole-souled, wifely devotion.

As a mother, how much the Queen's example has altered the relations between mothers and their children! Fifty years ago, what did a fashionable mother know of her children, either when they were infants in the nursery, or later, when they were in the school-room? Nurses and governesses had it all their own way. Sometimes they were good; sometimes they were bad – and too often engaged upon the recommendation of some fashionable friend, who wanted to get rid of them. The mother saw her babies once a day, sometimes not even that, and accepted as gospel whatever she was told – was perfectly satisfied if the children had pretty manners, were tolerably graceful, could play a little, dance a little, and speak a little French.

The Queen's views of motherhood altered all this. When it became known that all the details of the nursery were her especial care; that every spare moment was spent with her children; that sanitary regulations were insisted upon; that a high character and high standard was required of the nurses and governesses; that time was not to be wasted, every honest effort being instantly recognised; and that no public or other duties neutralised the Queen's sense of true motherhood: – she at once set an example which was largely followed. Other mothers felt ashamed of neglected duties, and good wives and careful mothers became the fashion: something higher and better came into vogue.

There is also another matter which strikes all those privileged to know anything of Her Majesty's surroundings, and that is how completely the law of kindness prevails. It is well known that no one would venture to repeat an ill-natured story or a scandal to the Queen, and if you meet those whose lives in some measure touch hers, the same thing strikes every one; for how genuinely and unaffectedly they silence ill-nature, and take the kindest view of every action capable of being construed in two ways. It is not too much to say that sympathy with the poor and the highest interpretation of our duties in all the relations of life have received from the Queen's example an impetus and an inspiration which makes our womanhood something to be respected, and of which no handful of silly 'new' women can deprive us.

5

COLONIALS

The Boer War in South Africa gave the British cause to scrutinise the values of Empire. The *Queen*'s editorial on 5 January 1901 stated:

the loss of our South African Colonies might have been followed by an inclination on the part of the others to have done with such an unworthy and incompetent parent. We have changed all that; and the nineteenth century goes out leaving the British Empire united as it has never been in all its history, with its Colonies full of soldiers, bred on their own soil and disciplined in the severest way of our time. There could be no such link between the Colonies and the Mother Country as the blood of the Colonials fallen in the armies of England, after proving themselves the equals, if not the superiors, of the best troops in Europe.

The British had no conscience about colonial power. Lady Hodgson's feature 'Besieged at Kumassi' is steeped in the conviction that the British way of life is superior to that of the West Africans whose land her people had occupied and governed since 1886 and would continue to do so until 1963 when Nigeria emerged as a republic. Lady Hodgson is persistent in unquestioning discrimination between 'natives', black Britons and white rulers; her support for the social hierarchy arising from her entrenched sense of difference seems today unwitting and grimly comic.

British women's newspapers and magazines carried regular and frequent items about colonial life; several, such as *Womanhood* and the *Gentlewoman*, ran special competitions for their colonial readers, helping to maintain strong links with the 'Mother Country' and the community of women fostered by competition and correspondence columns of these papers.

Racism that went hand in hand with colonial expansion was endemic in the language and attitudes of the women's papers in both Britain and America, catering as they did to largely white, middle class readers. Whether it was in recipes for 'Nigger Cake', as the Chicago *Woman's World* called one of its Christmas cakes in 1914, or in the girl's rejection of a black-haired doll in preference for one that has 'curly golden hair and lovely blue eyes and . . . cheeks . . . so pretty and pink' (*Woman's World* (Chicago), December 1915, p. 22), racism was casual and apparently unconscious. The anxiety expressed in many of the articles written for white women about the oppressed plight of African or Asian women must be framed by the white woman's overriding sense of superiority. The series of six articles about 'Pioneer Women in India' run by *Womanhood* (December 1900–May 1901), the first of which is printed here, unusual in focussing on Indian women themselves, finds them noteworthy because they introduce Western models and break the Asian mould.

The Mexican fable, 'The Cricket and the Lion,' from the children's page of the American *Good Housekeeping* reflects by its placement within that journal the hegemonic infantilisation of ethnically different peoples, but it can also be read as a fable about how the colonised may eventually outwit the coloniser. The concluding item of this chapter is a reminder that the term 'colonial' could refer to the white pioneers of American history, and it suggests something of the attitude of the pioneer towards the Indian population.

'Besieged in Kumassi,' Lady Hodgson, *Lady's Magazine* (London), January 1901, pp. 21–32

On my arrival at Accra, in November 1899, I little thought what my sixth visit to West Africa had in store for me. The people, both European and native, gave me a charming reception; the streets were decorated from the landing place to Government House, and most pleasing and kindly-worded addresses of welcome were presented to me.

It was on this day that I learnt from my husband that he was shortly going to Kumassi, not for pleasure but for stern duty, and that he wished me to accompany him. Hammock-travelling at its best is most tedious and tiring, and the news of this contemplated bush journey of 150 miles did not, I must confess, appeal to me, and I was not sorry when the Governor found that he could not leave head-quarters so soon as he had intended.

The rains commence up-country about March, and then travelling becomes more tedious than ever, and is also injurious to health. In this way I hoped the journey would not take place. But my hopes were not to be realised, and arrangements were made for our departure on March 13th. Superstitious people pointed out that the 13th was a bad day on which to start, but I am afraid officialism knows nothing of superstition. The carriers were all dispatched early in the morning to enable them to reach the first halting-place in time for things to be made fairly comfortable, for the first night at any rate. And I suppose they *were*; but I had never slept in a tent in a native village before, and found that it was not all joy, and more than once I wished I were back in my comfortable room at Accra. However, with a twelve days' journey before one, it was not any good being faint-hearted after only a few hours' travelling.

Besides ourselves we had with us the Governor's private secretary, Captain Armitage, Dr. Chalmers and Mr. Wilkinson, acting-Director of Public Works. We all appeared, whatever we felt, very cheerful when we met at dinner, which was served in the open, with hundreds of eyes looking at us.

We moved on next morning at seven, and for twelve days we travelled from seven a.m. until about three or four in the afternoon, halting in the middle of the day for a couple of hours' rest and for luncheon, the spot selected always being a shady one, for the sun is very fierce in the open, and hammock-travelling warm work.

[. . .]

The natives are somewhat reluctant to sell food stuffs, sheep, chickens, etc., to a white man passing through their villages, so that a fair amount of tinned provisions has always to be taken when travelling in the bush. A carrier will bear on his head from fifty to sixty pounds when hired, but thinks nothing of from eighty to a hundred pounds when he is on his own job.

There is not much variety in bush travelling. Some days are more irritating, tedious and tiring than others, perhaps from the stupidity of servants, carriers, and hammock-men, or from the stings of insects, which abound in the forest and also in the dirty villages where we had to pass the night. . . . We received a great ovation at every place we came to, the chief and all his followers coming to the entrance of the village to welcome us, playing before us with native music, beating of drums, horn blowing, and firing salutes in honour of the Governor's visit. The dancers of the village would come in front of our tent, and treat us to their performances, in many cases very grotesque and weird.

Presents would be brought in the shape of a fowl, eggs fruit, etc., for which we had to pay handsomely, for, according to native custom, it is not etiquette to receive a present without returning its equivalent, and if you are a 'big man' you are expected to deal handsomely by the giver.

Well, at last . . . I saw Kumassi ahead of us. . . . At the top of the first hill the Resident and all the officials of Kumassi received us and escorted us into the town, a pleasing ceremony taking place half-way up the other hill, where the Basel missionaries welcomed us and presented me with a magnificent bouquet of roses, the school children singing 'God Save the Queen' and holding banners with inscriptions of welcome upon them.

The top of the hill brought the Fort in view, and, passing under a prettily-erected triumphal arch, we turned into the fine broad road leading up to it. All the principal kings and chiefs of Ashanti had come to Kumassi to receive the Governor, and they were drawn up on either side of the road under their umbrellas of state. Their followers and attendants were very numerous, and it was estimated that there were not less than 6,000 natives to do honour to the 'Great White Queen's' representative.

As we passed along the route the kings and chiefs saluted the Governor by rising from their native chairs studded with brass nails and devices, and the big umbrellas were kept all the time revolving round and round over the king's head to denote pleasure and friendship.

We passed on to the Fort. . . . Shortly after entering it all the kings, chiefs, and followers passed in procession in front of the Fort, to again salute the Governor, who stood on the veranda bowing to them. This procession took over an hour to pass. The kings were carried in their palanquins on men's heads, and very stately some of them looked: their robes were gay, and their gold ornaments excited one's envy.

Behind each king and chief came all his officers of state, carrying various sticks or swords, overlaid with gold, denoting their official rank. The high executioner, whose post not long ago meant so much, was always an important person, with gold badges on his breast and upon his fierce-looking head, made more so by a black monkey skin cap. Looking from the veranda, the place seemed nothing but a moving mass of humanity, so dense was the crowd. The loud chattering of the people and the noise of native music were somewhat wearying, but the pageant was a grand sight, and one never to be forgotten. Drawn up in front of the Fort was a guard of honour of Hausa soldiers, and they lent not a little to the picturesqueness of the scene. After this ceremony was over and we had removed the stains of travel we all bore, we took a walk round Kumassi to acquaint ourselves with the place, of which we had heard so much.

The fetish grove, where the remains of the victims of the human sacrifices were thrown, as a grove exists no longer. The trees have been cut down, and the ground levelled. There were a few human bones still visible, but otherwise it presents no horrors to the eye; one could not, however, help thinking what a gruesome, terrifying place it must have been only a few short years ago.

There did not seem to be anything else of native interest to see except the fetish-tree, under whose branches so many horrible scenes have taken place. This was on the opposite side of the road to the fetish grove, so that the sacrificial officers had not far to go to dispose of their victims.

Everything seemed quiet and peaceable, but I was slightly disturbed in my mind, a few days after reaching Kumassi, by one of my servants saying he hoped there was not going to be trouble, and he thought we had better get away quickly. I asked him why he had thoughts of trouble, and he said that they (the servants) had noticed very bad fetishes on the road into the town, and on the day before we reached there. I laughed at him, but he said, 'Ah, missus, I know the Ashanti people; they behave too bad, they be very treacherous!'

Naturally I thought the Acting Resident, Captain Davidson Houston, would have his finger on the pulse of the people, and would know if any trouble were brewing so that I never gave the bad fetishes another thought.

So the days wore on, hot and oppressive. An expedition had been sent into the country to the north-west of Kumassi, the Governor having information that the people had been collecting ammunition and guns, and had large stores of them, and so it proved. It was also made clear to us that they were to be used against us, for the troops were fired upon and attacked by large numbers of natives and with great difficulty got back to Kumassi. It at once became clear that the situation was the reverse of pleasant. The slumbering rebellion aroused itself. Every endeavour was made to calm the agitation, and the powerful Kings of Mampon, Juabin, and Aguna were brought over to our side, together with lesser kings and several influential chiefs.

All these were brought away from Kumassi with us. There were palavers for a few days, until it became apparent that further negotiations were futile, and they were broken off. The rebels were now under arms, and we had taken stock of our position. On April 18th a small detachment of Hausas arrived from Accra, and reconnaissances of the rebel posts were made. So things went until April 25th, when the rebels became aggressive. Early on that day they showed signs of activity by killing the water carriers of the Basel missionaries when drawing water from the springs, so it became necessary to withdraw the missionaries from their houses and to place them in the Fort.

Besides the Fort, the Government has built Hausa officers' and doctors' quarters, and a good hospital and prison. The rebels closed round the mission house, and the officer commanding the troops had to take notice of their presence. A Maxim gun was run out of the Fort and got into action, but the rebels, who were in thousands all around, would not give way, and another gun had to be brought into play upon them. Still they held their ground, forcing back our Hausa soldiers gradually, until they (the rebels) had gained possession of the Hausa cantonments and the other Government buildings, which all lie in the same direction – behind the Fort.

It was a terrible day, and fighting went on from 10.30 a.m. until dusk, when the rebels began to show themselves in front of the Fort, about 600 yards away. The machine guns from the Fort were fired at them, and after a while they thought the back of the Fort was a pleasanter place than the front. There were guns also in the back bastions of the Fort, but these could not, owing to buildings, be so effectually used as the guns from the front. The scene by noon was almost a curious one.

The people living in Kumassi, who are not Ashantis, are known as 'strangers.' They came there to trade from various parts, and are greatly disliked by the Ashantis, especially the civilian Mohammedans, who are keen traders, and make money wherever they settle. So all these people, knowing what their fate would be if left to the tender mercies of the rebels, together with the loyal Ashantis, gathered round the walls of the Fort for protection. There were about 3,000 of them. They brought all their worldly possessions, dogs, monkeys, parrots, every conceivable thing. The noise from these refugees was incessant, and this added to the terrible anxiety of our position, nearly wore us out. One of the officers was ill with fever, and the incessant noise was telling upon him. Repeatedly we asked the refugees under his window to make less noise, but all in vain! When the day came we sighed for the night, hoping that some of them would sleep, and when the night came we longed for the day, so that in occupation we might not notice the constant chattering (a native's voice never being melodious at the best), crying of children, and all the other various sounds and noises.

The unpleasantness from this mass of people, all huddled together, can better be imagined than described! The windows had to be kept shut, for it was better to be stifled than to inhale so much humanity. All sorts of horrible and also amusing things took place under one's very eyes, and this went on for ten days. For two nights the poor refugees were without any shelter, but they gained courage on the third day, and went a short distance from the Fort to cut poles to make shelters for themselves. In about three hours or so a complete village had sprung up round the Fort walls. The shelters had to be kept by order to a certain height, so that, if necessary, the guns could be used from the Fort without injuring the people round it.

But to return to the rebels. After they had caused the Europeans to concentrate in the Fort, and had driven the 3,000 odd refugees under its walls, they looked round for the next mischief they could do, which was to set fire to the thatched mud huts of the 'strangers,' and the thatching on the Hausa cantonment huts, and Kumassi was a pitiful sight that night! Tongues of fire leapt up to the skies, calling, let us hope, for vengeance upon the heads of the rebels, who were returning evil for good.

I forgot to mention that all the sick from the hospital were brought into the Fort, and the prison-doors thrown open. Some of the prisoners worked round the Fort, some went off to the rebels.

Very little sleep was to be had that night, for we were all thinking of our plight, and how we were going to pull through. We feared, too, that at any moment we might be attacked, and were doubly on the alert towards dawn, which is one of the favourite times for the Ashantis to attack their enemies.

The next day (Thursday) was a very depressing and sad one, for we could see the rebels running backwards and forwards between the cantonments and the hospital and other houses as busy as bees. A few shots were fired at them, but it was thought advisable to do no more than let them see we were watching their movements. A strong escort of Hausas was sent later in the day to the hospital, to see if any of the drugs and medical comforts could be recovered, as the flight from there had been so hurried that many things had to be left behind. The rebels evidently thought there was some fetish attached to the hospital, for they had hardly touched anything beyond taking the doors away and a few chairs, so, fortunately, most of its stores were recovered. The water that day, and for many others, had also to be fetched under a strong escort.

The gates of the Fort were closed, and all those obliged to leave it on duty had to climb down a rope ladder over one of the bastions.

It was a miserable, heart-breaking day. Fancy being within five minutes of your enemy; a merciless, blood-thirsty one, hating the white man, and with a great bitterness in his heart against him for having taken his country and put down all customs dear to savage nature – human sacrifices, slave-dealing, and a few other pleasantries of that description.

I have seen some of the people who were tortured in days gone by; they make one ill to look at. Some without noses, some without ears, others with disfigured and distorted faces. Horrible! horrible! And to feel that such things would happen to us, did we fall into their savage hands!

That night the rebels kept up a wild song and beating of drums – a sign, we were told, that they meant an attack; and there *was* a night alarm! It came to nothing for they saw we were ready for them, and they did not feel quite brave enough to face the big guns so soon again. The sentries passed the word all down the line that the rebels were coming. The sleepers in the Fort were up and doing in a moment. I threw on my dressing-gown, and made for the veranda to see what was happening, although it was pitch dark.

An old Hausa on duty on the veranda to keep the refugees from swarming up the posts, which they had tried to do several times, pushed me back. He neither spoke nor understood much English. All he could say on this occasion was: 'No come out, no come out; Ashanti man come.' Two of my servants also came rushing into my room, presumably to look after me, but really, I think, to gain confidence by being with me. They held my hand, and tried in their own way to assure me if the Ashanti man came the Hausas were quite able to fight him back. The alarm was soon over, and those not on duty retired again to rest.

Early the next morning (Sunday) the rebels tried to set fire to the Medical Officer's quarters. This was too exasperating, and it was determined to try and save the building. A constant watch was kept upon this building and others, and when the rebels were seen to be up to some devilry shots were fired at them; I am glad to say the buildings were unharmed, and used again by us a little later on. Having been prevented from doing this mischief, they turned their attention to something more important, for they attacked the Fort! This attack was wonderfully exciting! The rebels opened fire from a loopholed hut, with a terrific fusillade.

The Fort guns were on them in a moment, and a seven-pound shell burst in their midst, causing them to precipitate their attack. . . . The fight lasted about a couple of hours, when we came off the victors, and not a rebel was left alive in Kumassi. We buried 130 of them next day, and saw many others being taken away during the fight. This battle gave us food, for the rebels, by the quantity of food-stuffs, gunpowder, and guns we captured, had evidently come to stay in our midst. Food was getting scarce, even in these early days, and the sight of so much native food greatly rejoiced the eyes of the Hausas. They behaved most nobly through this trying time, and did their duty like true Britons (black ones).

The old Hausa on the veranda, whom I have mentioned before, on this occasion called me out to him to show me a dead Ashanti on the road. The old man was delighted at the sight (and so was I), and kept on saying, 'See him! see him!'

This poor old Hausa afterwards got wounded in one of our other fights, and I feel that I had something to do with his disobeying orders and so taking part in it. He was an old man, who had been on duty at the gaol in the peaceful days, and being considered too old for active work now, was detailed for sentry duty on the veranda. I chaffed him one day, and I said I did not think he was able to shoot an Ashanti, as they ran too quickly for him. This chaff evidently disturbed his peace of mind, for in the next fight he crept after the troops and appeared when the fighting began. He got slightly wounded and was delighted with himself, showing me his wound with the greatest pride, as much as to say, 'Now, I have surely righted myself in your eyes!' For disobeying orders, he was never allowed on the veranda again, and I quite missed my faithful old friend.

But I have wandered away from our Sunday fight, of which we were all so proud. The native allies fought well, and the friendly kings who were with us in the Fort led their men bravely into the thick of the battle. The Kings of Nkwanta and Aguna had the greatest number of fighting men with them, and always were well to the fore. On this occasion the latter was carried back to the Fort, after the battle, on men's shoulders, all the black ladies swarming round him to shake hands. He looked very fine in his war-coat, a sort of jumper sewn back and front with any number of charms and fetishes.

During the fight the rebel slugs were flying about all over the Fort; one hitting a lamp close to where I was standing. It was most exciting to run from room to room to see from various points how things were going.

[. . .]

At the end of two weeks I went out of the Fort for the first time. The sight was a very interesting one. On either side of the road was a complete village of low and small huts, the people occupying themselves with their every-day work, having apparently forgotten the great danger to which they had so recently been exposed. Those who had goods for sale had formed a bazaar on each side of the road, and very picturesque it looked. Women were pounding foo-foo, others grinding corn, children playing about, and all looked quite happy and contented. We bought some native bracelets, by way of commemorating my first walk in besieged Kumassi; but I am sorry to say we lost those interesting (to us) articles, with many other things on our way to the coast. My camera and negatives were also lost on this trying march, greatly to my regret, for the photographs would have been of the greatest interest and quite unique. Things went on fairly quietly, the rebels contenting themselves by shooting any courageous person who went beyond the boundary line of safety, and keeping all food supplies away from us.

Food was now getting very, very scarce, not only for the Hausas and natives, but for the Europeans. In the early days, a few head of cattle were killed by the Mohammedan butchers, and sold at siege prices. After they were finished, the four cows belonging to the Government, and which were great pets of the residents, had to be used one by one. Fresh-meat day was a great event, and the four cows were made to last until May 25th. After this we had nothing but the one pound tin of inferior corned beef, and still more inferior biscuit.

Every morning my cook appeared for the orders for the day, as if he had just arrived from market with his usual supply of good things. At first we used to look at each other and laugh, when the ration was produced, and between us devise some means of disguising its unpalatableness; but, towards the end, my heart felt so heavy that even a little joke about rations was irksome, and I used to say, 'Take it away, Henry, and cook it as you like.' Signs of starvation began now to appear, and the terribly haggard, wan faces that were everywhere to be seen were heart-rending. We could do nothing for these poor refugees out of our slender stores! Expeditions were sent out to get food if possible, but they always returned unsuccessful, so closely were we invested.

[. . .]

The people tried to help themselves by going out at night in search of food, but many never returned. Then, as the days went on, the poor things got too weak to wander very far. It was pitiful to see them searching the ground over and over again for roots, etc. Leaves of trees were picked and made into a kind of soup. Rats, lizards, everything in fact that seemed or looked eatable, was used. Naturally, the people began to die off very fast, and the scenes were terrible to witness! Men sitting about the road and under trees would just fall forward, dead! Others again from starvation went raving mad, and would frantically beat themselves, yelling and shrieking! At last their strength would give way, their shrieks end, and death claim them.

There were always men at hand to help these poor creatures, detailed by the authorities to do so, but of what assistance could they be without the means of giving nourishment, which was an impossibility? All was done that was possible, but there were so many claiming assistance, that, had all been considered, the medical supplies of drugs, brandy, etc., would not have gone very far. The Kings had to be looked after. One poor old King, not being used to the luxury of tinned beef and hard biscuit, became seriously ill. His life was saved by milk and brandy. I went to see him with the Governor, and found the fine old fellow very tottery. The doctor had given the milk and brandy to him, but his followers did not know how to mix the milk, tinned milk, like many other things, being beyond their ken. I asked for a glass, water, and a spoon, which were all brought, more or less in a dirty state, and very native in construction. The milk was soon mixed and the brandy added, and the old King pronounced it good.

In doing this I had soiled my fingers, and, while fumbling for my handkerchief, my soiled fingers were enveloped in the end of a man's cloth (the cloth being his native dress), and carefully wiped! This seemed to give him great pleasure, but I am not sure that I derived quite so much from his attentions!

The children received every morning a pint of soup made from the crumbs left in boxes of biscuits, and what scraps could be collected from the various tables; but the soup was of the poorest, as may be imagined; yet the children, poor wee things, cried, and showed great impatience until their tins were handed to them. Many of them died, while others went over to the rebels with their mothers. Women and children were welcomed by the enemy, for they were turned into slaves! But, possibly, slavery with food is better than freedom with starvation.

There was one poor woman, so gentle and nice, who every morning used to bring her two children for the soup; she was so worn and tired that my pity for her was great, and I always watched for her, and gave her what little I could spare. One morning she was not there, nor her children, and on inquiry I was told she had gone to the rebel camp. I cannot blame her, but it gave me a pang to think of her desertion from the right side.

A very amusing thing happened one morning towards the end of our stay. The King of Aguna was seen to be very agitated and excited; the reason of it was his two wives had deserted him during the night, and joined the rebels; we very unkindly laughed heartily over the poor King's fix. He tried to get them back, but, finding this impossible, he soon consoled himself with others. The King was very fond of a drop of comfort, and bemoaned his fate when it was quite unobtainable. He paid us several visits, and always about the time he knew a little spirit might be had, but as he thought nothing of three-quarters of a tumbler of it raw, we had to point out to our kingly guest that this was a large share, and suggested to him that if he helped himself so liberally his visits must be fewer!

[. . .]

We all hoped against hope for relief before the time when provisions would end, and the dreaded march out take place, cutting our way as best we could through the rebel lines.

We daily heard rumours without number of the relieving column being close to us, but they were all from natives and not to be depended upon. We had had no news since the 29th of April, and now it was nearly the end of June. We were weak and run down, but still tried to appear cheerful and as if it were the easiest thing in the world to get out of Kumassi, knowing full well that we were offering our lives for the upholding of the flag.

[. . .]

On our march out, we heard from native rumour, which we hoped to be untrue, most disquieting reports of the tardiness of the relieving column, and began to wonder if three weeks would be sufficient for them to reach Kumassi, and save the Fort. Many more experiences could be written, but I think I have said quite enough to show the terrible time we had in Kumassi, and it must not be forgotten that this siege took place in one of the worst climates in the world. Only black troops, many young and inexperienced and recently joined, were with us. But they all did their duty, as I flatter myself everyone of us did, nobly and cheerfully, never once letting agonising thoughts come uppermost. Weakened as we were for want of food, and the mental strain telling upon our health, we yet tried to keep each other going, looking upon the bright side, hoping, waiting, longing for the relieving troops which never came, and doing our best to maintain the flag and the honour of our country.

'Some Ladies of South Africa,' Marie A. Belloc, *Lady's Realm*
(London), January 1900, pp. 371–6

From the days of the Lady Anne Lindsay, to whom the ballad-loving world owes 'Auld Robin Gray,' the English-speaking women have played a very great part in South African life, and never more so than during the last few years, when the opening up of the gold-field country has introduced a new and powerful element not only in South African, but also even in London Society. Perhaps this is the more curious when it is remembered that South Africa's dominating personality, Mr. Cecil Rhodes, is a bachelor, and that Government House, Capetown, under the *regime* of Sir Alfred Milner, is also lacking in one of those gracious official hostesses who have done so much all over the world to weld together the many racial strands which compose the human side of the Empire.

It would, however, be a great mistake to suppose that Capetown is lacking in feminine influences. When entertaining distinguished 'home' and colonial visitors at Groote Schuur, Mr. Cecil Rhodes is often helped to do the honours of his beautiful house by his sister, Miss Rhodes, who is said to be as remarkable a woman as her brother is a man. She is, like him, very unconventional, but her unconventionality is wedded to much shrewd common sense. She has become an authority on South Africa and its many difficult and complicated problems, and probably no Englishwoman has seen more of the inside of the country. She resided for a time at Bulawayo, and in her own house, which is situated not far from that of her brother, near Capetown, is a fine collection of hunting trophies and native curios. Miss Rhodes is very fond of country life: as a younger woman she was devoted to her English home, and was rarely seen in London Society; now, however, when she and her famous brother happen to be in Europe at the same time they are often lionised, as far as they will allow themselves to be, together, and Miss Rhodes' company is as eagerly sought as that of Mr. Cecil Rhodes himself.

[. . .]

South Africa has been designated as 'the country of Olive Schreiner,' and it must be admitted that so far the elder sister of the present Prime Minister of Cape Colony is the only notable writer Afrikanderland has produced. Since

Mrs. Cronwright Schreiner placed her powerful pen virtually on the side of the Transvaal it has become the fashion to speak of her as being to all intents and purposes a Dutchwoman. As an actual fact, the Schreiner family are in no sense Dutch. The grandfather was a German pastor, who settled in London in early youth, was naturalised there, and married an Englishwoman. In due course the family emigrated to Cape Colony from this country, but they have never had any direct connection with the Transvaal. Olive Schreiner's husband, Mr. Cronwright, is, it seems, of Dutch extraction, and this, of course, may have influenced her views; but it must be admitted that she was always intensely Afrikander in sympathy, though there is probably no South-African-born woman now living who has more friends and correspondents in the United Kingdom.

'The Story of an African Farm' was written when the author was still in her teens. Mr. George Meredith came across the manuscript and immediately realised the high qualities of the work; indeed, so struck was he by the story that he did what he is said to have done in the case of no other writer – he asked 'Ralph Iron' to come and see him in order to discuss the novel with her. Although the book is now far more topical than it was at the time of its publication, 'The Story of an African Farm' created an immense impression, and within a year of its appearance something like a hundred thousand copies were sold.

Since her marriage Mrs. Cronwright Schreiner has lived in a lovely Dutch homestead, which has been described by an enthusiastic visitor as an idealised edition of an African farm. Like her brother, she has always been keenly interested in politics. At one time she was an admirer of Mr. Cecil Rhodes; indeed, when 'Trooper Halkett of Mashonaland' appeared, an amusing skit was circulated in Capetown, supposed to have been written by Mr. Cecil Rhodes after the perusal of the book:

> Dear Olive, though you've ceased to be
> For some time now a friend to me;
> Though you explode at me and mine,
> I'm sending you a valentine
> In memory of olden days,
> Ere blame had taken place of praise.
>
> I've read your story – every scrap;
> It's too – well, Schreineresque (verb. tap);
> And, what with margins and big print,
> It seems to me there's not much in't!

In connection with what may be called literary South Africa two of the most valuable contributions to the history of the Rand and of the Reform Movement have been written by women, their work in each case gaining much in value and interest owing to the fact that each is the wife of one of the four members of the Reform committee who were condemned to death at the conclusion of the lengthy proceedings which followed the Jameson raid.

Under the modest title 'Some South African Recollections' Mrs. Lionel Phillips published last autumn a vivid account of her personal memories of the Reform Movement. The book is dedicated to the writer's three children, Harold, Frank, and Edith, and it was mainly written in order that they may, as they grow up, realise what actually occurred during the most momentous period of their parents' lives.

Mrs. Lionel Phillips is an Afrikander born, and so regards African problems from a very impartial point of view. Again, in no sense can Mr. and Mrs. Lionel Phillips be said to belong to the group of millionaires who have been so often taunted with making their immense fortunes on the Rand and then eagerly departing to spend them elsewhere. Mr. Phillips was once called 'the king of Johannesburg,' and during the whole of his early married life he and his family lived in the Transvaal; indeed, he built himself a beautiful house close to the 'Goldreef City,' and filled it with valuable works of art, which were, of course, brought at immense expense from Europe.

Now, as is natural in the circumstances, Mr. and Mrs. Lionel Phillips have removed their household gods to London, where they have lately taken a charming house in Mayfair, and Mrs. Phillips has already a leading place among those South African hostesses who form a characteristic section of English Society.

[. . .]

Already feminine pens have been busy in putting on record the events of the last few months. Lady Sarah Wilson, the youngest of the late Dowager Duchess of Marlborough's brilliant daughters, has been acting for some time as one of the special correspondents of the *Daily Mail*, and her letters from the besieged Mafeking gave a valuable, because amateur, view of how the whole situation struck an intelligent European having no direct interest in what was going on.

Lady Sarah, not content with being a war correspondent, also actively assisted in organising arrangements which were made for nursing the wounded. When, accompanied by her husband, she left England for a two months' tour in South Africa, she little thought that in four months' time they would find themselves in a beleaguered town. One of her earliest and most interesting experiences after her arrival in Mafeking was being present at the trial trip of an armoured train.

'Women's Medical Work in India,' Mrs Frank Penny, author of
'Caste and Creed,' *Monthly Packet* (London), September 1891,
pp. 260–65

No profession was opened to women more reluctantly than that of medicine. Only twenty years ago the obstacles placed in the way of the intrepid woman who wished to become that doubtful individual, a lady-doctor, seemed almost insuperable. The majority of men and women looked askance at the strong-minded young person who dared to attack the mysteries of anatomy, or presumed to master the science of medicine and surgery. Public opinion, backed by the personal prejudices of those who stood in a prominent position in the profession, endeavoured to show, firstly: that women were not fitted by nature to become surgeons, and that it would unsex them; secondly: that they were not needed, the field being already filled adequately by the men. The first objection has long since been proved fallacious; and we have only to look at India and Burmah to see that the second is equally false.

In our eastern colonies there is an illimitable opening for the lady-doctor. She need have no fear that she is encroaching on the rights of the sterner sex. It is a recognised fact that *medical aid to the women of India can only be given through women.* The whole channel with all its ramifications through which medical aid alone can flow *must be feminine.* If the aid cannot reach the female portion of the population through women it is refused; or administered in such a second-hand way as to render it practically useless. In the presidency towns there are a few, a very few, exceptions to this rule amongst the pariahs. But with the wealthy middle classes and the higher castes, in both town and country, the rule holds rigidly.

Of late years, under the auspices of a philanthropical government, several agencies have been at work to introduce the qualified lady practitioner. The missionary societies were amongst the first to recognise the importance of such a movement. They sent the lady-doctor to be the pioneer of the minister and catechist. They established dispensaries, at different centres, and made the cure of the body preface the salvation of the soul. But the skilled medical aid thus offered so freely was not always accepted. Close upon the heels of the doctor came the missionary; and the presence of the latter was not acceptable; the door of zenana and harem was too often rigorously closed.

This difficulty was recognised by India's rulers; and attempts were made in three or four centres to give women medical assistance, perfectly free of any religious teaching. The attempts were isolated and dependent on local charity; but so far as they went, they were successful.

At this juncture Lady Dufferin stepped in with a gigantic scheme – for founding female hospitals and wards all over the empire, where caste women could be treated without violating any of their national prejudices – for providing lecturers to teach native women in India to be doctors, hospital assistants, and nurses; and for introducing and establishing lady-doctors to attend hospitals, as well as to practise privately. Lady Dufferin's scheme was so practical, so well planned, that its success has been assured from the very beginning. It absorbed or affiliated all other attempts, and spread like a network over the whole country. Native princes, fearing no interference with their jealously guarded religious superstitions, have followed the example thus set; hospitals have been built by them in their capitals; lady-practitioners have been invited to become resident physicians, and to form classes for hospital assistants and midwives, and to practise privately amongst the richer portion of the population. Lady Dufferin's Association willingly undertakes to find candidates for any bona fide post that the native ruler may wish to fill.

Lady-doctors in India are thus divided into two classes; (a) those who work from a purely missionary spirit, and who use their profession as a means to a higher end; (b) those who undertake the work for secular reasons, regarding it solely from a business point of view. Appointments may be heard of (a) by applying to the secretaries of the missionary societies; and (b) through the Secretary of the National Association for supplying female medical aid to the women of India – in other words Lady Dufferin's Fund.

The time required for completing the medical course is five years at Edinburgh, and seven at the University of London. If the student prefers it, she can study in London, and go to Edinburgh for her examination, thus completing her course in the shortest possible time. But the woman who intends going out to India will do well not to hurry over her studies. It is of the greatest importance that she should be thoroughly proficient in obstetric practice, especially in operative midwifery. Innumerable cases will come before her of patients suffering from the most dangerous conditions incident to maternity; due to maltreatment by ignorant native practitioners, and the deplorable custom of child-marriage. Extra time devoted to this subject will be well spent.

[. . .]

But something else is needed besides the medical qualifications for taking up work in India. A woman must be physically strong, or her health will not bear the strain. The hospitals are necessarily built in the very midst of the people they are intended to benefit. The resident surgeon will find herself obliged to live in the most thickly populated part of the town, where the air is foulest and hottest. The Europeans, if there are any, will be some distance away in cantonments. Her time will be fully employed in seeing patients, diagnosing diseases, performing operations, attending confinements, and in teaching classes of native students. When her hospital duties are over, she will be obliged to pay her visits to patients at private houses. She will drive out in a close carriage through insanitary streets, where the open drains defy the doctor. She will enter the small ill-ventilated rooms to which rich and poor alike cling with fatal perversity; and she will once more have to combat the disheartening ignorance and obstinacy of those who tend the patient. Still more frequently will she find that she is expected to set right the irreparable damage done by the native midwife. During the hot months of March, April, and May she must stay at her post, whilst her countrywomen, the wives and daughters of the English officers, fly to the hills. It needs a strong constitution to endure such a life with its hard work and comparative loneliness.

A woman also requires tact – the instinctive tact which is the outcome of true nobility of mind. She is brought into close contact with a sensitive, quick-witted people, keenly alive to all the little courtesies of good-breeding, though they may not practise them themselves. She has to deal with prejudice, strong and deeply rooted, prejudice against herself as a foreigner, and against her system; which is in every detail exactly opposite to the practices of the native doctor. She will see the commonest laws of hygiene systematically disregarded in spite of all she may urge to the contrary. She must keep her temper and be gentle and tender in the face of obstinate perverseness; she must be courageous and persevering in the face of exasperating ignorance.

The Englishwoman who goes out to India, whether to work as a missionary or as a paid doctor, should always bear in mind that she is in a heathen country. She occupies a responsible position, for she stands as an example of Western civilisation and thought before the eyes of thousands of her Eastern sisters. The Oriental is essentially religious in his character; and this is especially the case with the women. A contempt is felt for those who have no faith. In the old days, when there were fewer clergymen and ladies in the country, and when Englishmen too often stooped to the level of the Mahomedan and Hindoo in their mode of life, the people were wont to speak contemptuously of the conquering race as 'kaffirs without religion.' Now the tone of society is better; and, though he may not understand it, the native knows that the Englishman has a religion; and he respects him for it. Lady Dufferin's Association requests its doctors not to interfere with the religions of their patients; it asks that the subject may not be mentioned. But it does not require an absence of all religion in the doctor herself; it does not expect her to set at naught the teaching of her childhood, and extinguish within herself the Christian instincts of generations.

Medical work in India should undoubtedly be taken up from the highest motives, whether the doctor works on purely business lines, or whether she labours conjointly with the missionary. She must possess the enthusiasm of a lover of the science, and also the desire to do good to her fellow-creatures and benefit suffering humanity. For whether she preaches Christianity openly or not, the lady-doctor must of necessity be the pioneer of a higher civilisation, and of a far holier creed than those which now hold India and her millions in their embrace.

'Pioneer Women In India: Being Outline Sketches Of
Their Work And Life. I,' Mrs Diver, *Womanhood* (London),
December 1900, pp. 47–8

Of Indian women in general, of their woes, their strivings, and their progress,
an infinite deal has been written during the past ten or fifteen years. But of
those few individual women who, by such supreme efforts of will and intellect
as we of the West can but feebly estimate, have succeeded in emerging from
the homogeneous mass of Asiatic femininity, singularly little is known, even
among those whose interest in the subject is more than skin-deep. In this
and the following papers, then, an attempt will be made to give brief outline
sketches of the lives, struggles, and ultimate achievements of these gentle, but
determined, heroines of modern India. It is this same priceless gentleness,
underlying always her strength of brain and will, that constitutes the chief
charm of the cultured eastern women. Lady Dufferin, when writing on this,
her favourite topic, asserts that it is impossible to read the life-history of any
one of them 'without pride and pleasure in the fact that so much talent,
perseverance, and determination should be found combined with so much
gentleness, and with so many truly feminine qualities: for one might have
feared that women who had to break through the hard and fast rules of caste
and custom would have lost their more lovable characteristics in the struggle.'
Let our pioneers of the West consider these words, and ponder them well,
for there is little doubt that, in these days of independence, of pushing
and striving among all ranks and sexes, the gracious, old-world flower of
gentleness runs sore risk of being completely trampled out of the feminine
character.

But to return to our main theme. The progress of feminine enlightenment
in India has, all obstacles duly considered, made truly wonderful strides since
the memorable year of grace 1829, when Lord William Bentinck struck
the first blow in the cause of women's welfare in India by abolishing the
practice of 'suttee' throughout all British provinces. Whether the Indian
widow herself derived much benefit from this reform may appear doubtful to
those who know anything of the death in life to which she is doomed by way
of a merciful alternative; but, at all events, the law was of great importance,
inasmuch as it acknowledged the independent value of a woman's life apart
from that of the man to whom she was allied. To the Rev. H. Ward, a Baptist
missionary, is due the honour of having been the first to enlist the sympathies
of English women in the degraded and neglected state of their Indian sisters;
and it was his earnest appeal which led to the embarkation, in 1821, of Miss
Cook, the first of a long, long line of devoted women who have given
themselves up, body and soul, to a stupendous, though surely not an entirely
thankless, task.

Since those early days changes, many and wonderful, have come to pass.
The indefatigable white woman has succeeded in imparting a small portion of

her own zeal for progress to the sternly repressed wives and daughters of the East; and it is obvious, except to the veriest pessimist, that the mass has at last begun to move from within. The India of to-day is rich in colleges for girls; its women may, if they be so minded, enter any of the learned professions, and compete for University degrees; in fact, strange as it sounds, the Indian Universities actually threw open their degrees to women three years before those of England could be induced to do so. Madras – always to the fore in matters educational – led the way in 1876; in 1878 Calcutta followed suit; and not until 1879 did London consent to countenance this daring innovation.

It became speedily evident, however, that owing to the prevalence of early marriages, and the rigidity of 'purdah' law, schools and Universities could reach only a small proportion of India's countless women. This discovery called into existence a new band of workers, namely the lady visitors to zenanas, through whose persevering efforts much that appeared wholly impossible has been successfully achieved. In this matter, as in most others, the missionary societies took the lead, and prepared the way for later workers, both English and American. But it should be remembered that the mere presence of an Englishwoman in a zenana does not, in itself, meet all the requisites of the case; more especially when, as is most frequent, the inter-course between guest and hostess is limited to signs and smiles, garnished with a few set phrases, previously learnt off by heart. And since, even in these days, comparatively few high-caste Indian ladies know more of English than a dozen or so of broken phrases, it behoves those who wish to make a practice of zenana visiting to give a larger share of their attention to languages and dialects than they have hitherto been wont to do.

It is a mighty task this of enlightening women crushed and crippled by centuries of ignorance and seclusion, but, despite the groans of the pessimist, it will not ultimately fail. That the women themselves are genuinely grateful for the efforts made on their behalf the following extract gives ample proof: 'Were it possible to entertain a doubt on this subject, it would be dispelled by such a sight as that which was witnessed in Calcutta in December, 1888, when nearly eight hundred native ladies came together at Government House to present to Lady Dufferin an address, signed by over four thousand women in Bengal, expressing their deep regret at her departure from India, where she had proved herself such a true friend to them, and their grateful appreciation of all she had done for them. Such a sight had never been seen before, and it was one never to be forgotten. The great throne room in Government House was filled from end to end with women of all ages, most of whom had never in their lives before been inside a European house, while many of them had never seen a European face; and to all it was strangely new and exciting to find themselves in a crowd. Only a small number of them could speak English, yet all showed themselves willing to converse by signs and smiles, where words were wanting. They were all overflowing with curiosity with regard to their new surroundings, as well as animated with real gratitude to the English lady, who, during her four short years of residence among them, had initiated and carried out a scheme fraught with so much benefit to them and their children. Such a gathering as this must do a great deal towards the breaking down of the wall of seclusion and exclusiveness with which Indian women are surrounded; and there can be little doubt that more frequent opportunities of social intercourse with cultivated Englishwomen would prove most helpful to them.'

The Parsees are living witnesses to the truth of this last statement. The bestowal of education upon women of the Purdah caste is, in truth, but the thin edge of the wedge; a means to a larger end, an effort to implant in their hearts those stirings of discontent which are the invariable forerunners of all progress.

It was this conviction, that in the purdah system lay the root of all evil, which induced the charming Maharani of Kuch Behar – despite her own natural shyness, and her instinctive disinclination to oppose the established customs of her race – to set an example of courage and good sense, which a very fair number of her countrywomen have since been emboldened to imitate.

It is meet, therefore, that, although not the earliest of India's pioneers, she should be accorded the foremost place in our small portrait gallery of eminent native women.

'Cruelty of Hindoo Child-Marriage,' H.B.B., *Woman's Journal*
(Boston), 16 February 1901, p. 52

The lecture of Dr. Emily Brainerd Ryder, at the last Fortnightly in Boston, Feb. 13, greatly stirred the sympathies of her large audience. Well might it do so! The condition of the Hindoo woman is a slavery almost inconceivably abject, complicated as it is with the additional restrictions of caste and creed. It seems amazing that suicide has not become universal among the Hindoo women, and that the race has not become extinct. Such would be the case if most men were not better than the law.

The domestic life of the Hindoos, who comprise a population of more than one hundred million, has been, until recently, practically unknown to the British Government, or to European residents in India. Only recently have women physicians been able to enter the homes and prescribe for their inmates. And even now they can only do so at a distance, not being allowed to come into contact with their patients, who are absolutely secluded from the outside world, brought up in ignorance, married in infancy, or at latest before they reach nine years of age, absolutely subservient to their husbands to whom they may not speak unless spoken to, not permitted to eat with them, or to have any food except what the husband leaves on his plate. They cook his food, wait upon him in silence, and are under the absolute domination of their mothers-in-law; severed from their own parents, unable to read or write, taught that they have no souls and are born women as a punishment for sins committed in a prior stage of existence, only to be atoned for by uncomplaining submission and with no privilege of escape except by suicide.

If a husband dies it is believed that he owes his death to the sins of his wife, who is therefore held responsible for it by his relatives, to whom she remains enslaved. Formerly she was burned on the funeral pile of her husband. Now, since this has been prohibited by the British Government, she is made to suffer a living death equally terrible. The system of patriarchal households, where children, grandchildren, and parents live under the government of the oldest man and woman, practically reduces all but the heads of the household to complete subserviency. Even grown men must bring their earnings to the head of the family, to be spent by him for their food and clothing, these to be distributed to the various members of these complicated congeries of families. Every caste is kept absolutely distinct, and cannot practise any trade but its own. All the sewing, weaving, and tailoring is done by men. There is nothing left for the women but domestic drudgery in total seclusion. The daughters are separated from their parents for life when they enter the households of their husbands, whom they have never seen or known before.

Such slavery as this is far below the former conditions of the negroes on Southern plantations, or of the inmates of Mohammedan harems. It seems like an inferno, yet it is the lot of millions of women.

Do our remonstrants, who affirm that women should be governed by men, imagine that if the Hindoo mothers had any freedom of thought or action they would consent to have their young daughters thus torn from them forever? Do they imagine that any woman had any hand in ordaining such a religion and such social usages as these? I think I never saw an assembly of women so thoroughly convinced of the need of taking their own part as that which heard this startling and pathetic lecture, which will make suffragists wherever it is delivered. We commend Dr. Ryder's lecture to universal consideration.

'The Cricket and the Lion. As Told by an Old Indian Woman from Mexico' translated by Katherine A. Chandler, [children's page] *Good Housekeeping* (Springfield, Massachusetts, New York, Chicago), July 1902, p. 20

One day the Lion was out walking in the wood. As he was stepping near an old rotten log, he heard a tiny voice say: 'O, please don't step there! That's my house and with one step more, you will destroy it.' The Lion looked down and saw a little Cricket sitting on the log. He roared: 'And is it you, weak little creature, that dares tell me where to step? Don't you know that I am king of the beasts?'

'You may be king of the beasts, But I am king of my house, and I don't want you to break it down, king or no king.'

The Lion was amazed at such daring. 'Don't you know, you weakling, that I could smash you and your house and all your relatives with one blow of my paw?'

'I may be weak, but I have a cousin no bigger than I who could master you in a fight.'

'O, ho! O, ho!' laughed the Lion. 'Well, little boaster, you have that cousin here to-morrow, and if he does not master me, I'll crush you and your house and your cousin all together.' The next day the Lion came back to the same spot and roared: 'Now, boaster, bring on your valiant cousin!'

Pretty soon he heard a buzzing near his ear. Then he felt a stinging. 'O! O!' he cried. 'Get out of my ear!'

But the Cricket's cousin, the Mosquito, kept on stinging and stinging. With every sting, the Lion roared louder and scratched his ear and jumped around. But the Mosquito kept on stinging and stinging. The Cricket sat on the log and looked on. At last he said: 'Mr. Lion, are you ready to let my house alone?'

'Yes, anything, anything,' roared the Lion, 'if you will only get your cousin out of my ear!'

So the Cricket called the Mosquito off and then the Lion went away and never bothered them any more.

'The Colonial Dame, Her "High Living" and her Noble Life,'
Mrs Ella Morris Kretschmar, *Good Housekeeping* (Springfield,
Massachusetts, New York, Chicago), November 1902,
pp. 301–5

What a jewel Miles Standish lost, and John Alden won! And oh! Priscilla, Priscilla, how history cheats you! For you must always live in our minds – and hearts – as only a Puritan maiden, distractingly lovely and shy, yet so ensnared to love that you forced your reluctant lips to speak the brave, difficult words which were the price of your happiness. We love the picture: your demure gown, folded hands, flushed cheeks, averted gaze and the low words to self-tortured John: 'Why don't you speak for yourself?' Who ever thinks of you as a well of housekeeping knowledge so profound that no one could teach you more? Who picture you in your masterful role of director-in-chief, and even master cook, of that first Thanksgiving feast, seven days repeated, with an hundred and fifty guests, ninety of them ravenous Indians? Who associates your love-lit eyes with the practical glance of the alert housewife, your slender hands with marvels of pastry, marmalades, cheeses, herb teas – or perhaps the necessary beating of your Indian 'help'? But never mind! Nobody thinks of Paul Revere's fine engravings or other mechanical exploits. He 'did' his midnight ride, while you – you asked a question, and you both are immortal. Besides, come to think of it, Madame Priscilla Moullin Alden, in your wisdom and skill you were only one of dozens, aye hundreds, of remarkable women in your own and sister colonies who accomplished remarkable things, under unparalleled conditions, during a remarkable period. Just how remarkable no one can form an adequate conception who has not studied colonial conditions more carefully than the high school graduate or the casual reader. It is our habit once a year to give a few glances backward, prompted by Thanksgiving day associations, but we do it with as scant and hazy an appreciation of the real history of those times as we give to the wondrous significance of Christmas. To follow the experiences in detail of the average (mind! the average) colonial woman, is to be overwhelmed by wonder, admiration, envy of her powers, courage, endurance, selfless love and loyalty, of her wisdom, skill, dauntless determination, and withal her unmarred charm of femininity.

Oh, 'New Woman!' you who face the twentieth century with the secret, self-complaisant reflection that you are the highest product of your sex, look back with honest impartiality to the woman of colonial days – and grow humble. You are priding yourself not a little because you are a graduate of Smith, of Wellesley, Vassar, or some other great college, that you can stir your clubs with scholarly theses or easy-flowing words, that you are proficient in domestic science, informed politically, that you are travelled; in short, are a brilliant, cultured, attractive woman, drilled to meet the taxing exigencies of modern life. Pardon me if I draw your attention to the fact that all your life-equipment may be acquired by any woman of average endowments – opportunity permitting. Your real fiber has never been put to a straining test. Have you the vast courage required for pioneering? Could you lend your fine instincts to the cheerful making of candles, cheese and medicines? To washing and carding wool, spinning, weaving and knitting, to eternal mending, brewing and baking? Could you stifle your yearnings to quietude while you churned, wove clumsy carpets, and did a hundred other homely things? And if you bore the test, would yet have spirit left for dancing minuets, for making yourself a charming, ever-hospitable hostess, for keeping in touch with the greater affairs about you, and finally for insuring to your children (as only a mother can insure) the gladness of childhood, spite of dangers, ever surrounding you?

'Colonial Days' to most of us, until we inquire closer, means an early period of our history, having certain fixed social and economic conditions. In reality it means almost the gamut of possible human experiences, condensed within a period of somewhat less than two centuries. It includes starvation, hardships incredible, sumptuous luxury and elegance, coarsest homespun and stiff brocade, with all that lies between. But *know* that whether starving or feasting, in homespun or brocade, a 'colonial woman' means but one thing: the most capable, versatile and courageous woman that ever lived. She faced her list of experiences, the recital of which fairly appals us to-day, but so courageously that we find her quite light-hearted from first to last, having such spirit 'left over' for gaieties that, as we read her life, we catch ourselves enjoying the 'good times' of her day.

[. . .]

In each colony, after the awful hardships of the first few seasons, the comforts of living increased with amazing rapidity. Even in the darkest days, fish and game were to be had by all who were able to hunt, cast a line or set a net; and there was always more or less corn – sometimes an abundance. In summer there was a fine supply of wild fruits – huckleberries, blackberries, strawberries, grapes, plums and cranberries; also pumpkins, beans and peas, cultivated by the Indians. At the first Thanksgiving dinner (1621) the turkeys which graced the board were finer than you, dear madame, can possibly find for your Thanksgiving dinner this month.

[. . .]

So promptly did all the colonies set about the cultivation of everything enjoyed in their mother countries that Johnson wrote in 1634: 'All can now have apple, pear and quince tarts instead of pumpkin pie.' At that time there was also an abundance of peaches, cherries, watermelons, turnips, carrots, cucumbers, potatoes, sweet potatoes, beets, lettuce and radishes, in addition to the vegetables before named. The Indians, at the very first, taught the colonists not only how to cultivate corn, but also how to make the many good dishes they prepared from it: hominy, samp, mush, pudding, hoecake, johnnycake, etc. They also inducted them into the succulent delights of roasting ears, and taught them to bake beans, the honor of which dish has always rested with New Englanders. [. . .]

6

WAR

New Century celebrations in Britain were clouded by the Boer War (1899–1902). Public life was profoundly affected by this crisis and home life thrown open to the vicissitudes of distant armies.

Lord Roberts returned to England from South Africa on 3 January 1901; Shakespeare's *Henry V* had just opened at the Lyceum Theatre in London. The reviewer for the *Lady's Pictorial* linked the two events:

Henry is above all else a warlike figure in a drama of war; and there is at least this much psychology in the revival, that it could not have been presented at a more appropriate time than now, when the air is charged with patriotic and military ardour, and when a great soldier is home again to receive well-earned honours at the hands of his Sovereign and fellow countrymen. . . . So absolutely is Shakespeare a writer of all time, that some of the passages might have been written to-day, with South Africa substituted for France.

That women were keen to be more than spectators in the theatre of war is illustrated by the material selected here, although it was not until the outbreak of the first World War fourteen years later that their involvement became more integrated with the general war effort.

American participation began in 1917. Until then American women's papers, in keeping with the policy of the *Ladies' Home Journal* to avoid disquieting subject matter, had largely neglected the subject. Olive Schreiner's 1914 article carried by the *Woman's Home Companion* was a rare exception. The more usual distance maintained by American women's papers is epitomised by the following advert from the *Woman's World* (Chicago) for February 1915:

OVERSTOCKED

Hand Painted Dresser Sets Just Received From The War Zone.

On account of the war in Europe, our annual shipment of hand-painted china was lost in transit and we were unable to advertise it for the holidays.

To our surprise, a few days after Christmas, the cases containing this beautiful ware began coming in, and we must arrange to dispose of it at once. This is a rare opportunity.

DO NOT DELAY YOUR ORDER

But two years later luxury was out and thrift was in. Women's papers were devoted to comfort and exhortation, promoting the reader's domestic role into nation-saving significance, while assuring them that 'if wars depended on women there would never be a war' (*Ladies' Home Journal*, June 1917, p. 7).

The illustration which accompanies this section is the front page of the Pankhursts' war-time suffrage paper, *Britannia*, on 8 February 1918. This was the first issue to come out after women in Britain over the age of thirty had won the vote, and it shows how the victorious campaign to liberate women became immediately linked to the campaign for military victory.

'Women's Work in South Africa. Interview with Mrs Richard Chamberlain,' Edwin Collins, *Womanhood* (London), December 1900, pp. 50–51

'Yes – if you really think I can do some good by saying what I and other women did, and would have done in South Africa, I am quite willing to be interviewed,' said Mrs. Chamberlain. I had pointed out to her how it was in the interests of humanity and Imperial defence that, since public opinion is potent to effect reforms, she should continue to expose the abuses by which noble-minded, sympathetic and generous women had been prevented from minimising the horrors of war, applying science to the saving of life, and inspiring our troops with confidence. When our soldiers were struck down in fighting for their Queen others, akin to her in character as well as sex, were ready to fight for them and shield them from the invisible army of pestilence that no physical courage can cope with, but that can be conquered by thought and tact allied to tenderness.

[. . .]

Sensitive, refined, and womanly in the very best sense of the word, the cousin of the most musical and passionate of Victorian poets expresses herself clearly and tersely without exaggeration or the faintest suspicion of sensationalism. If, then, her statements are long and the facts stated sensational, that is the fault of the facts and of those who are responsible for the condition of affairs they reveal.

'Let me say at once,' said Mrs. Chamberlain, 'that I do not hold the Government or the War Office responsible for the scandalous maladminis-tration of the hospitals, nor for the sacrifice of life and the suffering entailed by the refusal of civilian aid and the obstacles placed in the way of women anxious to help. Two persons are, in my opinion, to blame, whose names I

"Britannia," February 8, 1918.

FOR KING • FOR COUNTRY • FOR FREEDOM

Britannia

With which is incorporated
"The Suffragette."

Official Organ of the Women's Party
Edited by CHRISTABEL PANKHURST

No. 35. Vol. VI. FRIDAY, FEBRUARY 8, 1918 Price 1d. Weekly
REGISTERED AT THE G.P.O. AS A NEWSPAPER

A CALL TO WOMEN!

The great Suffrage Victory has come to inspire us and equip us for the task of helping to win Victory for our Country and our Allies.

Let us remember that our Suffrage Victory will not be final until the War is won, because Germany, at once if completely victorious, and in the near-future if successful in getting a compromise Peace, would sweep away for ever the votes of British women as well as of British men.

To-day we have got the vote. But to-morrow we shall have neither a vote nor a country to vote in unless we win the war.

Besides, how could we be content to have gained the vote while the small nations allied to us and the populations of all territory invaded by the enemy are martyred and trampled to the earth by the savage aggressor from whom we are pledged to rescue them, just as they, by their heroic fight and infinitely generous sacrifices, have helped keep us and our country safe from the dreadful horror of a German invasion.

The vote that we now possess and must defend on the Home Front or against the foreign enemy is more than a right; it is a trust. The vote is a means of raising the social condition of the masses of the people, and of so arranging the national life that the United Kingdom may become a pioneer among the nations by its prosperity, harmony, and spiritual advance. The vote is a weapon to be used bravely and faithfully in the great Crusade in which our Country and our Allies are engaged.

We call upon all women to whom this ideal of citizenship appeals to unite with us under the flag of the Women's Party!

For the Women's Party,

EMMELINE PANKHURST. ANNIE KENNEY.
CHRISTABEL PANKHURST. FLORA DRUMMOND.

4, William Street, Knightsbridge, S.W.1.

4 Britannia, front cover

would greatly like you to publish.'* [As I do not wish to run the risk of two libel actions, I am sorry I cannot oblige Mrs. Chamberlain in this. The law of libel is the strongest safeguard to sinners in high places. – A.S.B.]

'During my three years' experience as lady visitor at the Guards' Hospital in Rochester Row any matters of which I complained to headquarters were looked into and remedied. In South Africa, when I or others complained, this was the signal for our exclusion from our sphere of usefulness; but while I was not at first entirely excluded, others, women as capable, and as willing as myself, and entirely disinterested and self-sacrificing, but with less personal influence, were not only prevented from doing good, but were treated with arbitrariness and discourtesy.'

'At Cape Town there was not a shadow of excuse for the sick and wounded being deprived of any single necessary or even luxury conducive to their well-being, and thus, indirectly, to the safety of our Empire and the prestige of our service. The Base Commandant walked about with plenty of money at his disposal and plenty of stores, and Cape Town was literally full of trained and accredited nurses, anxious to give their services, and of officers' wives and resident ladies ready and eager to help with money and with the supply of anything needed by officers or men to alleviate their sufferings and smooth the path of convalescence. Yet in the hospitals not only were they short of everything, but refused to accept even pillows and other things urgently needed. Wives of officers, whose names I could give you, would fully corroborate this statement from their own experience. If the head of the Army doctors had had forethought when he found that they were short of Army doctors, and that plenty of civilian medical and nursing aid was available, he would have sent the Army surgeons to the front and run the base hospitals on civilian lines. My first idea in going out to South Africa was to start a civilian hospital for the soldiers, for which purpose I could have obtained unlimited funds at the time. Such hospitals were subsequently sent out; but my offer was persistently refused!'

'Somewhat like the refusal of mounted Colonial troops at the beginning of the war,' said I, 'and the preference for infantry!'

'No.1 Hospital at Wynberg was built over the outflow of the sewer, and was full of bad odours and vermin, but it so pleased the chief official that he increased the accommodation there. So inadequate was the provision made for patients that they were short of absolutely everything except drugs. I supplied sheets, which they were short of. Their only pillow was the small, hard regulation pillow, and men with rheumatic fever were put down with nothing but these hard pillows. I supplied pillows for these and other needful cases. There were practically no water-beds, no air-cushions, no hot-water bottles, and men, no doubt, lost their lives from collapse through these deficiencies alone. They were short of bed-pans also, and even soap and sponges I had to supply, and the civilian doctors had to buy chloroform for themselves. When I went, there were no screens to put round dying men, and they had to die in the sight of other patients, and one of the greatest difficulties I had was to be allowed to place a screen in each ward. Feeders, medicine cups, and cups and saucers were very short, with the result that feeders which had been used by typhoid patients were frequently used for other persons without being washed. We could not obtain buckets, etc., for sanitary precautions, such as disinfection of sheets and linen. Most serious of all, there were no means for obtaining a handy and constant supply of hot water for fomentations, poultices, hot-water bottles, etc.' To this latter cause Mrs. Chamberlain partly attributes the terrible conditions of dirt she described in her evidence.

'The nursing staff was so inadequate,' said Mrs. Chamberlain, 'that if you took the day and night nursing sisters together it came to one sister having charge of 175 patients at a time, and this while there were plenty of trained nurses from Johannesburg Hospital idle in Cape Town; but the medical authorities steadfastly set their faces against obtaining or accepting civil aid of this or any other kind. The nurses who were there were so overworked that I believe it was through exhaustion that many of them died and many were invalided home, while the superintendent, having to use all her energies in doing the work of an ordinary sister, had to leave the nurses without proper superintendence. This I consider an important point. In No.1 Wynberg there were nine nurses and 700 patients.'

In order to show how every effort was made to suppress reports of the true state of affairs, and also how women were prevented from doing all they would and could have done, Mrs. Chamberlain described to me how convalescents, whose presence in the wards not only retarded their own complete recovery, but also was most injurious, if not fatal, to serious cases requiring quiet, were forbidden to go to the garden of a lady who had a house near the hospital and used to invite the men to take tea there.

'Why,' I asked, 'were you excluded from the hospital at which you had been doing such a self-sacrificing and useful work?'

'No reason was given,' replied Mrs. Chamberlain. 'Indeed, no reason was ever given to the ladies whose services were refused; but the moment there seemed to be any danger of reports reaching England which would open the eyes of the public to the true state of affairs, and the moment anyone ventured to make a complaint, however justified, the possible witness or the actual complainant was silenced by intimidation, dismissal or exclusion.'

'The ladies at Cape Town who would have provided luxuries as well as necessaries for all the men in hospital, milk, fruit, flowers, etc. and who offered to write their letters for them, and otherwise minister to their needs as only women can, were not permitted to do so. Had these Cape Town ladies alone been allowed a free hand they could, and would, have made the hospitals as good as any English hospital.'

[. . .]

Neither the limits of space nor the scope of WOMANHOOD will allow me to give in detail a tithe of the facts and views set forth to me by Mrs. Chamberlain, but I hope that I have said enough to show how valuable and necessary is the aid of such women in military hospitals, and how urgently needed is the influence of all women who read this magazine to bring about reforms that would remove the obstacles now placed in the way of such aid being given.

'Woman And War,'[1] Olive Schreiner, *Woman's Home Companion*
(New York), November 1914, p. 23

We have always borne part of the weight of war, and the major part. It is
not that in primitive times we suffered from the destruction of the fields
we tilled and the houses we built; it is not that in a comparatively
insignificant manner, as nurses of the wounded in modern times, or now
and again as warrior chieftainesses, and leaders in primitive and other
societies, we have borne our part; nor is it even because the spirit of resolution
in its women, and their willingness to endure, has in all ages again and again
largely determined the fate of a race that goes to war, that we demand
our controlling right where war is concerned. Our relation to war is far more
intimate, personal, and indissoluble than this. Men have made boomerangs,
bows, swords, or guns with which to destroy one another; we have made the
men who destroyed and were destroyed! We have in all ages produced, at an
enormous cost, the primal munition of war, without which no other could
exist. There is no battlefield on earth, nor ever has been, howsoever covered
with slain, which it has not cost the women of the race more in actual
bloodshed and anguish to supply, than it has cost the men who lie there. *We
pay the first cost on all human life.*

There is, perhaps, no woman who could look down upon a battlefield
covered with slain but the thought would rise in her, 'So many mothers' sons!
So many young bodies brought into the world to lie there! So many months
of weariness and pain while bones and muscles shaped within! So many hours
of anguish and struggle that breath might be! So many baby mouths drawing
life at womens' breasts – all this that men might lie with glazed eyes and
swollen faces, and fixed, blue, unclosed mouths, and great limbs tossed!' And
we cry, 'Without an inexorable cause this must not be!' No woman who is a
woman says of a human body, 'It is nothing!'

No tinsel of trumpets and flags will ultimately seduce women into the
insanity of recklessly destroying life, or gild the willful taking of life with any
other name than that of murder, whether it be the slaughter of the million or
of one by one. And this will be, not because with the function of maternity
necessarily goes in the human creature a deeper moral insight or a loftier type
of social instinct than that which accompanies the paternal. Men have in
all ages led as nobly as women in many paths of heroic virtue, and toward
the higher social sympathies; in certain ages, being freer and more widely
cultured, they have led further and better.

Nor will women shrink from war because they lack courage. Earth's women
of every generation have faced suffering and death with an equanimity that no

---

1 Reprinted from 'Woman and Labor,' by Olive Schreiner, by courtesy of the Frederick A. Stokes
Company. Copyright, 1911, by Frederick A. Stokes Company.

soldier on a battlefield has ever surpassed and few have equalled; and where war has been to preserve life, or land, or freedom, rather than for aggrandizement and power, women have in all ages known how to bear an active part, and die.

Nor will woman's influence militate against war because in the future woman will not be able physically to bear her part in it. The smaller size of her muscle, which might severely have disadvantaged her when war was conducted with a battle-ax or sword and hand to hand, would now little or not at all affect her. If intent on training for war, she might acquire the skill for guiding a Maxim or shooting down a foe with a Lee-Metford at four thousand yards as ably as any male; and undoubtedly it has not been only the peasant girl of France who has carried latent and hid in her person the gifts that would make the great general. If our European nations should continue in their present semi-civilized condition a few generations longer it is highly probable that as financiers, as managers of commissariat departments, as inspectors of provisions and clothing for the army, women may probably play a very leading part, and that the nation which is the first to employ women may be placed at a vast advantage over its fellows in time of war. It is not because of women's cowardice, incapacity, nor, above all, because of her general superior virtue that she will end war when her voice is fully and clearly heard in the governance of states: it is because, on this one point almost alone, the knowledge of woman, simply as woman, is superior to that of man. She knows the history of human flesh; she knows its cost; he does not.

In a besieged city it might well happen that men in the streets might seize upon statues and marble carvings from public buildings and galleries and hurl them in to stop the breaches made in their ramparts by the enemy, unconsideringly and merely because they came first to hand, not valuing them more than had they been paving stones. One man, however, could not do this – the sculptor. He who, though there might be no work of his own chisel among them, yet knew what each of these works of art had cost, knew by experience the long years of struggle and study and the infinitude of toil which had gone to the shaping of even one limb, to the carving of even one perfected outline, he could never so use them without thought or care. Instinctively he would seek to throw in household goods, even gold and silver, all the city held, before he sacrificed its works of art!

Men's bodies are our women's works of art. Given to us power to control, we will never carelessly throw them in to fill up the gaps in ambitions and greeds. The thought would never come to us as women, 'Cast in men's bodies; settle the thing so!' Arbitration and compensation would as naturally occur to her as cheaper and simpler methods of bridging the gaps in national relationships, as to the sculptor it would occur to throw in anything rather than statuary, though he might be driven to that at last!

This is one of those phases of human life – not very numerous, but very important – toward which the man as man, and the woman as woman, on the mere ground of their different sexual function with regard to reproduction, stand, and must stand, at a somewhat differing angle.

The twenty thousand men prematurely slain on a field of battle mean to the women of their race twenty thousand human creatures to be borne within them for months, given birth to in anguish, fed from their breasts, and reared with toil, if the numbers of the tribe and the strength of the nation are to be maintained. In nations continually at war, incessant and unbroken child-bearing is by war imposed on all women if the State is to survive; and whenever war occurs, if numbers are to be maintained, there must be an increased child-bearing and rearing. This throws upon woman as woman a war tax compared with which all that the male expends in military preparations is comparatively light.

The relations of the female toward the production of human life influence undoubtedly even her relation toward animal and all life. 'It is a fine day, let us go out and kill something!' cries the typical male of certain races, instinctively. 'There is a living thing, it will die if it is not cared for,' says the average woman, almost equally instinctively. It is true that the woman will sacrifice as mercilessly, as cruelly, the life of a hated rival or an enemy, as any male; *but she always knows what she is doing, and the value of the life she takes*! There is no light-hearted, careless enjoyment in the sacrifice of life to the normal woman: her instinct, instructed by experience, steps in to prevent it. She always knows what life costs, and that it is more easy to destroy than create it.

For the vast bulk of humanity, probably for generations to come, the instinctive antagonism of the human child-bearer to reckless destruction of that which she has at so much cost produced will probably be necessary to educate the race to any clear conception of the bestiality and insanity of war.

'How Can I Do My "Bit"? An Editorial Answer to the
American Housewife,' *Ladies' Home Journal* (Philadelphia),
June 1917, p. 26

When a country is at war the economic and domestic conditions are absolutely in the hands of the women who stay at home. It is then that the finest and best in womanhood blossoms forth, and it all shows itself in her efficient conduct of the home and of her children.

If ever the American housewife has the chance to show her domestic efficiency it is now and in the months to come. Prices, already high, will undoubtedly be higher. Labor, scarce enough now, will be scarcer, trans-portation, already congested, will be more congested. And in the face of these problems that will touch, personally and directly, every housewife the average income will shrink as taxes increase and as men are taken from their wage pursuits to serve their country.

The American housewives' problem will be high prices and reduced incomes. . . . The American woman must learn thrift. She must get away from the notion that prodigality is the sign of the aristocrat and that it is mean to be thrifty. We have cooked by wasteful processes: we have served in overabundance, we have thrown away what others have used: we have taken no thought of lean times to come. But the lean times are here and they will be leaner yet before we are much older. It is here that every American woman can do her 'bit.' The time has come for her to study her job of running her home as a business, and to place it on an intelligent and systematic basis.

Let no woman decide that because she is 'only one woman' she can do little or nothing. She can do much. She can do all, so far as her own problems are concerned, for only she can solve them. Others may advise or help, but she alone can directly solve. And the finest work will be done quietly by the individual woman. That is always so. It is for each woman to solve intelligently the problem of her own home and family. And each woman should. There is no choice in such times as these. The woman who does is a help to her country: the woman who does not is a detriment.

'His Christmas Letter to His Mother. The Letter of a
19-Year-Old Ambulance Driver "Somewhere in France",'
Ladies' Home Journal (Philadelphia), December 1917, p. 12

Dear Mother: I am leaving Paris for the Front to-morrow. Not allowed to say exactly what my destination is, but it's somewhere in the Verdun sector. I have had a wonderful time in Paris for the last two weeks. We have been entertained a great deal. We lived in a regular palace which was inhabited by Benjamin Franklin when he was ambassador to France. That's the way these French people do things. We are Americans, trying to do our 'bit' for France, so they look around and present us with an enormous chateau, which is probably the richest in American history in France. Paris is the wonder spot of the earth. Never saw so much beauty scattered round loose in my life – not even in the front choruses of musical comedies!

But things are about to break. I feel as I used to just before the whistle of a big game; but this is bigger than a big game, and it will all be over by the time you get this. The morning paper will probably have about two lines on the second page. I have just been out in the rain grooming my car, and I think she'll keep going.

I'm so keyed up I can hardly sit still to write. All I can think is a deep prayer that my bus will keep going. I think every big gun in the world is going and I can hardly hear to think. My lamp rattles and jumps so when a big one goes off I can hardly see to write.

It has started for sure! Gas masks and 'elmets. 'Ell's poppin', mother! Think of this and then that what I started out to say to you was 'Merry Christmas and a Happy New Year!' Of course you know how impossible it is to even get a card out here!

Just back! (Have to write in snatches, you know.) I made three trips to the *'poste* with the number' and had one rather painful experience. I was given a man who was shot almost to pieces. He was conscious and O, Lord! with every yard of the twelve-mile drive he shrieked and groaned till I was just off my base. I finally got to the relay *poste*, and when they were taking him out of my car he passed away, poor chap!

I know that's a 'punk' beginning for a Christmas letter. But don't, for the love of Mike, think that occurrences like this, fearful as they seem, depress me for a moment any more. They can't. You can't let 'em. I have come as near to developing an optimistic fatalism as it's possible for a half-baked intellect to achieve. Don't misunderstand. I don't look gloomy and murmur resignedly 'The fates have so decreed, so it must be, despite me.' Far from such. It's 'Well, we may be able to save the next by good driving, so to it! and work like you know!'

This letter is supposed to be a Christmas present; I can't imagine finding anything worse in my stocking, unless it's a hole. But way down in my boots somewhere I have a strong hunch rattling around loose that the best present I can give you, mother, is to make you realize how completely successful is this expedition of ours. It's wonderful.

[. . .]

Last night I had a very exciting run, as the Germans dropped a curtain of fire on the road just after I had passed. It was a beautiful sight – FROM HALF A MILE AWAY. When I came back the curtain had stopped, and I had to run out into the fields and follow a labyrinthine trail to miss the impassable shell holes. I sure was glad that Frank (I call my car Frank) didn't fail me then, because there were some new shell holes when I came back to the *poste*. I must stop writing now for a while; I must get some sleep before I go on duty. I had hoped to send you some little thing for Christmas, but *c'est impossible* – and when the big day rolls round don't say to yourself 'I hope he isn't blue to-day,' because I won't be. I shall be on duty all day Christmas, working too hard to be blue.

7

GIRLS

'Hooligan girls,' 'fin-de-siècle girls,' 'Girton girls,' 'bachelor girls', 'new girls': whether the waywardness of girls was represented as progress or threat, it was always a topic for news. The articles in this section offer a variety of comment on the subject of girls, and together illustrate the age range of those who qualified as 'girls'. Correspondence from the *Woman's Signal* in 1898 about the kind of primary education appropriate for girls, depending on their future, and an article from the *National Review* in 1901 about aspirations and ideals of American school girls, illustrate the more youthful definition of 'girl'. Other articles, about the activities of young women, 'girls', mature and independent but crucially unmarried, illustrate a deep-rooted linguistic infantilisation of women. There is discomfort evident in the discourse of 'The Girl Ranchers of California' – about sisters aged nineteen and twenty who have inherited their father's ranch and continue to manage the estate – which suggests an ideological anxiety about the social status of women such as these. They are 'Amazons' and 'Dianas', though 'not . . . the traditional pastoral heroine'. A mythological framework is invoked to place these unconventional sisters within a sphere that can still be given a female gender.

Whenever the subject of girls came up the question of marriage was not far away. The *Woman's Home Companion* ran discussions of this subject in 1914, and by July the tide began to turn. In January 1914 Anne Bryan McCall concluded 'the normal girl looks forward to marriage, plans for it, hopes for it, and this is as it should be. . . . But whether we marry or not, the richest life for a woman is still that of service, and to prepare ourselves for marriage is after all to prepare ourselves for better, fuller service' ('The Girl Who Does Not Marry,' p. 5). In July Christine Herrick pronounced in her piece 'A Girl's Rights. Should the Girl with a Comfortable Home Earn Her Own Living?' that 'the girl of to-day, with the unfortunately logical tendency which she has learned at school or college is by way of asking: 'How does my case differ from that of my married sister or of my brother? . . . Why should my single-hood or my sex hold me to a life of domesticity, diversified by society and philanthropy?' (*Woman's Home Companion*, p. 16).

THE NEW GIRL.

When the New Girl and Cupid first met,
How the little god sighed with regret !
  "I suppose, now," he said,
  "I must aim for the head,
And my old-fashioned methods forget."

But she dodged, and the shaft went astray;
So the moral is this, one would say,
  He must send his best dart
  At the New Maiden's heart
In the dear old Arcadian way.

Anna Mathewson.

5 'The New Girl'

'Manual Training in Girls' Schools,'
Mrs Arthur Francis, *Woman's Signal* (London),
3 November 1898

When asked to open this discussion on Technical Education for Girls and Women, I begged to be allowed to speak to you on what is its necessary foundation – viz., Manual Training in all our Girls' Schools, both Primary and Secondary. For want of such training in early life much of our present technical instruction fails to produce its proper and adequate result, because the students lack the foundation which alone can enable them to profit fully by the skilled teaching which is now open to all.

Those of us who advocate manual training are often reproached with trying to lower the standard of general education; we are told the years are all short in which our children have to gain their intellectual training. This reproach arises from a misunderstanding of our aims. Ruskin has nobly said that 'Education is the leading human souls to what is best and making what is best out of them,' and we who advocate manual training as an essential part of any systematic education are content to abide by that definition. We do not believe that our schools are to be regarded primarily as training grounds for domestic servants or even for wives and mothers. We do wish so to train our girls that first and foremost they shall be good and capable women, competent, well trained persons, able to take care of themselves and of those whom God may entrust to their care in after life. Adequately to fulfil human relations demands a complete person; and it is because we are convinced that a system which strives to train only the brain can never produce a complete person, that we beg for a training of hand and eye side by side, and in conjunction with the brain.

We fully endorse the statement that children are sent to school to prepare for life, not to be taught to earn a living. I have heard it insisted that our aim in education is to teach a child to think, but surely that is only half our work; we should also train her to give expression to that thought in action. The aim of education should be 'complete living,' as one writer tersely puts it.

Manual training certainly tends to give us the power of using our knowledge to some practical end. It ought to be part of any complete intellectual and moral training, not superseding literature, but being subordinate to it.

In the formation of character it plays a valuable part. Nothing is so good for the moral sense as a pride in the production of good, sound, honest work. Children so trained are early in life encouraged to do something and finish it. The undeveloped mental power of the young child is, of course, not capable of sustained or concentrated attention, except through its bodily activities. Manual training properly carried out accepts this fact, and turns it to good account. The average child shows its want of character in its lack of purpose and steady perseverance. If left without guidance it suddenly takes up some interest, and as suddenly drops it – without reason; thus the weak, emotional nature, having no higher interest than the passing moment, becomes weaker. Bring the child's bodily activity into play, let the brain and hand and eye work in conjunction under intelligent guidance, and the steady progress of any piece of hand work, begun and completed with due care, calls forth a strength of purpose, perseverance and diligence which is astonishing in a young child.

Some children can learn little or nothing except through the medium of hand and eye. There is the child of whom we say 'she does not take to lessons,' whose brain is not naturally receptive nor capable of lively interest in abstract ideas. She is not necessarily stupid; rather would I say we are stupid and limited in our educational methods, in that we look for a successful result through the same means on widely differing material. Let that child be put to some work, which shall employ and train both hand and eye, and she will often show great and surprising aptness in handiwork.

If you want a visible proof of the intellectual power gained through manual training, take two children – any two – one of whom has had some sort of training for hand and eye, and one who has had none. One will follow you with close attention, ready to observe the smallest detail of your diagram, perhaps to draw one like it, and to grasp your explanation with intelligence. The other will not be quick to notice small detail, will probably omit much of it if asked to reproduce your illustration, or if required to construct will assuredly be clumsy in handling. No power is of more use to us through life than that of attention, of being able to concentrate all the mental powers at a given time on a given subject. This power is often conspicuously absent in adults; and all teachers have experience of children to whom the habit of attention is unknown, and who appear to make no effort to gain it through a literary source. For such an one manual training will do wonders, for it not only trains and strengthens the habit of attention, but it is a perpetual test of it. In carving, for instance – take a piece of the simplest kind – the moment the mind wanders from the tool the result is failure, and probably a cut finger. Cutting out and fixing a pair of sleeves demands the same close attention and thought. The power of attention is visibly tested in both cases.

Briefly, we claim a place for manual training in the general education of our girls of all classes, on the ground that it cultivates practical intelligence, strengthens the memory and tests and trains the powers of attention. Its moral effect is excellent, as it develops a love of order and neatness, caution and dexterity, and a respect for good and thorough workmanship.

'Domestic Economy in Schools,' Mary C. Tabor,
Woman's Signal (London), 15 December 1898, p. 383

Madam, – I was exceedingly glad to see your remarks on the attempt of the Women's Industrial Council to discourage the teaching of cookery, laundry, and housewifery in our elementary schools. As you justly observe, to limit such teaching to ex-standard VII. scholars, is practically to shut out the whole school population from this most vital and invaluable part of a girl's education. The housewifery classes under the London School Board are not intended to fit girls for 'domestic service,' as these objectors assume, but to prepare them for the ordinary, inevitable life of womanhood. Sooner or later 90 per cent of girls in our elementary schools will be at the head of working-class homes, doing the work of them with their own hands. Nothing can be of more importance to these girls, or tend more to the dignity, comfort, and content of their after life, that they should learn how to do that work intelligently and well, with precision, method, and despatch; in short, with satisfaction both to others and themselves. The London School Board, in my opinion, has done no more valuable work than the institution of these cookery, laundry, and housewifery classes for girls. The training given in them is educative in the best sense of the word, and it would be matter for profound regret if they were to be interfered with in any way at the instance of an outside and irresponsible body.

'Some Recollections of My Schooldays,' Sarah Grand,
Lady's Magazine (London), January 1901, p. 42

When I hear the person who is tenderly sentimental on the subject of her schooldays refer to them as the happiest time her life, I always wonder if she thinks them so because of what she remembers of them, or because of what she has forgotten. The tendency of human nature is to allow unpleasant things to lapse from the memory. The days to which we look back as beautiful days, as landmarks in life which indicate the brighter spots, usually have their drawbacks; but such drawbacks we chase involuntarily from our recollection when we can: or else they become an addition to our pleasure in the retrospect by adding a touch of humour to the position, so that the impression that remains with us is wholly happy.

My own memory has never played me any such trick with regard to my schooldays. An attempt to recall them brings with it a dreadful sense of lassitude – that is the most imperative, the most poignant recollection I have of them. The length of each day and its deadly dulness; the remorseless routine; the constant wearing effort; the inevitable weary striving to accomplish one uncongenial task after another; the aching sense of something to be done that must be done, in the mood or out of the mood – and it was usually out of the mood with me. As I was not happy there, I will not give the name of the school, but it is still flourishing. It has kept up with the times too, I understand, and is doing excellent work in the way of education.

In my day, the work it did was also excellent, but more in its effect upon the formation of character than upon the cultivation of intellect. That, however, was not the fault of the school, but of the whole system of education then in vogue for girls. Unfortunately for me my time was just before the reformation. I was one of the last victims of the old stultifying restrictions.

But I did not remain. I married at sixteen – the great inducement being that I should be able to study thoroughly any subject I liked, learn languages so that I could speak them, and music so that I could play it, have the command of good books, and escape from routine.

I did my work conscientiously all the time I was at school, but it was always a weary effort, and most disheartening, for I despised the sort of work I had to do, and at the same time found it hard. I was fourteen when I went to school, and had only a slight acquaintance with the multiplication table and the first four rules of arithmetic, my ideas on the subject of spelling were original, and my handwriting was likened unto that of the old gardener who kept his accounts with a burnt stick on the whitewashed wall of a shed.

But my writing was rather worse than the gardener's, because it had been cruelly cramped in view of the scarcity of paper, and the pressure of ideas which sought incessantly for written expression. For, although I was very backward in the kind of lessons which we learnt at school, my intelligence had been developed in other ways. I had had the run of a good library, and been read to and talked to by people of taste and capacity all my life, so that when at last I was sent to school, I was cultivated in some respects beyond my years, and had acquired the habit of conversing intelligently on topics which other girls of my age would have been at a loss to comprehend. But this only made it all the worse for me.

It was long before I could shake off the baleful impression which those two years at school had made upon me, long before I could be persuaded to believe that all schools were not prisons in which captive children were made to suffer agonies of mental misery; and even now one of the worst dreams I have is about school. I dream they have sent me back.

Nevertheless, I do not blame the school, and if I had a daughter I would send her there, only I would send her early. That was the mistake that was made in my own case; I was not sent early enough. It was an error of judgement. It would not have mattered so much in these days, perhaps, because the education of girls is more intelligently directed; but at that time it meant a martyrdom to a girl of my temperament.

We had none but the most babyish books; our recreation in the grounds was limited to monotonous walks up and down the gravelled paths; we had no games of any kind – nothing to develop our physique at all but the making of our little beds every morning and an hour's 'deportment' once a fortnight. When we were taken out to walk for exercise, we went in classes, each like a sorry caterpillar, moving reluctantly.

We were only allowed to write to our parents, and but one letter a week. Every alternate week the letter was 'public,' that is to say, the head mistress had the right to read it. The public letters were careful compositions, written out on a slate, first of all, and then transcribed with infinite pains.

In our private letters, as they were called, we were able to expand a little, but they were limited in length, and, as we had a whole fortnight to write them, our thirst for intimate expression was never slaked. That was a real hardship to some of us, and the consequence of it was that many of the girls wrote clandestinely to their own mothers, although they lost caste with the other girls for doing so, for deceit of any kind was strongly discountenanced among us.

The present lady principal of the school, Miss L., was the head girl when I was there, she being in that proud position at sixteen, if I remember rightly, while I, her junior by only two years, was among the little girls in the sixth class. Miss L. left that year, having learnt all that the school could teach her, and went elsewhere to continue her education. I went out to the East when I married, and heard little of any of my school fellows until I published 'The Beth Book.'

Then, to my surprise, there came a shoal of letters from my contemporaries, who had at once identified the 'St. Catherine' of the book with the old school. Some of them thought I had coloured the picture unfairly to suit the exigencies of the story.

Miss L. tells me that my conduct during my last 'half' is chronicled in the record of the school as 'unsatisfactory.'

Her own impression of her school days is very much the opposite of mine, but then she was sent there early. Besides, there is a difference of temperament which must make my record everywhere more or less unsatisfactory compared with such a record as hers – the record of one who does the work of an arduous and responsible position in the most admirable manner. I may say that her good work keeps her still at the head of the school, while I, alas, am only in the sixth.

'The Girl Ranchers of California,' W.F. Wade,
Lady's Magazine (London), June 1901, pp. 633–6

A traveller who had penetrated to the rocky fastnesses of Mendocino County, California, not long ago reined in his horses at a point known as Big Rock, where one of the Eel River tributaries comes cascading down the mountains to its own rollicking music, to watch the passing of a great flock of sheep. The special interest of the spectacle lay, in fact, not in the sheep, but in the shepherds in charge of them. They were astride spirited mounts, one of which also carried, slung behind the rider, the body of a panther.

The wide Mexican sombreros shaded good-natured, sunburnt faces, which hardly belonged, however, to typical men of the mountains, and the voices which replied to the traveller's questions were too musical not to make strange the owners' occupation and appearance. They were, in fact, girls – well-known personages, with the story of whose lives the country resounds.

It was almost twenty years ago when Jacob Lahm married a wife, and with her came to this northern wilderness to establish a home. He was the pioneer on his ten thousand acres of virgin forest-land, stretching along the mountain range. His domain had to be cleared not only of the gigantic redwoods, the pines and firs, but also of the bears and panthers native to it. So Jacob Lahm, before he could be a stock-raiser, had to be a hunter and trapper.

No doubt his children ought to have been boys. But in point of fact, they were girls. And Jacob Lahm, realising that feminine qualities alone could never meet the necessities of existence in that remote and wild country, set to

Gussie Lahm makes an early morning start.

Louise Lahm.

6 'Louise Lahm' and 'Gussie Lahm makes an early morning start'

work to graft on the gentleness and modesty of his girls the independence, resourcefulness, practical wisdom, strength, courage, and hardihood of the frontiersman.

Some months ago their father died, and the care of the ranch fell upon the daughters, Miss Gussie and Miss Louise Lahm. They are respectively nineteen and twenty years old, and they have full management of an estate which is worth, perhaps, ten thousand pounds.

These young women now, therefore, devote their time to the practical affairs of stock-raising, and the varied details of a mountain farm. Their five thousand sheep, together with their droves of horses and cattle, look to them for care. They brand the increase of the sheep, supervise the shearing and market the wool. Ploughing, harrowing, sowing and harvesting are in the list of their agricultural employments.

Tracking, trapping, and shooting game are their avocations. The riatas at their saddles are used by hands that can lasso a wild horse or a steer with unerring success. In the late autumn months, when the grass is short, the stock are fed in the corrals, but at other times they stray, and must be driven in at night. It may not be the idyllic picture of the traditional pastoral heroine, but it is, none the less, a pleasing one to see the great flock of silly sheep and bleating lambs running before their modern shepherds and their dogs.

Your shepherdess of song and fable is a lovely little fairy with a ribboned crook. With yawning difference, these modern Californians have guns, and are clad in the Amazonian garb of coats and knicker-bockers.

During the season in which the cares of the ranch are lighter they may indeed don skirts and join the pupils in a district school miles away. They are more likely to change the duties of farm superintendence for a far-ranging search after missing sheep, or a hunt for the enemies of the flocks.

The range upon whose side stands the Lahm ranch stretches for twenty miles, and there is little of it that is not familiar to these young women. From the time they were old enough to hang on by clinging to a horse's mane, they have been as much at home galloping astride over these mountains as a *debutante* of last season in a to-day's drawing-room. Between the ranges run canyons covered with chaparral, manzanita, and oaks whose acorns tempt the sheep – canyons in the depth of which many a straying beast gets lost. Then when the count at feeding-time shows a shortage, the girls clap saddles on their broncos, pull their leather-trimmed sombreros down, and are off to find and bring back the missing. The search may last till midnight; it may take them miles away from home, over wild passes and by the brink of precipices, perhaps through the blinding fury of a storm. The frightened sheep may have sought shelter in the dangerous depth of some ravine, but these intrepid rescuers are ready to risk their lives wherever the piteous bleating calls them.

More exciting excursions are those upon which the Lahm girls are called when the skulking enemy prowls too freely upon the flocks. If he be a coyote, steel traps need only be placed at such points as are most likely to be passed by his predatory feet. If he be a bear – his tracks will show – these Dianas set aside a day and a night, take the hounds, and hunt him to his death.

They are absolutely fearless, and think no more of tracking a 'grizzly' than of hunting a deer. Long residence in the wild forest-land has trained their eyes and ears to startling acuteness, and in addition to being dead shots they possess the keen sight and ready aim of the practised huntsman. Their excursions often lead them into deadly peril, and were it not for their skill in the use of fire-arms they might have long since fallen a prey to the many dangers they have passed through unscathed.

The Lahm home is bric-a-bracked with innumerable trophies of its daughters' valorous deeds, skins of lynx and panther, of cinnamon bear, testifying to a prowess of which backwoodsmen might boast. The beautiful panther which caught the eye of the traveller at Red Rock (sic) measured eleven feet, and weighed one hundred and thirty-two pounds. The sisters have shown that women, given equal chances with men in the matter of out-door education and uncivilised environment, can fairly compete with them in the management of a large and important ranch. Had they been reared amid the comforts and refinements of English home life their latent capabilities for sport and agriculture would probably never have been developed, and they might have fallen victims to lethargy or an occasional *crise de nerfs* with the rest of us. As it is they have had the ideal education for their hardy and adventurous lives and have nobly fulfilled their father's expectations.

In the saddle, out under the sky by day and night, on the wind-swept plateaux and in the dark under-wood of the ravines, life apparently has its own interests and its sufficient excitement for these girls of the golden West.

'The Ideals of the American School-Girl,' Miss Catherine Dodd, *National Review* (London), June 1901, pp. 610–23

Readers of the *National Review* will remember that an attempt was recently made to compare the ideals of English and German school-children by considering their answers to two questions:–

Which would you rather be, a man or a woman – and why? Which man or woman of whom you have ever heard or read would you most wish to be – and why? The same two questions have been set nearly 600 American school children with interesting results.

The sets of paper about to be considered came from schools in New England and the Western States. The contrasts between the two are in some particulars very marked, so it is well to consider them separately. The American school girl is more interesting than the school boy, chiefly on account of her individuality, the variety of her aspirations, and the loftiness of her ideas; and this paper deals only with her. There is a monotony in the desires of the young human male. His demands for money, power, pleasure, and fighting are fairly universal all the world over; in fairness to the German boy, however, we must admit that he sighs for the ideal and scholarly distinction, and he rarely allows himself to express any desire for either money or pleasure, but he has less of the human boy and more of the ungrown man than other school boys. The German school boy never plays – this makes him serious; and he never sits in the same class with girls, and therefore is sometimes beaten by them, hence, like little Martin Yorke, he despises 'womenites.'

Very striking is the contrast between the lively American school girl, with her limitless ambitions and cheerful confidence in herself, and her placid, pliable, pious German sister, who is content to be patted and moulded into the comfortable shape which masculine taste demands. The American school girl follows Emerson's counsel and insists on herself. Wrong-headed she may occasionally be, but nobody can accuse her of meekness. Her nature is strong, she bristles all over with impulses, feelings, and prejudices, but she never sits down in a state of pulp and allows herself to be moulded.

'Never imitate,' says Emerson, 'your own gift you can present every moment with the cumulative force of a whole life's cultivation, but of the adopted talent of another you have only a half possession.' The American school girl does not imitate. She gives herself as she is, with a refreshing spontaneity, and she forms a more interesting study than the prim little German in consequence. The German school girl is self-conscious. The superiority of her male relations overawe her, and she is full of sentimental yearnings to be, and do, and suffer all that these magnificent beings demand. Domestic life in Germany may be fitly described as Jove mated with Martha, only a regenerated Martha, patient and uncomplaining.

From the New England school girls there were nearly 100 papers; of these only 15 per cent wished to change their sex. Eighty five per cent were content with themselves as they were, urging as reasons that the lot of women was preferable to that of men.

In England 34 per cent wished to be men, urging that men had a better time, more glory, and more money than women. In Germany half the girls were not allowed to answer this question at all because such speculations might unsettle them, and several of those who were allowed to attempt it remarked soberly, 'It is wicked to wish to be a man.'

There is more discontent with a woman's portion in England than in New England, while in Germany there is apparently absolute content; but men teach in the German Secondary Schools, and the first lesson they wish girls to learn is that of submission, and as from her babyhood the girl courts masculine approval she learns this easily.

Even in America, which, judging from these papers, is an earthly paradise for women, there are a few who rebel against their sex and envy man's power over circumstances. These are the practical damsels. They want to make money, and to have a wide choice of work on equal terms with men and to have an easier time: – 'I want to be a man, because men are stronger and can make more money.'

'Man has a choice of many professions; if a woman goes into professions like lawyers, men are jealous, besides she does not get so much to do.'

'Men can be poets, and I want to be a poet like Shakespeare.'

'Men can travel more than women, and they do not need much luggage, because women have a lot of dresses which is a bother.'

'Men needn't do housework, and all other work is nicer than this.'

These remarks are just and to the point. One damsel of thirteen says, forcibly: 'I wish most to be a man, because this is a man's world, and I want my share of it.' She sums up the whole gospel of the Woman's Suffrage in this pithy sentence.

The 85 per cent who are true to their own sex may be classed as follows:–

Twelve per cent are self seeking. They are convinced that a woman's lot is easier than a man's, therefore they prefer it.

Fourteen per cent despise men, and believe women to be superior.

Twenty-four per cent are cheerfully philosophic, and accept the inevitable.

Thirty-five per cent are convinced that women have a respectable career before them.

Among the self-seeking ones we get the following reasons:–

'It is better to be a woman, because women travel more, and they spend more money, which they do not have to earn.'

'Women have no hard work to do and men have.'

'Women have more enjoyment than men, and they go to parties.'

'Women have better chances in life than men, and they can teach better.'

'Women wear nicer dresses and more colours.'

'Women are treated more politely than men, and they do their hair nicer.'

'Women is not punished so much as men, for the law is not hard on them.'

All this is comforting to the feminine mind, and if in truth the American women have 'better chances in life,' 'no hard work,' 'more polite treatment, and more lenient laws,' then is this country indeed a woman's paradise.

Fourteen per cent, are strong-minded, and they despise men in consequence. In Germany no heresy was breathed against masculine superiority. Strong-mindedness is not a characteristic of German girls or women, on the contrary they glory in their inferiority.

There is a severity in the New England girl's view of men, she compares them with women greatly to the advantage of the latter in manners, morals, and mental endowments.

Here are some of the pithy conclusions and condemnations on mankind:–

'A woman has better sense than a man.'

'Women learn things quicker, because they have more intelligence.'

'Women are always better than men in morals.'

'Women are more use in the world.'

'Woman has more religion than man has.'

'Women are quicker than men, and they can control their temper.'

'Women just has patience, when she is crossed, but men uses bad language.'

'Women bring up children, and the child is father to the man,' is the crowning testimony to woman's superiority by these young moralizers. Those of us who know the travelled American child in hotels and boarding-houses will agree that the child is certainly father to the man in a way which Wordsworth never contemplated.

Twenty-four per cent are well-balanced and cheerful. They accept the inevitable and make the best of it.

> 'I would rather be a woman, because I have to be.'

> 'I wish to be a woman, I can't help it.'

> 'I am satisfied with the way I am, and it would make no difference if I wasn't.'

> 'I wish to be a woman because God gave me no choice.'

> 'I would rather be a woman, because I cannot be anything else, and I mean to be as good as a man anyway.'

These papers show a commendable philosophy, and a steady determination to make the best of doubtful circumstances. There is no time wasted in vain regrets. 'Discontent,' as Emerson says, 'is want of self-reliance,' and the American girl scorns futile repinings. She goes upright, and insists on herself. Thirty-five per cent take life seriously. They crave for the joy of vigorous action and of adequate expression. They long to assert themselves to some notable result. The teaching profession has many attractions for the American school-girl. 'I want to be a woman because I wish to be a teacher, it is the noblest profession there is.' Others aspire to be doctors, nurses, Sisters of Mercy, and millionaires. To minister to the sick and preach the Gospel are aims which always appeal to ardent young natures. There are others who aspire to be painters, poets, politicians, professors, singers, and writers, and they express themselves very confidently that women are good at these things.

'I would rather be a woman,' writes one, 'because it is more important to be a woman than a man. Men have had chances of being great in all history, but women have not. Now women has better chances, and they will show the world what they can do. I should like to be great poet or a philosopher, like Plato.'

These aspirations contrast very strikingly with those of the meek little German girl. She humbly hoped to be pious, and a good housewife. She dared not aspire to politics, letters, art, or even music or literature.

Custom and national opinion bind the German woman closely to her kitchen, and in time she learns to like it, and to seek no other destiny. '*Nach Freiheit strebt der Mann, das Weib nach Sitte*,' says the poet, and the German girl believes it, while her bolder American sister demands both freedom and glory. Only once does a New England girl mention maternal duties. 'I wish to be a woman to educate my children; it would be my aim to make the girls brave and the boys good.'

The New England girl is engagingly frank as an idealist. She admires goodness and longs to enable it in all sorts and conditions of life, but she is by no means insensible to the glories of position and wealth. She refrains, however, from making these an end in themselves, she prefers to regard them as a means to an end, thus: – 'I wish to be Queen Victoria,[1] because she is the greatest Queen that ever was, she has beautiful jewels, and she can do much good.'

Again: – 'I should like to be the Duchess of Marlborough, because she is noble and has a high position, and she can help the people.'

The distinction of notoriety is not despised by these ambitious school-girls, thus: – 'I wish most to be Mrs Harriet Beecher Stowe, because many people all over the world admired her, and she freed the slaves.'

In considering the heroes of these American girls, we get the following: – George Washington and Miss Helen Gould head the list. The former, whose incapacity to fabricate a plausible fiction has made him a pattern for childhood, is still the hero *par excellence* of the American school-child. 'I want to be like George Washington,' writes a little maid of ten, 'because he was the greatest man in America, and he never told a lie.'

Miss Gould's wealth and good works excite much admiration. 'She has more money than anyone else, and she does good with it always,' writes one fervent admirer. The greatness of Washington and the wealth of Miss Gould come first; the veracity of the former and the benevolence of the latter are secondary considerations.

Louisa Alcott, the author of *Little Women*, comes third in the affections of the New England school girl, and truly she merits the loving admiration of all English-speaking school girls. To be thirteen years old, to have a half-holiday, and one's first introduction to *Little Women*, is an ideal state of things which rarely recurs in a lifetime. 'I would rather be Miss Louisa Alcott then anyone else, because she wrote Little Women, which is the nicest book in the world,' is a sentiment which will meet with agreement from those who remember their school girl days.

Queen Victoria and Rosa Bonheur come next in the esteem of these young people. The goodness and greatness of the English queen appeals strongly to them. 'She is the greatest Queen that ever was,' writes one, 'except Queen Elizabeth, and she is ever so much better.'

Rosa Bonheur, as an artist, is greatly admired. 'It must be beautiful to paint animals so well,' writes one. Washington's wife Martha, Mrs Beecher Stowe, M. E. Wilkins, Mrs McKinley, the Duchess of Marlborough, Mrs Vanderbilt's daughter, Mr Moody, and Longfellow are among the ideal personages of the New England school-girl.

---

1   These papers were written in November, 1900.

Several things strike one in glancing through these pages. *Firstly*, the heroes are all real personages, and tolerably modern. There is no instance of a character from literature, poetry, or remote history being held up for admiration.

Secondly, the New England girl shows no desire to fight for her country. She includes no names of Generals or warriors among her list of heroes. The province of protecting the country is evidently exclusively relegated to men.

Thirdly, the admiration shown by the American girl towards her own sex is marked and sincere. There are very few men's names among a long list of women to be emulated.

Comparing the New England school-girl with her English sister, one notices that the latter has a good deal of the adventurous spirit which the former lacks. She longs to be Nansen, and discover the North Pole; to be Columbus, and fund out new continents. She includes Wellington, Nelson and Napoleon among her heroes, and yearns to be a General and fight for her country. Again, the English school-girl has some imagination; she lacks, perhaps, the level-headedness of the Boston girl, for she includes Portia and the Sleeping Beauty among her heroes. The German girl is infinitely superior to the American, as well as the English, in the matter of sentiment and imagination. She invariably chooses her ideal of womanly excellence from history and literature. Queen Louisa, the Holy Elizabeth, Perpetua, a Vestal virgin, and the mother of Goethe are her favourites, and she chooses them for their piety, devotion, and domestic virtues. No man's name is found on the immaculate list of holy saints, pious queens, and devoted matrons whom she longs to resemble. To sum up, the New England school-girl is a practical young person with many virtues. She aches to do good, and she never undervalues herself. She is firmly persuaded that 'it is more important to be a woman than a man,' and she is determined to get her 'share of the world,' in spite of the men who own it.

The school girl from the Western States is an attractive little person, unreserved and cheerful. Her unconsciousness of sex, her enthusiasm for goodness, her fearlessness, her spontaneity, and her frankness respecting her own merits are among her characteristics. She possesses an engaging exuberance and unconventionality which is lacking in her more level-headed New England colleague, and she forms a startling contrast to the mild and impressionable German girl. Yet the piety of the school girl from Indiana is as sincere as that of the prim little German, and it is one of her greatest charms. The German nature, overflowing with sentiment, finds it hard to comprehend the cold, practical, eminently pious nature of the American, and one readily understands the perplexity of the German woman quoted by Mr Bryce, who described the American girl as *'fuchtbar frei,'* but she was compelled to add *'und fuchtbar fromm'* [*sic*]. It is precisely that naive mixture of freedom and piety which makes the American girl so charming.

There were 205 papers from school children in the West. In considering the answers to the first question, we find that only 14 per cent of these girls wish to be men, and the remaining 86 per cent, are quite content to be women.

A variety of reasons are given for wishing to be a man. Some wish to get through life easily:–

'I would rather be a man, because they have an easier time'; and 'I wish to be a man, because they have not so many responsibilities as a woman.'

Then there are those who rebel against duties which bring no material reward, thus:– 'I would rather be a man, because they don't haft to be shut up in a house, and haft to cook and wash dishes, but they does regular work they is paid for.'

There are those, too, who are sceptical as to the perfect equality of sexes in their country. Here are some examples:–

'I wish to be a man, because he always gets work quicklier, and he gets more wages.'

'I want to be a man, he has chances of being better known and being somebody.'

Some ardent souls wish for political and military distinctions.

'A man is best, he can be President, and go to war, and have offices for his country, and a woman cannot'; and another, who has little faith in her own sex, says, 'I would rather be a man, because he can fight for his country, and a woman can only talk.'

The 86 per cent who are content with a woman's portion may be classified as follows:–

35 per cent believe that their sex is superior.

25 per cent wish to escape the *monotony* and *pettiness* of men's lives.

17 per cent believe in woman's work for its own sake.

14 per cent are cautious and evade a direct reply, but they allow one to infer that the balance is in favour of a woman's lot.

These papers are certainly remarkable, and form a curious contrast to those from England, Germany, and New England. In the first place, the percentage of those who believe in the superiority of women is very high. In Germany there were none, in England about 4 per cent, in New England 14 per cent, and in Indiana 34. The obvious inference is that the women in this State are made of very good material.

Again, whereas in the other cases a certain proportion have preferred to be women in order to escape the trials and difficulties of men's lives, 20 per cent of these Western damsels wish to be women to escape from the *pettiness* and *monotony* of *men's* lives. In England the contrary was the rule.

A cursory glance at these papers convinces one that Providence is entirely on the side of the women in this part of the world.

Vanity is not a characteristic of these girls; only two mention physical attractions. One says:– 'It is nicer to be a woman, because they have long and beautiful hair'; and another remarks, 'Women have finer shapes and nicer waists than men.' Among the reasons urged to convince of woman's superiority, we get the following:–

'I want best to be a woman, because I know many good women, and it is hard to find good men.'

Again:– 'Women are more noble than men. Portia was noble and Cordelia, but Lear and Bassanio had many faults.'

Ruskin[2] says the same thing, and he proves it in the same way from literature. Chaucer, he would have us remember, wrote a 'Legend of Good Women', but no 'Legend of Good Men.' Spenser's Knights are sometimes deceived and vanquished, but Una and Britomart are invincible. Shakespeare had no heroes, only heroines; Rosalind, Cordelia, Isabella, Hermione, Desdemona are faultless, and of the highest heroic type of humanity; moreover, he shows that the catastrophe in each of Shakespeare's plays is caused by the folly of a man, and the redemption, if there be any, by the wisdom and devotion of a woman.

Surely, when Ruskin, Chaucer, Shakespeare, and the little Indiana school girl agree on this point, it is time for men to take a humbler estimate of themselves.

A glad, confident note shows itself in the assertions of these little maidens which brings hope to those of us who wait wearily for the good time coming, yet one cannot help pitying the men, now that their universe is tottering.

> 'I want to be a woman, because theirs is best; they get a good education, while the boys quit school before they ought to.'

> 'A woman has more show in society, and, as the law is now, men cannot be school-teachers, and of all occupations I like teaching.'

> 'I would rather be a woman, as they have better chances in life as teachers in public schools.'

After this one feels inclined to doubt the New England girl's statement that 'this is a man's world.'

The Indiana school girl is sweeping in her condemnations, and judging man from a religious and utilitarian standpoint, she considers him more or less of a failure. She says:– 'Women are more godly than men, and they can do better things.'

---

2 *Sesame and Lilies.*

'I would rather be a woman any day; men get drunk and steal, and they can't work or make children's clothes or do anything useful.'

'Women do not take to bad habits like men, they have moral courage.'

'Women are more industrious than men are.'

We refrain from quoting more examples. A sufficient number have been given to show the inferiority of men all along the line.

Twenty per cent could not endure the dreariness and monotony of men's lives. Women's lives, it appears, are rich in incident, full of possibilities, surprises, and chances. Men's lives, on the contrary, are dull and commonplace. This will be a revelation to those of us who have not lived in Western America.

'Women have many more pleasures and a happier life than a man.'

'Woman can go about to many places and see things; a man has to stop in a hot office.'

'Women are able to take care of themselves, and have a good time.'

'Women have good chances in life; they can be in any profession; or if they do not want to be, they can marry and do nothing.'

'Women are better educated than men; they travel more, and enjoy things better.'

Truly the American woman has much to be thankful for. The Eastern prince who remarked that if he were not himself he would choose to be born an American woman, was not lacking in intelligence.

Seventeen per cent desire to be useful as women. They have no wild ambitions, and no desire to jostle with men for elbow-room. Teaching is their favourite ambition. 'To teach school,' 'to teach in Sunday School,' and to 'be a music teacher' appeal to many of them. Some would rise to wilder heights and be musicians, painters and authors. One little girl of eleven says, 'I should like to write books. This is the best thing in the world.' There are a few timid, domestic-loving souls, even in Indiana, and the moderation of their aspirations more than makes up for the eccentricity of their spelling. Here are some of them. 'I would rather be a woman when I am grow, I like to stay home with my parents.' 'I wood rather be a woman, becourse I like to do hous-work like all woman.'

'I should rather be a woman, because I could take care of the hose-whold goods.'

And one small maid, who like St. Theresa and Dorothea Causabon, courts martyrdom, writes, 'I would rather be a woman because they suffer more than men, and it is blessed to suffer.'

Fourteen per cent are very prudent little persons. They admit both sides, with masculine caution, and evade giving any deliberate opinion in the end.

'A man make a lot of money, but a woman has more goodness,' is a non-committal statement.

'I was born a girl, and I shall have to be a woman, so there is no use in crying over spilt milk,' is a philosophical way of looking at it.

But I liked best the Mrs Poyser-like severity of the following:– 'A man can work harder, and a woman has more sense, if I wanted to be a man it would be no use, and men swear and spit on floor, so I have not lost much.'

A curious and somewhat involved speculation from a twelve year old reformer opens up wide vistas:– 'Girls grow into women, and I must. If girls grew up into men, there would be better men, for girls are better than boys.' One wonders what effect it would have on boys to bring them up as girls. Froebel went to a girls' school, and was thankful for it. He says he owed to this training the first awakening of spiritual life within him.

There is a tendency at present in favour of teaching girls the same subjects as boys, and giving them nearly as much freedom. This is called modern education. The reverse system of introducing the regulations and limitations of a ladies' boarding-school into the education of boys, so far as I know, has never been tried. There is a compromise which we call co-education, under which system boys and girls sit in the same class-rooms and study the same subjects. England is very timid in adopting it. Germany declines tampering with it, and rigidly separates the sexes both with regard to schoolroom and subjects. America believes in the system, and has adopted it with distinct advantages, it is affirmed, to both boys and girls.

'What Shall We Do With Our Daughters?' Dr Frank Crane,
Woman's World (Chicago), January 1914, p. 11

The New Question

This is a new question. Formerly the only question was: What shall we do with our sons? He had to select an occupation. It was he who had 'an aim in life.' All his school and college career was a preparation to fit him to be a doctor, lawyer, preacher or business man. But as for the girl, she had no choice. It was understood that but one thing was in store for her. She was to be somebody's wife, keep house and bring up children. That and that alone was 'her being's end and aim.' If she married well everybody congratulated her. She was successful, just as successful as a man is when he triumphs in the mercantile or professional field. She merged herself entirely into her husband's personality. This was symbolized by her dropping her own name and taking his. Any person who gave an opinion that this was not the ideal duty of every woman was looked upon askance.

The Old Idea of Educating a Girl

The education the girl received was such as to equip her for the business of wifehood and motherhood. If her folks were plain people she was taught to cook, sew and sweep. Such accomplishments would recommend her to the seeking male. She must needs be hard-working, economical, satisfied to stay at home, milk cows, look after the chickens, drive close bargains with the grocer, and attend to the children, of whom she was to have as large a number as possible. If her parents were well-to-do, she was trained in such manner as to catch a husband with money. She was sent, to a 'finishing school,' where she could be properly polished and made to shine in the eyes of society's young men. She was sent abroad to say she had been abroad. She was carefully dangled and chaperoned in those circles where the husband-fish are supposed to be plentiful and to bite freely.

Where the Old Idea Broke Down

This theory was not without its good results. Many happy and useful lives with developed under it. But the difficulty with the system was that not every woman was suited to marriage, not every marrying woman could find a suitable mate, and more and more young women began to rebel against the idea of waiting upon the whim and pleasure of men, waiting to be chosen as a blackberry on a bush waits to be picked. Furthermore, it had a tendency to cause her to make an unworthy match. In her fear of being an old maid she would marry a man to whom she was wholly unsuited. She would be inclined to accept the first offer. She would cheapen herself. She would descend to arts and tricks not consistent with high character. Besides it rendered the men egotistic, and sometimes tyrannical. The whole system was vitiated with quite too many shipwrecks.

The New Spirit of the Times

Added to this, there has come, within the last generation, a change in the Spirit of the Times. There has been a remarkable development of independence among the women of the civilized world, noticeable not only in America, but in Europe. It has had many forms of manifestation. Thousands of young women have invaded business, and are employed in offices as stenographers, typists and bookkeepers. The profession of school-teaching has been monopolized by women. More and more women are engaged in private business, such as storekeeping and clerkship. The majority of our magazine literature is written by women. The graduating classes of our high schools are girls three to one, showing that the feminine sex is going in more for that work which calls for education, while boys still slump out before graduation, and are satisfied with inferior occupation. Women's clubs have multiplied; hardly a small town is without one; and the women are studying political economy, literature, art and all the things once supposed to be the peculiar concern of men. There are as many famous actresses as actor stars. There is the suffragette movement in England, the feminist cause in France, the Woman's Rights campaign in America. In many of the states of America women have equal franchise with men. There are even woman juries, woman policemen, woman political officials.

Good Effects of the New Movement

The only issue then is: What will be the influence of the modern emancipation of women upon marriage and the family life? In the long run it will be good. Things will adjust themselves to the new conditions. One beneficial effect will be the demand for a higher standard among men. The independent young women will scorn the dissolute suitor, even as a self-respecting young man now hesitates to take to wife a woman with a shady past. This 'double standard' for men and women will cease. The more independent economically a woman is, also the more likely she is to make a better choice of a life-partner. Many and many a girl has married because it was that or starvation – or worse. If she can support herself in decency and comfort by her own efforts, a girl is not going to marry until she is reasonably sure that such a step will increase her happiness. In fine, the modern self-supporting young woman is far more likely to drive a better bargain in the marriage mart than did her helpless, dependent sister of yesterday.

Better Trained Women, Better Marriages

There are many tragic homes, many a dull, drab life where a woman's soul is crushed, her spirit broken, her heart dead, all under the cover of marriage, simply because she has been under the ancient grip of old notions of utter subservience. A woman is not a man's slave: she is his equal. The modern woman is going to assert this. The outcome will be more happiness all around. Will there be fewer marriages? Will there be fewer children? We need not trouble ourselves about such matters. They are in the hands of Nature, or better say God. There may be fewer sordid marriages, fewer brutal matings, fewer wretched economic refugees; but what marriages there are will be more and more intelligent, eugenic, idealized and productive of daily contentment, in proportion as the woman is FREE to choose or reject.

WHAT SHALL WE DO WITH OUR DAUGHTERS?

What to Do with Our Girl

What, then, shall we do with our girl? We must educate her; train her hand and head, so that she will be no mere 'commodity' in the marriage market. We must encourage her, as well as her brother, to have some 'aim in life,' some occupation in which, if need be, she can earn an honest living. She must not be a helpless dependent. Her body and soul are hers to GIVE to the right man, never to SELL. We must teach her, preferably in the sanctity of the family, the laws of sex. We must no more confound ignorance with innocence. We dare not send her out into the world a lamb among wolves. We must teach her that while the time will never come when the noblest, happiest career for a woman is elsewhere than by the side of the man she loves, and ruling over their children in the home, yet the best preparation and insurance for this, is to be so equipped that when the time comes to say yes or no to the demand of love there shall be no economic pressure, no social influence, nothing to stain the perfect purity of the uncompelled choice of the heart.

8

CHRISTMAS

Christmas magazines were richly illustrated and brimming with tips and clichés for the festive season. Rituals and recipes were rehearsed; even the fiction was customised, summarised by the editor of the *Gentlewoman*'s children's page who was assessing results of a story-writing competition: 'the majority of you find such difficulty in getting away from the stereotype characters and plots of the season. I cannot tell you how many unhappy mothers and grandchildren have been forgiven by a stern grandparent and driven away into wealth and happiness on Christmas Eve. Several heroes, too, reported dead have returned to their families. This is all very natural, but I don't like you to kill quite so many good little children by either starvation or snowdrifts. A Christmas story may be pathetic, but I really think it ought to end well' (12 January 1901, p. 63). The journalist's quest for the new could yield comfortably to the guaranteed pleasure of the familiar.

No Christmas issue was complete without reference to plum pudding. 'Mrs. Beeton's Unrivalled Plum Pudding' was made as follows:

Stone and chop a pound and a half of the best muscatel raisins, wash and dry a pound and three-quarters of currants, and cut six ounces of citron peel into thin slices. Mix these with a pound of sultanas, two pounds of moist sugar, two pounds of bread-crumbs, and two pounds of finely chopped suet. Moisten with sixteen well-beaten eggs; strain these into the pudding. Add a gill of brandy, and if the pudding is not sufficiently moist, add a little bottled beer. Turn the mixture into a well-buttered pudding mould; cover with a buttered and floured cloth, and boil for ten hours. If preferred, the pudding may be cooked first for six or seven hours, and when required for table boiled again for three hours. When the pudding is turned out decorate it with blanched and sliced almonds, and stick a sprig of holly in the centre. It is generally sent to table alight with burning whiskey or rum. Pour the rum round the pudding on the hot dish, and apply a match to it outside the dining-room door (*Woman's Life*, 15 December 1900).

How labour intensive the season was for women is illustrated by all the articles reprinted here, from Elizabeth Cady Stanton's romanticised *Mayflower* account to the final facetious piece about Christmas cards.

Seasonal gifts were as overt in their promulgation of stereotype as the seasonal fiction. The author of 'Filling the Xmas Stocking' for the Chicago *Woman's World* in December 1915 illustrates this: 'The little girl who loves to pin bits of cloth about her dolly's shoulders will go into ecstasies over a shoe box or a doll's trunk full of pieces of cloth, bits of lace and ribbon. But her happiness will be quite complete if you tuck down in the bottom of that receptacle a set of paper patterns such as you set by for yourself of simple garments that will fit the doll. . . . And the best of such a gift is that it develops ability along a line that will be of lasting benefit to her' (p. 22).

In Britain the centuries closed and opened on 'the saddest and dreariest Christmas Day within the memory of many living, and perhaps to be only equalled . . . by the heavy Christmastide of 1855, when the country was on the rack with anxiety for men far away in the Crimea, even as it is now for those in South Africa' (*Queen*, 6 January 1900). But a latent opportunity for novelty in this situation was seized by the tipster on 'How Children Can Decorate The Christmas Table' in the *Woman's Life* of 9 December 1899. Imperialist ideology was brought to the dinner table which was literally to be decked out as a battle zone, Union Jacks flying from forts made of Christmas crackers. 'The tablecloth can be spread early in the morning and let the boys take all the trouble of its decoration for Christmas off our hands. Let them draw up their soldiers in battle array, build forts of the crackers, hedges and ambuscades with the holly.' The inspiration for this came from 'these little "generals" . . . poring over piles of old daily papers containing plans of recent battles and skirmishes.'

'Christmas on *The Mayflower*,' Elizabeth Cady Stanton,
Woman's Journal (Boston), 29 December 1900, p. 411

While yet at sea, the mothers began to discuss the probabilities of reaching land by Dec. 25, and having some little celebration for the children, as they had half a dozen on board of the right age to enjoy some holiday performances. The foremothers who came from Holland had imbibed Dutch love for festive occasions, and were more liberal in their views than the rigid Puritans direct from England, who objected to all the legends of old saint Nicholas. But Elder Brewster, then seventy-nine years old, and loving children tenderly, gave his vote for the celebration. Accordingly, as they sailed up the beautiful harbor of Plymouth, the mothers were busy in their preparations for the glad day. Knowing the fondness of Indians for beads, they had brought a large box of all sizes and colors, which they were stringing for the little Indians, as they intended to invite a few of them to come on board the ship. The mothers had

225

also brought a barrel full of ivy, holly, laurel, and immortelles to decorate their log cabins. Of these they made wreaths to ornament the children and the saloon.

As soon as the *Mayflower* cast anchor, Elder Brewster and his interpreter, and as many of the fathers and mothers as the little boats would hold, went ashore to make arrangements about their cabins, to visit the squaws and invite the children. The interpreter explained to them the meaning of Christmas, the custom of exchanging gifts, etc., and they readily accepted the invitation. Massasoit was sachem of the Wampanoags and chief at this point. The yellow fever had reduced his tribe, once estimated at thirty thousand, to three hundred, now scattered all along the southern coast of Massachusetts.

When the Pilgrims landed there were only a few huts at that point. But the noble chief Massasoit was there, fortunately for our little colony, consisting only of one hundred and two, all told – men, women, and children. Massasoit was a splendid specimen of manhood, honest, benevolent, and he loved peace. When Christmas dawned, bright and beautiful, he came on board with two squaws and six little boys and girls, all in their ornaments, paint and feathers, the children in bright scarlet blankets, and caps made of white rabbit skins, the little ears standing upon their foreheads, and squirrel tales hanging down their backs. Each one carried a small basket containing beech and hickory nuts and wintergreen berries, which they presented gracefully to the English children standing in line ready to receive them. The interpreter had taught them to say 'Happy to see you,' 'Welcome,' and 'Farewell,' in the Indian tongue. So they shook hands and received the natives graciously, presenting them, in turn, with little tin pails filled with fried cakes, almonds and raisins, some bright English pennies, a horn and a drum. The mothers tied strings of beads around their necks, wrists, and ankles, with which they were greatly pleased.

They went all over the ship, and asked many questions about all they saw. When Massasoit proposed to go, the mothers urged him to stay to dinner, but he declined, saying that they did not understand English customs in eating, and that the children would not know how to use knives, forks, and spoons. Moreover, he said that they never ate except when they were hungry, and the sun was still too high for that.

The exchanging of presents was a very pretty ceremony, and when they were ready to depart, the good elder placed his hands on each little head, giving a short prayer and his blessing. While all this was transpiring, the squaws asked the foremothers to give them beads, which they readily did, and placed wreaths of ivy on their heads. As they paddled away in their little canoes, the horns and drums sounded.

Then the mothers decorated their tables and spread out a grand Christmas dinner. Among other things they brought a box of plum puddings. It is an English custom to make a large number of plum puddings at Christmas time, and shut them up tight in small tin pails and hang them on hooks on the kitchen wall, where they keep for months. You see them in English kitchens to this day. With their plum puddings, gooseberry tarts, Brussels sprouts, salt fish and bacon, the Pilgrims had quite a sumptuous dinner. Then they sang 'God save the King,' and went on deck to watch the sun go down and the moon rise in all her glory.

The children took their little baskets to their berths, the last objects of interest on which their eyes rested as they fell asleep.

'Cookery. Menu for a Christmas Supper,' *Woman at Home* (London), December 1899, pp. 341–2

Roast Sucking Pig. Chestnut Sauce.
Grilled Goose.
Game Fritters. Filleted Teal.
Savoury Potatoes. Stuffed Cucumber.
Pears in Jelly. Spanish Cream.
Queen Tart.
Cheese Meringues.
Indian Craipe Toast.

SUCKING PIG

Truss like a hare (after wiping thoroughly and stuffing according to taste), and rub over with clarified butter or fresh salad oil before roasting. When done enough cut off the head before the pig is taken from the fire. Take out the brains and chop them up quickly with the stuffing; add the gravy which has dropped from the pig and a little more stock. If preferred the brains may be stirred into melted butter instead of gravy, or they may be put under the head on the dish. A sucking pig to be eaten in perfection should not be more than three weeks old, and should be dressed the same day it is killed. Average cost, 6s.

CHESTNUT SAUCE

Peel off the outside skin of the chestnuts and put them into boiling water for a few minutes; take off the thin inside peel, and put them into a saucepan with a little white stock and a strip of lemon peel, and simmer for half an hour. Rub the whole through a hair sieve with a wooden spoon, and add a quarter pint of milk and seasoning. Let it simmer (not boil) for a few moments, and serve quickly. Cost, about 8d.

GRILLED GOOSE

Dip the cooked pieces (legs and back are most suitable) into warm butter, and score them, season with salt, cayenne and mustard, and a pinch of sage; coat the breadcrumbs and again dip into butter. Lay them on a gridiron (greased) and turn them about until heated through and well browned. A good sauce is made by boiling up a glass of claret with a chopped shallot, a sage leaf, and a morsel of French mustard. It is then strained and mixed with enough hot brown sauce to thicken it. Cost, including sauce 5s.

GAME FRITTERS

Take any kind of cold roast game (about 1lb), and free it from skin and gristle; chop finely with half a dozen mushrooms, three shallots, and the rind of half a lemon. Season with salt, pepper, grated nutmeg, sweet thyme and marjoram. Mix thoroughly, then add 4 eggs well beaten, and shape the mixture into balls. Dip in prepared butter, and fry in clarified butter. Cost, about 3s.

FILLETED TEAL

Half roast the birds, cut into fillets and stew for ten minutes in brown gravy, flavoured with lemon juice. Pour the gravy over the birds and serve mushroom sauce with them. Garnish with watercress and form the fillets into a pyramid. Cost for two birds, 3s. 6d.

SAVOURY POTATOES

Rasp 12 medium sized potatoes, cut off a small piece at the top and scoop out the centre, but be careful not to break them. Prepare a stuffing with a mixture of breadcrumbs, chopped parsley, thyme chives and shallots. Season with salt and pepper, and moisten with a spoonful of milk and yolk of egg.

Fill the potatoes with the stuffing, and brush with oiled butter; bake in a moderate oven for twenty minutes. Cost 1s.

STUFFED CUCUMBER

Scrape the green rind off two large cucumbers, cut into pieces about three inches in length, stamp out gently the centre with a round cutter.

Fill with stuffing of cooked beef or veal, breadcrumbs, and two eggs well beaten. Cover the ends with thin slices of bacon, which tie on with a string; let them stew gently with a little stock until quite tender. Cost, inclusive, 2s.

PEARS IN JELLY

Ingredients required are: half packet of gelatine, 1 large cupful of sugar, 6 large pears, 1 lemon, a pinch of cinnamon, and a cupful of cold water. Peel, core, and slice the pears into very cold water. Before they can change colour pack them very closely in a glass or stone jar, with just sufficient water to cover them, put on a loose lid, that the steam may not crack the jar, set in cold water almost up to the neck, and cook until the pears are clear and very tender.

Soak the gelatine for two hours in a cupful of cold water, add the lemon juice and peel, sugar and cinnamon. Make hot and pour over the pears. Leave to set and serve with

SPANISH CREAM

Beat the yolks of 6 eggs with 8 tablespoonfuls of sugar. Have ready an ounce of gelatine soaked in three pints of milk for an hour. Stir this in the egg mixture, and let it simmer for a short time; then take off the fire and stir in the whites of the eggs beaten to a froth. Flavour with lemon or vanilla. Cost of jelly and cream, 3s.

QUEEN TART

Cover a tart pan with puff paste, stew some apples very soft, and rub them through a sieve; sweeten them and put them in the paste; make a custard with half a pint of good milk, flavoured to taste; when it boils stir in the yolks of three eggs, and pour over the apples as soon as it thickens.

Beat the whites of 8 eggs to a very stiff froth, and spread it over the custard, sift fine sugar on to it, and bake in the over for about 20 minutes. Average cost, 2s.

CHEESE MERINGUES

Whisk the white of 3 eggs to a stiff froth, stir in gently three tablespoonfuls of Parmesan cheese, a pinch of salt, and a little cayenne pepper. Have ready some boiling butter, drop the mixture from a dessert-spoon into the butter. Fry a light-brown colour. Cost about 9d.

INDIAN CRAIPE TOAST

Take 3 well-beaten eggs, a finely cut green chilli, pulp of 2 ripe tomatoes, an ounce of butter, and a little cream. Season with salt and pepper. Put in a stew-pan over a quick fire. Stir until set; spread on hot buttered toast and serve. Cost 8d.

COST OF SUPPER, One Pound, seven shillings and seven pence.

'How to Dress a Christmas Tree for Thirty Shillings,'
Woman's Life (London), 22 December 1900, pp. 130–32

Many children's parties will be in progress during this festive season, and no children's gathering at Christmas-tide is complete without the mystic tree, a veritable growth from fairyland.

Father Christmas, dressed up like his pictures, with his sack on his back, or Santa Claus, with his bag of toys, may be very fair substitutes, but they are never equal to the Christmas-tree in their power to produce a very deep delight.

There is the pleasure of preparation, too, on the part of the feast-givers, and the delirium of anticipation on the part of the small guests as the time draws near for the wonderful candle-bearing tree to be lit up.

The tree should, if possible, be kept in a separate room until the time for lighting it up. A recess, curtained off, will do very well; or a screen may be used to hide the enchanting branches until the time for showing it arrives.

The tree must be completely dressed before any of the guests come. It should contain at least one present each for the children – that needs no saying. If more than one gift is arranged for, then the number for each child must be equal. It is wonderful what jealousy is aroused even in small morsels of humanity by an unequal distribution of presents.

The presents must be labelled with the name of its recipient. The children are then given the exquisite joy of searching the gifts on a laden tree for their own names. The method of ticketing the gifts with a number and then indiscriminately giving the children numbers to correspond is disappointing, as the presents are invariably misbestowed, boys getting girls' gifts and *vice versa*. The numbering will do if the numbers are assigned with care, thus, 'Mary Jones to have No. 1 gift,' and so on.

Even a very little tree, lighted up with a few penny-worths of candles and decked with a few sweets, ornaments, and toys, will give immense pleasure, costing little. The writer has decked many trees for whole roomfuls of school children, and would like to detail the method of cheaply producing a brilliant tree.

Thirty shillings has been chosen as a fair estimate of the amount average people who give children's parties at Christmas might care to spend on the tree. Such a tree would serve quite twenty children. Of course, the amounts may be halved or divided into thirds, if the quantities named are proportionately lessened. A sixth of the sum is allowed for the tree itself, and about a fifth for toys. Most people who intend to have a Christmas-tree, however, prepare small, home-made presents for it, thus augmenting the number of toys. For instance, woolen balls are easily netted. The tinsel paper that comes with tea sometimes should be saved and wrapped round a tight little rag ball, which is then netted over with bright wool, and has attached to it a length of round elastic. These are very bright additions to the tree. Also small essence bottles may be saved from the kitchen, filled with sweets, and laid by, ready to be hung by their necks from the branches. Cachous or similar small sweets fill them nicely. Pretty cardboard boxes may be bought cheaply from drapers or confectioners. They may be covered with the bright scraps known as 'transfers,' and filled with chocolate or butterscotch. Scrap-books filled with bright pictures and tied up with bright ribbon make very acceptable toys also. Pin cushions, stuck with pins, are gay too.

The following is the list of articles required:

	s	d
3 doz coloured candles, farthing size	0	9
1 doz coloured candles, halfpenny size	0	6
1 doz glass ornaments, halfpenny size	0	6
1 doz glass ornaments, penny size	1	0
2 packets of frosting powder	0	2
Cotton-wool to imitate snowflakes	0	2
Wire to attach articles to tree	0	3
1 roll crinkled or crêpe paper to hide pot	0	4
Tissue paper in four colours	0	6
Narrow ribbon in assorted colours	0	6
2 doz sugar pigs, halfpenny size	1	0
1 doz sugar pigs, penny size	1	0
1 doz assorted animals, sugar mice, &c	1	0
½ doz Father Christmases, sugar or plaster	0	6
1 doz flags, gelatine composition	0	6
1 doz Christmas stockings, containing sweets and toys, penny size	1	0
½ doz stockings, twopenny size	1	0
1 doz muslin bags of sweets	1	0
1 doz apples, bright and red	1	0
1½ doz oranges	1	0
1 doz boxes of chocolate, assorted shapes, and threepenny size	3	0
Assorted toys of various sorts	6	0
1 box of coloured crackers	2	6

		s	d
	1	5	0
Cost of tree, six or seven feet, in pot		5	0
TOTAL	1	10	0

The toys should include horns, whistles, drums, boxes of marbles, boxes of soldiers, animals with woolly bodies and moveable heads, shuttlecocks – these can be bought cheaply in their season, just before Easter, and kept for the Christmas tree – books, games, and so forth. Holly berries may also be used to brighten the branches. The gay crêpe paper is pleated round the pot, and cotton wool is used to cover the earth in it. Flakes of the cotton wool may be scattered over the tree also, but as it is very inflammable care must be taken to keep it away from the tiny candles. Watch must be kept over the candles when they are lit in order that as they burn down no branch or toy may catch fire. The smallest size of candle will, however burn for an hour if there is no draught. The tissue paper is used to make fancy paper balls to hang on the tree, also to wrap up small mysterious presents.

'Amusing Xmas Games for Little People,' *Woman's Life*
(London), 9 December 1899, pp. 48–9

Penny Bun

'Penny Bun' is a game which necessitates a good deal of running about, and is therefore a great favourite with children.

One player comes to a shop to buy a penny bun. He finds the baker, and behind him, in a row, holding on to one another's dresses are the macaroon, the cheesecake, the sponge-cake, and all the other kinds of cakes.

But the buyer does not want any of them; he 'must' have the plain penny bun, which is at the very end of the row.

The baker will not be disturbed for such a small matter; he says the buyer must fetch his bun for himself. 'But where is it?' says the poor buyer. Then the baker says it is on the table, or under the carpet, or on the shelf, but the buyer is not satisfied.

At last the baker says: 'It is at the back of the oven,' off starts the buyer to seize his bun, and off starts the bun, running up the other side of the row to reach the baker. Of course, the cakes won't allow the buyer to pass through them, so he has to run all the way round.

If he catches the bun before it reaches the baker he takes the baker's place, and the bun becomes the buyer; but if he is too late he has to pay a forfeit and try again, while the little bun turns into the baker, and the last of the row becomes the bun.

The Surprise

All the children except one stand in a circle with their hands behind them, the palms turned outwards. All keep their eyes fixed on the ground, for if they looked up a forfeit would be the punishment.

The one who is left out runs round and round the circle carrying a handkerchief, which, after a time, he quietly slips into the hand of one of those in the circle, who, without saying a word, immediately touches with it another of the players.

The one touched must run away as quickly as possible, and is pursued by the handkerchief bearer, who has been on the look-out to see who would be touched by the handkerchief.

If the pursuer catches the runaway they change places, but if the fugitive can reach his or her place in the circle untouched the handkerchief bearer must pay a forfeit.

The players are obliged to pay the greatest attention to the game, for they must be prepared to run away at any moment, as they cannot tell to whom the handkerchief has been given. The 'Surprise' is a good name for this game.

Fox in the Den

A 'Home' is marked out at each end of the room or playground; one for the fox's den, the other for the chicken's yard. The fox hides himself under a rug in his den. Up comes the hen and her chickens, all in a row, holding on to one another.

'Pray, Mr Fox,' says the hen, 'can you tell me what time it is?'

The fox begins to count; 'One, two, three,' etc.; the hen and her chickens are quite safe until he says, 'Twelve o'clock at night;' then he rushes out to seize them and they all disperse, to run as fast as they can to their yard.

Sometimes the fox says, 'Twelve o'clock noon,' and they know they are safe, for he cannot venture out in the daytime. Sometimes he counts very slowly, and then suddenly calls out, 'Twelve o'clock at night,' darting at the same time out of his den.

As soon as a chicken is caught it has to take the fox's place, while the fox becomes one of the chickens.

Beating the Drum

All the players stand or sit in a row, each pretending to play some chosen instrument, such as the trombone, violin, or trumpet. The leader, either at the head or in front of the row, officiates with the big drum. Occasionally, for a variety, they all jump up and walk round in a ring.

During the whole game they sing in lively strains:

'Sandy he belongs to the mill,

And the mill belongs to Sandy still'

Suddenly the drummer ceases to beat his drum and begins instead to imitate the instrument of some member of his band, who must immediately cease playing his own instrument and start beating the drum.

As soon as he sees fit, the leader again begins beating the drum, whereupon the player, whose functions he has been usurping, goes back to his own instrument. All must keep their eyes fixed on the leader, for a forfeit must be paid by each player who fails to beat the drum or take up his own instrument at the right moment.

The song must be kept up without intermission, and no laughing is allowed.

'The Christmas Card Craze,' Mrs E. T. Cook, *Woman at Home* (London), December 1899, pp. 245–51

Little bits of paper	Of all the joys of Christmas Day,
Scattered through the land	One joy's as good as any
Make the postman crusty	That friendships may be tinkered, say,
And the shopman bland	At cost of but a penny.

Every year it is prophesied anew that 'Christmas cards are going out,' that the fashion is slowly but surely dying: but I for my part must confess that I see nothing of it. Indeed, much as I myself abhor these unmeaning bits of paste-board, much as I dislike to see them littering the rooms for weeks after Christmas (grimy, faded, and dirty with the 'decorative' (?) mistletoe and holly, till at length a merciful waste-paper basket receives them), yet, inconsistent as it seems, I too must confess if deprived of my fair share of them – to a feeling of something like shame, the feeling that 'one card does not make a Christmas.' Although this fashion of sending Christmas cards (to quote Montaigne), 'like all several, strange, and particular fashions, proceed rather of folly or ambitious affectation than of true reason,' yet, being but a very ordinary mortal, I strive, with Poins, to 'think as every man thinks'; nay, I flatter myself that 'ne'er a man's (or woman's) thought in the world keeps the roadway better than mine.' Therefore I yield to the craze, and dutifully send Christmas cards to my acquaintance. Therefore, again, on a 'drear-nighted' (and yellow-fogged) December, I sallied forth on their quest.

But, first, I must state that, being of an economical turn of mind, I did not go out to spend without duly considering whether any of my old cards would not, as the phrase goes, 'do send on.' I had got out my last year's hoards, and had cogitated deeply over them. But some were too dirty; many (alas!) had the sender's name thoughtlessly inscribed on them *in ink*! (it is a cruel thing to write on a Christmas card; if you are ever tempted to do so, let it be only with the erasible pencil!); some were too deeply religious; a few were meant to be comic; while the rest were of so gloomy a tendency that I could not prevail on myself to afflict my acquaintance with them! I do not know why my friends have always thought a desolate graveyard scene, with lurid storm-clouds, or a leafless branch with owls, to be especially appropriate to me. It is true that

I do not come of a long-lived family and that I am a good deal alone; but for these very reasons I fail to see why I should receive such gloomy offerings, coupled, too, with verses about 'a silver lining to every cloud,' 'resignation under affliction,' and the like, instead of just the old-fashioned and seasonable 'Merry Christmas.' I counted as many as twenty tombstones, to say nothing of owls, in my private collection, and put them aside, with the religious cards, for the children's hospital. Perhaps the children may be able to bear up against them, or they may have a less depressing effect when pasted into a scrap-book! I *did* also find, among my private hoards, three cards representing respectively three fishes (apparently sardines) of different sizes, two kangaroos holding sunshades, and five fat pugs sitting in a row on a stile. But these struck me as simply flippant; so I put them all away as useless, and, as I said, started bravely in search of new material. [. . .]

Well I reached home at last, but my troubles were, alas! not ended. In the sanctity of my own abode I examined my purchases, and discovered that in the hurry and flurry of the transactions (I was never 'a good shopper') I had somehow got hold of some very extraordinary cards – among others a fat woman bicycling in scarlet bloomers, a tipsy policeman swaggering down a street, an elephant trying to skate, and a greedy boy apparently suffering from too much Christmas dinner! These seemed hopeless! I don't know what was their final destination (their sending may, indeed have cost me several friend-ships, who knows?), but at the end of a long day's struggle with stationery and address-book, I was – joyful thought! – 'free' of Christmas, so to speak, for the space of another year!

And yet, am I *really* yet free to repose on my laurels? For Christmas Day approaches, and I know, alas! beforehand, that it will be my fate to receive cards from all the friends to whom I have omitted to send them, and to be forgotten by most of those to whom I *have* sent. Such is life! And I also know instinctively that my old Aunt Susan, whose income is in thousands, will 'save an honest penny' by sending me on a card sent her by somebody else. I may think myself lucky (as she is very blind) if it have not 'To dear Susan, with fondest love' already inscribed on it! Or perhaps, I may again, as last year – who knows? – receive a card back that I know for a fact to have sent to the generous donor the year before! Some cards, like the famous Ring of Polycrates, seem hard to get rid of. I hope it may not be my fate to receive back the bicycling female in bloomers; but as curses, like pigeons, come home to roost, so also may Christmas cards!

And then one may also expect minor evils. I have not forgotten that last year my parlourmaid went about with red eyes for a week because she darkly suspected her 'young man' of having sent her '*the* most insulting Christmas card I ever got,' while the cook spoiled the dinner in her fury at having been sent the picture of a drunken soldier in a red coat!

Perhaps, however, one can hardly call these great afflictions; and then there is another side to the Christmas-card craze. Friendships may be made and mended, as well as marred, by the judicious use of the Christmas card. The craze will surely never entirely disappear, for it is too convenient a way of picking up again the ravelled threads of acquaintance and interest to be lightly discarded. The repairing is really cheaply done at 1d., or to be lavish (and the 1/2d stamp for postage is in my opinion a mistake), 2d. the friendship! Surely these are cogent reasons for continuing the custom; if there chance unluckily to be a few quarrels, 'What else,' as the cockney says, 'can ye expect er Chrismus?' But apart from any other reason, 'What' (as an old charwoman of my acquaintance is wont to remark) 'would Christmas be without Christmas cards?'

9

ADVERTISING

Advertisements provided women's magazines and journals with essential income. 'It is from the high price charged for advertising space that the harvest is reaped. We shall be within the mark if we put the advertisements of the *Queen* at £1,000 a week. Its importance to trade may be gauged by the fact that while at the beginning of its career [1861], the outside sheet was let out for £10, the price has crept up, till it now commands £40 or even £50' claimed Evelyn March-Phillips in the *Fortnightly Review* of November 1894 ('Women's Newspapers', p. 663). But the balance between advertising revenue and cost of production had to be carefully struck: 'if a paper, which is sold under the cost of production, is made to pay by advertisements, every copy sold reduces the profits, so that circulation beyond a certain point would be fatal. On the other hand, if the trade is not satisfied that circulation is pushed sufficiently to recompense its outlay, the advertisements will fall off' continued March-Phillips. This was the case for every profit-making newspaper, whatever its readership.

Yet it seems that the aggressive marketing of both journal and advertised product selected women as targets particularly susceptible to tabloid page layout and the commercial 'information' offered in this way. There was sometimes little difference between the snippets of news, gossip or fashion talk typical of such papers as the commercial giant *Tit-Bits*, and the advertisements it carried. The easy assimilation of both newspaper text and advertisement was one way of coaxing the reader to buy both products. Equally, for journals catering to more intellectual readers, advertisements could masquerade as news features, textually and visually indistinguishable from real news items.

Three examples of these are given here, 'Ladies who Preach', 'Gentlewomen in Business' and 'Girls that Whistle'. These sophisticated adverts toy with the intelligent self-image of the projected reader and deploy tactics of 'new journalism', such as interviews and first-person authority coupled with intimacy, to strike a relationship with the reader. But while that relationship is struck initially with a type of woman who defies her traditional gender role by preaching, business, or whistling, the identity and valorisation of these defiant types and their counterparts in the reader, alter through the course of the advert. The independent woman is thoroughly parodied by the end: the advert tells her that she is incomplete without, for example, Pink Pills For Pale People. Furthermore, the advert has a disturbing narrative structure and message not unlike the story 'The Courtship of Lord Arthur Armstrong' (pp. 39ff.).

The likeness between journalism and advertising copy can also be seen from their function in facilitating dialogue between editor and reader. In December 1901 Edward Bok, editor of the *Ladies' Home Journal* decided to share some of his post bag:

Many of you have written that you do not like some of the corset advertisements which appear in THE JOURNAL. You say advertisements illustrated in the manner in which they are have no place in a home periodical which is open to the reading of both sexes. But there is another side to the question: the argument that a woman's magazine is essentially the medium of all mediums in which it is perfectly permissible to print such advertisements and present them according to modern ideas of illustration. The honesty at least of that decision will be perhaps better understood when it is more clearly known how far away from commercialism the advertising department of THE JOURNAL is conducted. To understand this, suppose you look over the advertising pages of any of the high-class magazines of to-day – the highest in standing, in your estimation, if you please. You will find in all of them page after page of advertisements which have been offered to THE JOURNAL and declined. Keeping within the safest limits of assertion, there is more than one thousand dollars of advertising to-day which THE JOURNAL could have each year by a simple nod of the head, but which it has refused year after year. You never see a patent medicine advertisement in THE JOURNAL, and yet this line of advertising is one of the largest sources of income to all the other magazines. Not another magazine refuses this type of advertising. You never find a liquor advertisement in THE JOURNAL, although scores are offered to it. Nor a mining, real-estate investment or financial advertisement. For the slightest objectionable wording the most profitable advertisement is rejected. All this advertising THE JOURNAL could have just as well as not. It is offered to it often enough. I mention these facts because they are not generally known to our readers, and principally to prove one fact: that the insertion of illustrated corset advertising in this magazine is not based on financial consideration. Right or wrong it is here because of an honest conviction of the department which governs such things that it should be there.

The high moral tone of this comment might make the reader feel good but it contradicts the statement made at the beginning of the same editorial that 'a magazine is purely a business proposition' and that as the editor succeeds or fails to attract subscribers so the 'magazine secures or fails to secure an

7 'Featherstone Bicycles'

advertising patronage.' At least the offending image of woman's body has a rational place in corset advertising, unlike its role in the man's bicycle advert from *Cosmopolitan* pictured here. The extravagant Mucha style image of the female form signals the objectification of woman's body that would become a dominant trope of advertising as the twentieth century wore on. The 'Ell-Arr' corset manages its point without representation of body or corset, although the 'new century' claim is as randomly significant as the link between ladies who preach and Pink Pills for Pale People. The languid and overdressed

NEW STATIONERY FOR THE NEW CENTURY.

EMBOSSED OR PRINTED
NOTE PAPERS.
WRITE FOR SAMPLES.

WEDDING STATIONERY.
VISITING CARDS.
DANCE PROGRAMMES.

SHARP WALKER AND Cº, 259, HIGH HOLBORN, LONDON.

The Cook's Right Hand.

Bovril is the cook's right hand. It adds a delicious savour to all kinds of "made" dishes, whether of meat, poultry, or game. With Bovril the most inexpensive dish becomes a luxury, and for making nourishing soups and gravies Bovril is in almost universal use.

Bovril possesses both stimulating and strengthening properties in the highest degree. It is warmth-giving and sustaining. A cup of hot Bovril between meals is an invaluable safeguard against the effects of cold and chills.

Begin the Century with it.

If you start the

New Century

right, by wearing a

New Corset

you will appreciate

New Comfort

such as only the

'Ell=Arr' Corsets

can give you. Their

New Features

are best seen in the

New Models—

"MĪPHANSI" Corset, 6/11.

"AZŪLĪKIT" Corset, 8/11.

❧

These tell of value in a

New Way.

❧

Ask to see them at your Drapers.

8 'New Stationery for
the New Century';
'Bovril'; 'Ell-Arr
Corsets'

eroticism of the model's pose for the 'Specialité Corset' does raise the question: for whom is it a 'dream of comfort'?   This was also the era when the advertising jingle began to develop, as for example in the infantilising nursery rhyme:

Mistress Mary quite contrary
How does your garden grow?
No doctor's bill for Cockle's Pills
Keep pretty maids all of a glow.
(*Gentlewoman*, 5 January 1901,
p. xl)

Whatever our cynical interpretation of these advertising styles may be today, in their own day they were welcomed by readers, not just as entertaining diversion but as useful information. 'They are my walk down Bond Street,' March-Phillips quotes one provincial girl as saying about advertisements, and

9 'The Specialité Corset'

she continues with the claim that the ladies' illustrated papers 'constitute a species of perambulating shop, in which the wares are set forth by means of print and picture.'

'Ladies who Preach', *Woman's Signal* (London),
20 October 1898, p. 255

Formerly a lady preacher was looked upon as little short of a phenomenon; and it yet remained somewhat of a novelty to hear that 'Miss Velvick, of St. Michael's, would occupy the pulpit of Bethersden Wesleyan Chapel on Sunday next.' Such an announcement made during a recent month drew large congregations.

The lady preacher, Miss Bessie Velvick, was seen and gave some particulars of her career, a few days before the event alluded to, to a newspaper man, at Tenterden, Kent, where her parents have dwelt (she said) for more than thirty years. The family are well known and evidently respected by their neighbours. Miss Velvick...had formerly been an officer in the Salvation Army, reaching the rank of 'captain,' but her health broke down.

'I was at the time in south Wales,' said Miss Velvick, 'and I fell ill from an accidental fall, causing injury to the spine. That happened in April, 1896; in the previous February I had an attack of scarlet fever, which had left my back weaker than usual. In consequence of the injury I was troubled with abscesses which formed on the spine. I went as an out-patient to the Swansea Hospital, and there an operation was performed that gave me some relief. The surgeons described the formations as cancerous abscesses. They told me that I had disease of the spine commencing, and that this caused the trouble for which they operated. Perhaps the worst of the whole thing for me was the effect it had on my nerves. I could not bear to hear an organ playing or to listen to singing, and even a loud laugh in my hearing would send me into a faint.'

'Naturally, you could not preach in such a state?'

'No; I kept on as long as I possibly could, but about twelve months ago I was obliged to give it up and come home. I should tell you that after my first treatment for spinal disease, I had an attack of brain fever, which left me in a very weak state, and with my nervous system sadly out of order.'

'But it is easy to see you have recovered.'

'Yes; my improved health is due to Dr. Williams' Pink Pills for Pale People, which I began taking about three months ago, at my mother's suggestion. I was so ill that people only gave me a few weeks to live. The case of Sims Blackman here (which you published) made us think about them, and his having been cured by Dr. Williams' Pink Pills some time ago, and having kept so well since, induced me to try them, as we knew him well. By the end of the month I was considerably better. Of course, the diseased bone cannot be replaced, but I can now work, and whereas at one time I was bent nearly double, and could only walk with the aid of crutches, I can now get along well enough without any help at all.'

Miss Velvick's ability to occupy so difficult a position as the pulpit is a tribute to the steadiness of nerves which (as she mentioned in the interview above) were once utterly shattered. The complication of disorders of which she was cured by Dr. Williams' Pink Pills, aptly illustrates the two ways in which this medicine predominantly acts, viz., as a nerve tonic, and as an agent for enriching the blood. Abscesses and spinal disease have repeatedly yielded to them, and they are an ideal tonic, having no purgative effect whatever. Among other diseases they have cured are paralysis, locomotor ataxy, rheumatism, sciatica, scrofula, rickets, consumption of the bowels and lungs, anaemia, muscular weakness, indigestion, palpitations, pains in the back, nervous headache, neuralgia, all forms of female weakness, and hysteria. If there is any difficulty in obtaining the genuine pills, with Dr. Williams' name, it is better to send 2s. 9d. for one box, or 13s. 9d. for six, to Dr. Williams' Medicine Company, 46, Holborn-viaduct, London. Readers should see that the round pink package bears in red ink the full name, Dr. Williams' Pink Pills for Pale People. It is important to secure the genuine pills only, and to avoid accepting substitutes (often illusively coloured and labelled).

'Girls that Whistle', *Woman's Life* (London),
15 December 1900, p. 77

and hens that crow ought *to have their heads chopped off*; so the old saying runs. We don't endorse it, of course. We've heard girls whistle and hens crow, but we never thought of chopping their heads off. Fancy taking a pretty girl's head off! And if the hen was a good layer, even though it did crow occasionally, there's no sense in taking its head off. Certainly, whistling in girls and crowing in hens is a bit *infra dig.*, still chopping their heads off is really too drastic. A desperate disease needs a desperate remedy. Page Woodcock's Wind Pills are not a desperate remedy, but they're safe remedy and most excellent for the cure of Indigestion, Wind on the Stomach, Biliousness, Costiveness, Liver Complaints, Sick Headache, Palpitation of the Heart, Nervous Debility, etc.

A lady said to the proprietor only a few days ago: 'I have used your Wind Pills for sometime. I suffer from a peculiar form of Indigestion and Wind, which, giving me severe pain near the heart, makes me imagine I suffer from Heart Disease. Nothing relieves me so quickly as your Wind Pills. I would not be without them on any account.' This lady's name is Elizabeth Hylton, 7, Clarkston's Row, Lincoln.

Page Woodcock's Wind Pills, being purely Vegetables, Tasteless, and Mild and Tonic in their action, may be taken with perfect safety by the most delicate of either sex. Children may safely take them in reduced doses.

Page Woodcock's Wind Pills are sold by all Medicine Vendors at 1/1 ½ and 2/9; post free for price by Page Woodcock, Lincoln.

'Gentlewomen in Business', *Lady's Magazine* (London), February 1901, p. 221

What work shall I take up? is a question of most absorbing importance to a very large number of gentlewomen to-day.

Most women have wonderful powers of organisation but are not aware of it. They have always been restricted to the management of their own homes, which to the uninitiated male seems a very simple affair.

Any woman who is able to keep in order her own house, manage her servants, bring up her children, please her husband and entertain her friends, can certainly succeed in business or philanthropic undertakings.

The same common sense is needed with preliminary knowledge of the work undertaken as in housekeeping, to make any venture a success. An apprentice-ship is necessary in any business or profession, and with a reasonable amount of capital and plenty of pluck, the wide-awake and energetic woman is certain to succeed.

Let us consider what has been, and is being done, by Gentlewomen in Businesses, more especially as those applied to those enterprises in which only gentlewomen are employed both as employers and employed.

We thus at once exclude those undertakings carried on for philanthropy, for fun, or notoriety, and come to those sober enterprises initiated to profit three classes, the foundress, the employees, and women in general.

There is no more striking instance of success in an undertaking of this character than that attained by Mrs. Jeanette Pomeroy. I am thankful to say that this lady, whose name and work are now held in such high esteem among women all over the world, is a British subject.

Some years ago she studied the Face in all its phases with a view to improving the Complexion: and also surgical electricity for removing superfluous hairs and growths. Being firmly convinced of the great need existing for Hygienic Treatment of the complexion, as well as the relief of thousands of women suffering from those terrible disfigurements, superfluous hairs. Mrs. Pomeroy started at first in a small way at 29 Old Bond Street, London, but her business increased so rapidly she soon had to take two additional floors, and train one assistant after another to cope with the ever-growing number of patients who demanded this successful treatment as well as those who besieged her rooms for Electrolysis.

In so extending the sphere of her work she was actuated by the resolve to endeavour to find employment for as many gentlewomen as possible in an occupation of great usefulness to their own sex. To meet the convenience of patients residing in Ireland, Mrs. Pomeroy last year opened Rooms at 39

Grafton Street, Dublin, and installed some very capable ladies trained to the work by herself. I should mention that Mrs. Pomeroy's Toilet Preparations which enjoy such world-wide popularity, are manufactured at 29 Old Bond Street, London, under her personal supervision, by a fully qualified chemist. They are the outcome of years of study, and are the purest and most wholesome, as well as the most sensible in the world, and are absolutely harmless.

Mrs. Pomeroy's wonderful skill, great experience, honesty of purpose, her straight-forward dealing, and her excellent advice bestowed free of charge, personally or by correspondence, on all who ask for it, have placed her in the premier position in the world of Complexion Specialists. She neither attempts the unattainable, or promises the impossible, and has no patience with women who are too lazy to obey the most natural laws of Hygiene and cleanliness, but think they can be transformed into images of Venus or Diana, and made stout or thin by some quack remedy at a few shillings a bottle.

A good complexion means good health, and if you would retain either, both must be studied. 'Old age is honourable, but a dirty skin is an abomination.' When a little care will obviate such a condition, surely some trouble should be taken, if but to ask advice of those who have studied the subject for our common benefit.

10

REFERENCE

A nineteenth century bibliography of suffrage journals from the
Englishwoman's Review: 15 January 1900; 15 July 1900;
15 October 1900.

AN AMERICAN PERIODICALS BIBLIOGRAPHY

*Denotes in progress

THE UNA, 'a paper devoted to the Elevation of Women.' Mrs Paulina Wright
Davis, Editor and Proprietor. Published monthly at Providence, Rhode
Island.

1868–70   THE REVOLUTION (Weekly). Published by Miss Anthony. Edited
          by Parker Pilsbury and Mrs Stanaton. New York.
1870*   THE WOMAN'S JOURNAL. Boston, Mass. Founded in 1870 by
          Lucy Stone. Published weekly. Edited first by Mrs Livermore, Lucy
          Stone, H.B. Blackwell and Alice Stone Blackwell.
1876   THE BALLOT BOX. Published and edited by the Toledo Women's
          Suffrage Association (Ohio). Managing Editor, Sarah R.L.
          Williams. Monthly, first No., May 1876. In 1878 changed hands
          and continued as THE NATIONAL CITIZEN AND BALLOT BOX.
          Published at Syracuse, New York. Matilda Joselyn-Gage, Editor
          and Proprietor.
1883*   THE WOMAN'S TRIBUNE. Edited and published fortnightly by
          Clara Beswick Colby. (Started at Beatrice, Nebraska). Washington
          D.C.
1883*   WOMAN'S EXPONENT. Salt Lake City, Utah.
1888   THE NEW CYCLE. Published monthly as the official organ of the
          Federation of Women's Clubs. Edited by Mrs J.C. Croly. New
          York.
1890   QUEEN ISABELLA JOURNAL, issued quarterly by the Queen
          Isabella Association, to promote the Interests of Women at the
          World's Fair, 1892. Chicago.

1898   NATIONAL SUFFRAGE BULLETIN. Edited by Carrie Chapman. Catt.

GREAT BRITAIN

THE WAVERLEY JOURNAL. Of this Journal Miss Bessie Rayner Parkes (Madame Belloc) wrote in her Essays on Women's Work, 1865 (page 61):–

It was in October 1856, that a stray number of a periodical, professing to be edited by ladies, caught my eye in the window of a small shop in Edinburgh. On making some enquiries at the office, I found it to be a paper of a very harmless but inefficient sort. The proprietor, however, wished to improve it, made an offer after some negotiation of the entire control of this periodical; and then it was I asked Mrs Jameson's advice as to the desirability of attempting to devote such a magazine to the special objects of women's work.

The negotiations, however, were not carried through, and Miss Parkes and her colleagues founded the *Englishwoman's Journal*, which started March, 1858.

THE ENGLISHWOMAN'S JOURNAL: published monthly, 1s. at the office of the *Englishwoman's Journal* Company, 19 Langham Place, London. First number, March 1858. In 1864 it became incorporated with the *Alexandra Magazine* (Jackson Walford and Hodder, Paternoster Row).

THE ALEXANDRA MAGAZINE AND ENGLISHWOMAN'S JOURNAL was suspended in 1866, but the *Englishwoman's Journal* revived under the title of

*THE ENGLISHWOMAN'S REVIEW of Social and Industrial questions. Edited by Jessie Boucherett, and published quarterly at the office of the Society for Employment of Women, 22 Berners Street. At the close of 1869 it amalgamated with *Now-a-Days*.

'NOW-A-DAYS. A monthly magazine which will comprise the two magazines hitherto known as "Woman's World" and "Kettle-drum"[1] with the addition of a Chronicle of all Matters affecting the Interests and Education of Women, both in England and on the Continent.'

But *Now-a-Days* was ephemeral, of a day. The *Englishwoman's Review* continued, starting a new monthly series. Edited by Caroline Ashurst Biggs from 1870 to her death, September, 1889; by Helen Blackburn and Antoinette Mackenzie from October, 1889, onwards. Quarterly, 1s.

---

1   *KETTLEDRUM, with which is united 'Woman's World,' a magazine of Art, Literature and Social Improvement. DUX FAEMINA FACTI. Monthly, price 6d. London: 49, Essex Street, Strand, W.C. 1869

JOURNAL OF THE WORKHOUSE VISITING SOCIETY. Edited by Miss Louisa Twining. London: Longman, Green, Longman and Roberts. Price 6d. Published every two months. Discontinued 1865.

THE VICTORIA MAGAZINE. Edited by Emily Faithfull, Victoria Press, Princes Street, Hanover Square, London. Published monthly. Price 1s. Started 1860. Discontinued about 1875.

THE WOMAN'S SUFFRAGE JOURNAL. Edited by Lydia E. Becker. Monthly 1d. Started March 1870. Closed August, 1890, after Miss Becker's death.

JOURNAL OF THE WOMEN'S EDUCATION UNION. Edited by Miss Shirreff and Mr George C.T. Bartley. Monthly 6d., at the office of the Nat. Union for Education of Women. Started January, 1873. Closed when the Union dissolved in June, 1882.

WOMEN AND WORK. A weekly Industrial, Educational, and Household Register for Women. Edited by Emily Faithfull. Price 1d. 1870 to about 1876.

THE LADIES' EDINBURGH MAGAZINE, being a new Series of the *Attempt*. Edinburgh: Maclaren and Macniven. January, 1875 to 1880. Published monthly. Price 6d.

WORK AND LEISURE. A magazine devoted to the Interests of Women. Edited by M.L.H. (Miss Louisa Hubbard). Monthly 3d. Hatchards and Co., London. Started in 1875. Closed in December, 1893, when the *Threefold Cord* became the organ of the Women Workers Union.

THE WOMEN'S UNION JOURNAL. Organ of the Women's Protective and Provident League. Edited by Mrs. Emma Paterson until her death in 1886. Monthly 1d. Started in February, 1876, at the then offices, 31, Little Queen Street, Holborn.

THE WOMEN'S GAZETTE AND WEEKLY NEWS. Edited by Miss Orme. Organ of the Women's Liberal Federation. Price 2d. Started 1888. Suspended about 1893.

THE WOMEN'S PENNY PAPER. Edited by H.B. Temple, 86, Strand, W.C. Published weekly. October 1888. Changed in 1893 to

THE WOMEN'S HERALD, a Liberal Paper for Women. Edited by Christina S. Bremner, and afterwards by Lady Henry Somerset, 27, Victoria Street, S.W.; and again changed in January, 1894, to

THE WOMEN'S SIGNAL. Edited by Lady Henry Somerset and Annie E. Holdsworth, and in January, 1896, by Mrs. Fenwick Miller. Suspended March, 1899.

A THREEFOLD CORD. A magazine for Thoughtful Women. Quarterly, 3d. F.

Kirby, London. Started 1891, modified in 1893 to be the organ of the Women Workers' Union. Editor, Miss Janes. Monthly 1d. Gave place in 1896 to

*AN OCCASIONAL PAPER of the National Union of Women Workers. Quarterly, 1d. 59, Berners Street, London.

*WOMEN WORKERS. Quarterly Magazine of the Birmingham Ladies' Union of Workers amongst Women and Girls. Started June, 1891.

IRIS. The Organ of the Women's Progressive Society. Price 4d. April 1892. Continued a few months only.

WOMEN'S SUFFRAGE NEWS. Edited by A.B. Louis. Published monthly. Price 1/2d. January, 1894. Suspended after six numbers.

*THE WOMEN'S INDUSTRIAL NEWS. Organ of the Women's Industrial Council. Quarterly. Started 1895.

*THE CHURCHWOMAN. Weekly. Price 1d. Started in September, 1895. 11 Ludgate Hill.

OUR SISTERS. A monthly Magazine devoted to the Interests of Women of every Class, Clime and Creed. Edited by Mrs Hooper. Started December, 1895, continued for three years. Price 1d.

*THE RATIONAL DRESS GAZETTE. Organ of the Rational Dress League. Published monthly, for Members only. Editors, Miss Swanhilde Bulan and Mrs. Hartung. 1898.

THE COLONIES

THE WOMEN'S SUFFRAGE JOURNAL. Edited by J.H. Theobald. *Sydney, New South Wales.* Monthly. Price 1d. Started June, 1891. Suspended May, 1892.

THE WOMAN'S VOICE. Edited by M.S. Wolstenholme. Monthly, 1d. *Sydney, New South Wales.* Started 1894. Continued for about two years.

*THE WHITE RIBBON; Organ of the World's Christian Temperance Union of New Zealand. Edited by Mrs. Sheppard. Monthly, 1d. Started 1894. *Christchurch, New Zealand.*

AUSTRIA

DER LEHRERINNEN WART. Zeitschrift für die Interessen der Lehrerinnen und Erzieherinnen, &c. Edited by Marianne Nigg and Dr. F.M. Wendt. Vienna. Started in 1889. In 1891 changed to

*NEUZEIT. Blätter für Weibliche Bildung Inchule [*sic*] und Haus.

*OESTERREICHISCHE LEHRERINNEN ZEITUNG. Organ des Vereines der Lehrerinnen. Vienna, 1893.

*FRAUEN-WERKE. Oesterreichische Zeitschrift zur Förderung und Vertretung der Frauenbestrebungen. Edited by Maria Nigg. Monthly, 20kr. Kornenburg. Started June, 1894.

*DOCUMENTE DER FRAUEN. Edited by Marie Lang. Bi-monthly, vi, i. Magdalenenstrasse, 12, Vienna. Started 1898.

GERMANY

*NEUE BAHNEN, Organ des allgemeinen Deutschen Frauenvereins. Edited (at first by Louise Otto) and Auguste Schmidt. Bi-monthly. Leipzig. Started 1865.

*DEUTSCHE HAUSFRAUEN ZEITUNG. Edited by Frau Lina Morgenstern. Weekly. Started 1874. Berlin.

DEUTSCHER FRAUEN-ANWALT. Organ des Verbandes Beutschen Frauen-Bildungs und Erwerb Verein. Edited by Jenny Hirsch. Monthly, 8 marks per annum. Berlin. Started 1879.

*DIE FRAU. Monatschrift für des gesammten Frauenleben unserer Zeit. Edited by Helene Lange. Monthly. Berlin. Started 1892.

*DIE FRAUENBEWEGUNG. Revue für die Interessen der Frauen. Edited by Minna Cauer. Bi-monthly. Berlin. Started 1895.

*FRAUENBERUF. Blätter für Fragen der weiblichen Erziehung, Ausbildung, Berufs und Hilfsthätigkeit. Edited by the Swabian Frauenverein. Stuttgart. Weekly. Started 1898.

*DIE GLEICHEIT. Zeitschrift für die Interessen der Arbeiterinnen. Edited by Frau Klara Zetkin. Stuttgart. Started 1898.

CENTRALBLATT des Bundes Beutscher Frauenvereine Bundesorgan. Edited by J. Marie Stritt. Bi-monthly. Started 1899

BELGIUM

*LA LIGUE. Organ du droit des Femmes. Brussels. Quarterly. Started in 1893.

CAHIERS FEMINISTES. Bi-monthly. Price 10 centimes. Secretary, Mlle. Gatti de Gaurord, Rue de la Montague 5, Uede-Stalle-lez. Brussels. Started 1896.

DENMARK

*QUINDEN OG SAMFUNDET. Organ of the Danish Women's Union. Copenhagen. Started in 1884, changed in 1900 from a monthly magazine to a bi-monthly paper.

FINLAND

*NUTID. Organ for Women's Unions in Finland. Helsingfors. Monthly. Started in 1894.

FRANCE

L'AVENIR DES FEMMES. Revue Politique, Litteraire et d'Economic Sociale. Edited by Leon Richer. Monthly. Paris. Started in 1869, changed its title in 1878 to –

LE DROIT DES FEMMES, continued until Mr Richer retired in 1891.

*JOURNAL DES FEMMES, Organe du Mouvement Feministe. Paris, 31 Rue Francoeur. Monthly. Edited by Maria Martin. Started in 1889.

*LA REVUE FEMINISTE. Bi-monthly. Directrice, Madame Clotilde Dissard, 41 Rue Claude Bernard, Paris. Started in 1895.

GREECE

*EPHEMERIS TON KURION. Edited by Callirroe Parren. Weekly. 27, Odos Panepistemion, Athens. Started 1887.

HOLLAND

*DE NAAISTERBODE. Organ of the Dutch Union of Seamstresses. 15th of the month. Price 3 centimes. Amsterdam. Started 1899.

ITALY

LA DONNA. An Educational Periodical of Contributions by Italian Ladies. Edited for many years by Gualberta Adelaide Beccari. Bi-monthly. Bologna.

LA RESSEGNA DEGLI INTERESSI FEMMINILI. Edited by Fanny Zampini Salazaro. Rome. Bi-monthly. Started January 1887, ceased in 1888.

LA VITA FEMMINILE. Organo del Movimento Femminile Italiano. Edited by Rosy Amadori, 37, Via Panisperna, Rome. Monthly. Started 1896.

NORWAY

*NYLAENDE. Christiania. Bi-monthly. Edited by Gina Krog. Started in 1885.

RUSSIA

JENSKI WIESTNIK (Women's Messenger). Appeared for a short time somewhere between 1862 and 1868.

*JENSKOIE DIELO (Women's Choice). Edited by Mrs Pieshkou-Tioufiaieva-Tolivierova. Started 1899 (probably still in progress).

SWEDEN

*DAGNY. Organ of the Frederika Bremer Bund. Stockholm. Edited by Lotten Dahlgren. Monthly. Started in 1885.

SWITZERLAND

LA SOLIDARITÉ. Edited by Marie Goegg. Geneva. Quarterly.

*REVUE DE MORALE SOCIALE. Quarterly 2s., a year 8s. Edited by Professor Louis Bridel, 1, Place du Port, Geneva. Started 1899.

SELECTED BIOGRAPHIES

Marie A. Belloc, 1868–1947. English writer, daughter of a French barrister, she began her career in journalism during the late 1880s under W.T. Stead, editor of the *Pall Mall Gazette*. She went on to publish over forty-one popular novels and three plays in the early twentieth century.

Helen Blackburn, 1842–1903. Irish-born pioneer of woman suffrage, she worked in London from 1874 as secretary to the central committee of the National Society for Woman Suffrage (founded 1867), and from 1880 to 1895 she was secretary for the Bristol and West of England Suffrage Society. She was the sole editor of the *Englishwoman's Review* from 1881 to 1890, when she was joined by Ann Mackenzie. From 1895 she devoted most of her time to care for her father. She published *Women's Suffrage: A Record of the Movement in the British Isles* in 1902.

Marie Corelli, 1855–1924. Popular English novelist whose florid romances were admired by Queen Victoria. These include *The Soul of Lilith* (1892), *The Sorrows of Satan* (1895) and *The Mighty Atom* (1896).

Charlotte Perkins Gilman, 1860–1935. American author of the semi-autobiographical *The Yellow Wallpaper* (1890, published 1899). Her feminist commentary on gender and society took many forms, amongst them *In This Our World* (1893), a collection of poems about womanhood, and the prose polemic *Women and Economics* (1898). She edited her own woman's magazine, the *Forerunner*, from 1909 to 1916, writing every item herself.

Sarah Grand (alias Frances Elizabeth McFall), 1854–1943. Irish-born novelist; she travelled for five years in the East, China and Japan in her early twenties, and served as Mayoress of Bath in 1923 and 1925–9. Her fiction champions the New Woman, most notoriously in *The Heavenly Twins* (1893).

Lady Jeune (Susan Mary Elizabeth Stewart-Mackenzie), London Society hostess, who also entertained at her country house, Arlington Manor, Newbury, Berkshire. In 1881 she married Sir Francis Henry Jeune (1843–1905) who was President of the Admiralty, Probate, and Divorce Division of the High Court from 1892. She was voted 'Lady High Chancellor' to serve in an imaginary cabinet of women by readers of the *Gentlewoman* in January 1901.

Louisa Lawson, 1848–1920. Australian journalist, founder of the pioneering feminist monthly, the *Dawn*, in 1888. She wrote or edited the entire contents of each issue for seventeen years until its close in 1905.

Mrs E. Lynn Linton, 1822–98. English novelist and journalist whose outspoken anti-feminism is expressed in her collection *The Girl of the Period and Other Essays* (1883). She wrote for the *Morning Chronicle* (1848–51), and later for the *Saturday Review* and *All the Year Round*. Her non-fiction includes *Witch Stories* (1883); her novels include *The True History of Joshua Davidson* (1872), *Patricia Kenball* (1874) and *The Autobiography of Christopher Kirkland* (1885).

Olive Schreiner, 1855–1920. South African writer praised by literary London for her novel *The Story of an African Farm* (1883). Reformist political argument includes *A Letter on the South African Union and the Principles of Government* (1909), and *Woman and Labour* (1911), while her attack on Cecil Rhodes and his treatment of blacks in 'Rhodesia' is contained in the novel *Trooper Peter Halket of Mashonaland* (1897).

Lady Henry Somerset, 1851–1921 (Lady Isabella Caroline Somerset). Married in 1872, separated from her husband in 1878, raised their child alone, inherited husband's estate in 1883. In 1889 she was elected President of the British Women's Temperance Association, resigned in 1903. She founded the *Woman's Signal* in 1894 which ran until 1898, promoting the dual causes of suffrage and temperance. In 1895 she founded the farm colony Duxhurst near Reigate for the treatment of women alcoholics, and worked there herself for 26 years. Her publications include the verse collection *Our Village Life* (1884), *Sketches in Black and White* (1896), and a novel, *Under the Art of Life* (1906).

Elizabeth Cady Stanton, 1815–1902. Leading American campaigner for the emancipation of women. Her three volume *History of Women's Suffrage* was published in 1881.

Annie S. Swan, 1859–1943 (Mrs Burnett-Smith). Scottish novelist, popular and commercially successful, publishing 162 novels in her own name and over forty under her pseudonym David Lyall. Her first novel was *Aldersyde* (1883), and ten years later her career in journalism took off when the editor W.R. Nicoll invited her contributions to dominate the new magazine the *Woman at Home*, subtitled *Annie Swan's Magazine*. She published her autobiography, *My Life*, in 1934.

SELECTED FURTHER READING

Ballaster, Ros; Beetham, Margaret; Frazer, Elizabeth and Hebron, Sandra (1991) *Women's Worlds. Ideology, Femininity and the Woman's Magazine*, London: Macmillan

Beetham, Margaret (1996) *A Magazine of Her Own? Domesticity and Desire in the Woman's Magazine, 1800–1914*, London: Routledge

Brake, Laural (1994) *Subjugated Knowledges: Journalism, Gender and Literature in the Nineteenth Century*, London: Macmillan

Brown, Lucy (1985) *Victorian News and Newspapers*, Oxford: Clarendon

Dancyger, Irene (1978) *A World of Women: An Illustrated History of Women's Magazines*, Dublin: Gill and Macmillan

Dougham, David and Sanchez, Denise (1987) *Feminist Periodicals, 1855–1945: An Annotated Bibliography of British, Irish and Commonwealth Titles*, Brighton: Harvester

Ferguson, Marjorie (1983) *Forever Feminine. Women's Magazines and the Cult of Femininity*, London: Heinemann

Fox, Stephen (1990) *The Mirror-Makers. A History of American Advertising*, London: Heinemann

Humphreys, Nancy K. (1989) *American Women's Magazines. An Annotated Historical Guide*, London and New York: Garland

Lawson, Olive, ed. (1990) *The First Voice of Australian Feminism: Excerpts from Louisa Lawson's* The Dawn *1888–1895*, Brookvale: Simon and Schuster Australia

Ohmann, Richard (1996) *Selling Culture. Magazines, Markets, and Class at the Turn of the Century*, London and New York: Verso

Reed, David (1997) *The Popular Magazine in Britain and the United States 1880–1960*, London: The British Library

Rendall, Jane, ed. (1987) *Equal or Different? Women's Politics 1800–1914*, Oxford: Basil Blackwell

Richards, Thomas (1990) *The Commodity Culture of Victorian England: Advertising and Spectacle, 1851–1914*, London: Verso

Scanlon, Jennifer (1995) *Inarticulate Longings. The Ladies' Home Journal, Gender, and the Promises of Consumer Culture*, London and New York: Routledge

Shevelow, Kathryn (1989) *Women and Print Culture: The Construction of Femininity in the Early Periodical*, New York: Routledge

Smart, C., ed. (1992) *Regulating Womanhood*, London: Routledge

Vincent, David (1989) *Literacy and Popular Culture: England, 1750–1914*, Cambridge: Cambridge University Press

Weiner, Joel, ed. (1985) *Innovators and Preachers. The Role of the Editor in Victorian England*, Westport and London: Greenwood Press

White, Cynthia L. (1970) *Women's Magazines 1693–1968*, London: Michael Joseph

Winship, Janice (1987) *Inside Women's Magazines*, London and New York: Pandora Press

INDEX